The Morality of Spin

The Morality of Spin

*Virtue and Vice in Political Rhetoric
and the Christian Right*

Nathaniel J. Klemp

ROWMAN & LITTLEFIELD PUBLISHERS, INC.
Lanham • Boulder • New York • Toronto • Plymouth, UK

4/2/13
WU
$70-

Published by Rowman & Littlefield Publishers, Inc.
A wholly owned subsidary of The Rowman & Littlefield Publishing Group, Inc.
4501 Forbes Boulevard, Suite 200, Lanham, Maryland 20706
www.rowmanlittlefield.com

Estover Road, Plymouth PL6 7PY, United Kingdom

British Library Cataloguing in Publication Information Available

Library of Congress Cataloging-in-Publication Data
Klemp, Nathaniel J., 1979-
 The morality of spin : virtue and vice in political rhetoric and the Christian right / Nathaniel J. Klemp.
    p. cm.
 Includes bibliographical references and index.
 ISBN 978-1-4422-1052-3 (cloth : alk. paper) — ISBN 978-1-4422-1054-7 (electronic)
 1. Communication in politics—Moral and ethical aspects—United States.
2. Rhetoric—Political aspects—United States. 3. Deliberative democracy. 4.
Christians—Political activity—United States. 5. Manipulative behavior—Political
aspects—United States. 6. Persuasion (Rhetoric)—Political aspects—United States.
7. Focus on the Family (Organization) I. Title.
 JA85.2.U6K54 2012
 172—dc23
                                                                2011045008

Printed in the United States of America

To Margi and Joe Klemp—For sending me on this journey and for all your support along the way

Contents

~

Acknowledgments

I started exploring the theory and practice of political rhetoric eight years ago. At each step along the way, many others played a key role in helping make this book possible. My advisors in the Department of Politics at Princeton provided invaluable guidance during the early stages of the project. Stephen Macedo, my primary advisor, helped me begin to carve out the structure and arguments of the book. He pushed me to ask questions that extended beyond theory to the actual practice of democratic politics.

Jane Mansbridge at Harvard University also played a pivotal role. She gave me detailed comments on each chapter draft. She also coined the title of this work. As she said during our first meeting together, "What if you called it *The Morality of Spin?*"

Alan Patten, Tali Mendelberg, and Philip Pettit also commented on chapter drafts and offered important advice along the way. Alan helped me refine the theory, Tali helped me sharpen the case studies, and Philip challenged me to expand my thinking about the idea of manipulation.

Many others at Princeton supported this project. I am grateful to Robert Wuthnow for his comments and for the research support offered by the Center for the Study of Religion. I am thankful to my fellow students at the time: Ian Ward, John Lombardini, Alex Zakaras, Michael Frazer, Eric Beerbohm, Michael Lamb, Larry Stratton, and Danielle Shani. I am also grateful to Glenn Stanton and others at Focus on the Family who met with me several times.

The faculty and students at Pepperdine University offered insights and support for the project. Lee Kats and the Dean's Office of Research helped support my research. I am also grateful to my colleagues in political science: Dan Caldwell, Robert Williams, Joel Fetzer, Megan Francis, Candice Ortbals, Brian Newman, and Chris Soper. Pepperdine undergraduate Catherine Morton offered valuable copyediting assistance at the end of the process. The advice of friends and family members like Dara and Chad Creasy, Judy and Jim Warner, Liz Essary, Thad Wong, and Jacob Klein also made this book possible.

Jon Sisk, my editor at Rowman & Littlefield, provided helpful suggestions and support during the final stages of the project. The comments from anonymous reviewers and copyeditors also helped in finalizing the manuscript.

I have published some of the arguments in this book previously in other books and articles. Parts of chapter 2 are drawn from "When Rhetoric Turns Manipulative: Disentangling Persuasion and Manipulation," in *Manipulating Democracy*, ed. Wayne Le Chiminant and John M. Parrish (New York: Routledge, 2010), 59–86. Chapters 3 and 5 were developed out of three earlier publications: "Beyond God-Talk," *Polity* 39 (2007): 522–44; "The Christian Right: Engaged Citizens or Theocratic Crusaders?" *Politics and Religion* 3, Issue 1 (April 2010); and Nathaniel Klemp and Stephen Macedo, "The Christian Right, Public Reason, and American Democracy," in *Evangelicals and Democracy in America*, ed. Steve Brint and Jean Schroedel (New York: Russell Sage Foundation, 2009).

I have dedicated this book to my parents, Margi and Joe Klemp. During good times and bad, they offered unconditional support and inspiration. I could not have done it without them.

Finally, I am grateful to my wife, Kaley. She spent hours pouring through each chapter; she helped me brainstorm ideas on our walks together; and she helped remind me that life is bigger than books, theories, and politics.

~

Introduction

The words "spin" and "rhetoric" have become ubiquitous in modern democratic politics. In everyday talk, these words describe the kind of partisan back-and-forth found on op-ed pages, political talk shows, and debates. They point to what most perceive as a pervasive modern democratic vice. To spin or use rhetoric is to speak in half-truths, exaggerations, and overly emotional appeals. It is to engage in strategic and cunning forms of political persuasion unworthy of our highest democratic aspirations.

The implicit sense of immorality attached to "spin" and "rhetoric" leads lawmakers and candidates to use these words to undermine the sincerity of the opposition. As then House Majority Leader Dennis Hastert declared in a 2005 debate over the "estate/death" tax, "You see, no matter what kind of spin our friends on the other side of the aisle try to use, the *death tax* simply isn't fair."[1]

The power of such accusations arises from the implicit claim that one's own position represents an authentic expression of truth while the opposition's rests on partial truths strategically crafted to maximize influence. Within such claims lies an alleged duality between the authenticity of the accuser and the crassly strategic motivations of the accused.

The irony, of course, is that all politicians and candidates appeal to a variety of rhetorical strategies to put their position in the best possible light and their opponent's in the worst. Political actors frequently appeal to fear and other emotions. They reframe policy positions and arguments to cater to particular audiences. They use cleverly devised slogans to spin their own vices into virtues and their opponent's virtues into vices.

So ubiquitous is rhetoric in modern campaigns that it has spawned a cottage industry of communications consultants and spin-doctors. Contenders for state and national office now spend millions of dollars on PR strategists and pollsters to refine their message and probe the potential vulnerabilities of the opposition. Once elected, they rely on focus groups and telephone surveys to test-market the efficacy of policy proposals and political speeches.

All of this points to an atmosphere of moral ambivalence that surrounds the modern practice of spin and rhetoric. At the level of principle, rhetorical speech is most often seen as disingenuous, inauthentic, and even morally dangerous. Yet at the level of practice, it is often accepted as an inevitable and necessary part of competitive party politics. If we are Democrats, we protest against the ways Republicans "spin" their message and yet accept and deploy the partial presentations of truth offered by candidates we favor, while not always understanding them as such. If we are Republicans, we do the opposite, castigating the "rhetoric" offered by Democrats without considering the moral status of our own party's message. The moral principle implicit in our political practices is thus deeply ambivalent: spin and rhetoric are morally objectionable when used by our opponents, but politically necessary when used by the political leaders that we support.

This sense of ambivalence not only pervades our modern everyday intuitions. It also arises in ancient discussions of rhetoric. Plato views rhetoric as an insidious form of "flattery."[2] He calls such speech "the ghost or counterfeit part of politics" because it produces "delight and gratification" without imparting real knowledge.[3] As Plato suggests, "The rhetorician need not know the truth about things; he has only to discover the way of persuading the ignorant that he has more knowledge than those who know."[4]

If Plato was rhetoric's first great critic, Aristotle was its first formidable advocate. In the *Rhetoric*, Aristotle argues that rhetoric is an inescapable and even beneficial aspect of politics. To engage effectively in political debate, "you must make use of emotions," he declares.[5] "You must make the audience well-disposed towards yourself and ill-disposed towards your opponent, magnify or minimize the leading facts, excite the required state of emotion in your hearers, and refresh their memories."[6] In short, you must spin your message in the most positive light, while spinning your opponent's in the worst.

The question of the moral status of rhetorical speech looms large in ancient discussions of rhetoric and everyday political conversation but is often overlooked in contemporary theories of political speech. Over the last forty years, political scientists have been captivated by the possibilities of ideal forms of deliberation. Such deliberative ideals put forth an important set of democratic aspirations. They clarify what political deliberation might look like under the best conditions and provide a lens for critically evaluating existing social practices. Yet as a result of their emphasis on ideal deliberative virtues and speech situations, they tend to neglect the moral qualities of the kinds of non-ideal political speech found in concrete political circumstances. Outside of what Simone Chambers calls "safe havens of deliberation,"[7] it is often difficult to find these ideals realized in modern politics.

What we often do find in the practice of democracy is a more strategic, even manipulative, mode of speech. In public debate, politicians, pundits, and activists often seek to win by putting their position in its best possible light and their opponent's in its worst. Even deliberative democrats like Bruce Ackerman and James Fishkin admit the scarcity of truly deliberative speech. In their words, "Politicians [now] formulate appeals from focus groups and 'pre-test' their positions with pollsters, constantly modifying them to increase their appeal to marginal voting groups. . . . The aim is to spin a message that will snare a majority."[8]

There is, therefore, a tension between deliberative practice and deliberative ideals. On the conceptual level, this tension arises in two areas, where the emphasis of deliberative ideals tends to depart from the realities of political speech. The first is the deliberative commitment to *reasoned* argument and debate. Many ideal theories of deliberation imply that deliberation should be based on rational argument alone, not appeals to emotion or other rhetorical techniques. As Jurgen Habermas puts it in *The Theory of Communicative Action*, "Participants in argumentation have to presuppose in general that the structure of their communication . . . excludes all force . . . except the force of the better argument."[9] For Habermas and Joshua Cohen, ideal deliberation consists of a rational exchange, free from emotional appeals and rhetorical tactics that distract from "the force of the better argument."[10] Other deliberative theories carve out a space for rhetoric, while implying that such speech is separate from deliberation. Gutmann and Thompson, for instance, argue that "nondeliberative means" such as the use of passionate rhetoric "may be necessary to achieve deliberative ends."[11] This position does not exclude rhetoric from the deliberative process. However, as Bryan Garsten notes, it implies that rhetoric occupies a kind of second-class status in the deliberative arena.[12]

Implicit within these ideal accounts is a claim that rhetoric either opposes or is somehow separate from reasoned argument. Yet what we find in the rhetorical tradition and the actual practice of politics is a more complex picture. Traditional accounts of rhetoric offered by thinkers like Aristotle and Cicero view rhetorical speech as an essential tool that often empowers, rather than opposes, the persuasive potential of reason. As Quinton Skinner remarks, "The need for rhetoric stems from the fact that, as Cicero repeatedly emphasizes, reason lacks any inherent capacity to persuade us of the truths it brings to light."[13]

The actual practice of democratic politics bears out Cicero's insight. In political discussion, it is almost impossible to find examples of purely rational, non-rhetorical speech that "excludes all force . . . except the force of the better argument."[14] Within even the most reasoned appeals to fellow citizens, we find traces of rhetoric: subtle appeals to emotion, metaphor, and other techniques of rhetorical persuasion.

In the rhetorical tradition and in politics, we see a radically different picture of the relationship between reason and rhetoric. On this picture, there is no inherent opposition or even separation between these two. In some instances, rhetoric can distract and disorient listeners from reasoned argument. In others, however, rhetoric can empower and enliven the practice of reasoned argument. The mere existence of rhetoric has little to do with the quality of deliberation. What matters is the more holistic relationship between rhetoric and reasoned arguments.

Second, ideals of deliberation often reject the inconsistencies that arise in rhetorical speech. In *Democracy and Disagreement*, for instance, Amy Gutmann and Dennis Thompson regard the rhetorical technique of *loci communes*—changing arguments and reasons to cater to particular audiences—as a violation of "civic integrity." Mutual respect, they argue, demands that in interactions with fellow citizens we adhere to the "principle of civic integrity," which requires "consistency in speech." As they put it, "We expect citizens and officials to espouse their moral positions independently of the circumstances in which they speak."[15] For Gutmann and Thompson, civic integrity demands that speakers express the moral grounds of their position consistently—that they hold their positions "for reasons of morality, not (only) for reasons of political advantage."[16]

In actual politics, however, lawmakers and candidates often use rhetoric to do the opposite. Rather than maintaining consistency, they seek to maximize "political advantage" by tailoring their rhetoric to the beliefs and values of each audience. Their rhetoric and spin thrive on some degree of inconsistency of speech.

Here again, the rhetorical tradition offers an important defense for the alleged vices of inconsistency. As Bryan Garsten explains, when shifting their rhetorical appeals across audiences, "speakers treat their listeners' existing opinions with a certain deference, and yet they do not cater to them. This respect for the actual opinions of one's audience serves to acknowledge the particular features of individuals—their histories, identities, commitments, and needs."[17] Garsten's point is that rhetorical inconsistency need not signal a lack of mutual respect. Instead, it is often a mark of ineffective communication and even disrespect when speakers fail to adjust their reasoning to each audience.

These two tensions illuminate the gap between deliberative ideals and real-world deliberative practice. In contemporary debates, these worries point to what Joshua Cohen describes as "the most important objection"[18] to ideal theories of deliberation. This is the worry that, as he puts it, "public deliberation is irrelevant to modern political conditions."[19] It is the concern that by focusing on political speech at its best, such ideals become too detached, too removed, from real-world political conditions. The problem is not simply that the rhetorical appeals of political actors often fall short of these deliberative aspirations, for political ideals will always stand beyond reality. It is that such theories fail to offer a robust set of conceptual tools for distinguishing the various moral qualities of non-ideal forms of speech. By focusing on speech at its best, in other words, such theories often fail to account for the distinctions between morally ideal, decent, and problematic forms of speech.

In response to this gap between deliberative ideals and practice, many theorists call for a rehabilitation of rhetorical speech. They argue that rhetoric helps "get an issue on the agenda for deliberation,"[20] that it promotes "communication across wide differences of culture and social position,"[21] and that "a politics of persuasion . . . is worth defending."[22]

Such theories play an important role in challenging the presumption against rhetorical forms of speech implicit in many deliberative ideals. Yet they also risk glorifying rhetorical speech and over-stating its moral and democratic virtues. In particular, existing theories of rhetoric lack nuanced distinctions between morally ideal, morally decent, and morally problematic forms of rhetoric. For example, Bryan Garsten's influential book *Saving Persuasion* emphasizes the importance of distinguishing between speech that persuades and speech that manipulates.[23] Yet his book focuses primarily on historical arguments for and against rhetoric. It does not offer the tools for conceptualizing manipulative speech or distinguishing various non-ideal speech types in practical politics.

The Argument

The Morality of Spin aims to further our understanding of the non-ideal realm of rhetorical speech. It asks, When does political rhetoric enhance and when does it diminish democracy? Answering this question requires a holistic examination of both the act of rhetoric (the speaker's words and intent) as well as the context of rhetoric (the deliberative setting in which it arises).

The argument works on two levels. The first concerns the moral quality of speech itself.[24] To distinguish the various moral dimensions of rhetoric, I argue for a three-fold distinction between "deliberative persuasion," "strategic persuasion," and "manipulation." These speech types illuminate the moral qualities of morally ideal speech (deliberative persuasion), morally decent speech (strategic persuasion), and morally problematic speech (manipulation).

Respect for other citizens' choices distinguishes such morally acceptable forms of persuasion from manipulation. Deliberative and strategic forms of persuasion allow listeners to choose freely, while manipulative rhetoric interferes with this capacity. By using covert or irrational appeals to distort the listener's capacity to choose, manipulative speech erodes individual autonomy and the democratic ideal of rule by the people. Lies, concealments, and other forms of manipulation subtly obscure relevant alternatives, distract us from the objectives we seek to achieve, and distort assessments of certainty.[25] By covertly altering our beliefs, actions, and choices, manipulative speech strips "we the people" of our sovereign authority, placing this power in the hands of manipulators.

The second level of analysis concerns the moral qualities of the deliberative context within which rhetoric is exchanged. In actual politics, deliberative, strategic, and manipulative rhetoric arise in a variety of deliberative contexts. On the one side, rhetoric may arise within "contestatory spaces," consisting of the fair competition of diverse interests. On the other, rhetoric may arise within "one-sided information spaces," where a single religious, moral, or political perspective is insulated from oppositional views.

These contextual conditions help determine the moral quality of political rhetoric. The diverse and competitive nature of contestatory spaces improves the moral quality of all three ideal speech types. Robust contestation helps to dissolve the many dangers posed by morally problematic forms of manipulation. Within such contextual conditions, rival interests have incentives to expose the manipulative tactics of the opposition, creating strong disincentives against manipulative speech.

The lack of contestation and debate in one-sided information spaces has the opposite effect. Such contestatory vacuums magnify the dangers of manipulative rhetoric. In these spaces, the primary antidote to manipulation—the risk of exposure—is no longer supplied by robust conditions of contestation. Such one-sided spaces also diminish the moral virtues associated with the most ideal forms of deliberative persuasion. They create enclave conditions that lack the deliberative checks and balances found in contestatory spaces and often cultivate polarization and intolerance.

The Method

This is primarily a work of political theory. It aims to expand our current understanding of the moral dimensions of political rhetoric and deliberative context. Yet it also attempts to ground these conceptual reflections in the real-world practice of democratic politics. I appeal throughout the book to a case study drawn from my own field research on the rhetorical practices of the contemporary American Christian right. In chapter 3, I examine the "two-tiered rhetoric" of three prominent organizations—The Christian Coalition, Colorado for Family Values, and Focus on the Family—to illuminate the qualities of deliberative, strategic, and manipulative speech. In chapter 5, I examine the deliberative context within Focus on the Family to highlight the influence of deliberative context on the moral quality of speech.

This mixture of theory and political anthropology has two primary benefits. First, the back-and-forth between theory and practice of this mixed method is a tool for theoretical construction. As Jane Mansbridge explains, "By looking at what happens to an ideal under stress, theorists can obtain what I think of as an 'exploded diagram' of its inner meanings and potentialities."[26] In this view, the actual world of politics is a theoretical testing ground. In juxtaposing moral ideals against real-world practice, we may uncover problematic assumptions or gain new and unexpected theoretical insights. In either case, this method deepens our theoretical understanding. The practice resembles John Rawls's "reflective equilibrium."[27] When comparing theory and practice, our aim is, as Rawls might say, to "work from both ends"[28]—to travel between the ideal principles of theory and the concrete realm of political practice. Like Rawls's "reflective equilibrium," this back-and-forth may confirm ideals, prompt revisions, or even prompt reevaluations of our intuitions.

Second, this mixed method illuminates the application of these theoretical concepts to concrete political practice. While understanding the moral status of political rhetoric requires rigorous theoretical reflection, understanding the implications of theoretical reflection for politics requires application. So my hope is that by examining the rhetorical practices of the Christian right, these conceptual categories will come to life.

A Definition of Rhetoric

While ubiquitous in modern political conversations, "spin" and "rhetoric" require some preliminary definition. "Spin" is a relatively recent addition to the modern political vernacular. Defined roughly, spin is a message consciously crafted to influence the beliefs and actions of listeners by putting information in its best or worst possible light. The *Oxford English Dictionary*, for instance, defines it as "a bias or slant on information, intended to create a favorable impression when it is presented to the public."[29] While the dictionary cites 1978 as the year the word "spin" was first used in a political context, the rhetorical practice of putting arguments or information in their most favorable light is at least as old as democracy itself.[30]

Throughout the history of western political thought, the term "rhetoric" has been used to describe such practices. Given its conceptual richness and history, I use the word "rhetoric" rather than "spin" throughout the book. While ancient thinkers like Plato, Aristotle, and Cicero disagree as to whether rhetoric is a virtue or a vice, they all point toward a similar definition. In the "Gorgias," Socrates defines rhetoric as "the artificer of persuasion," to which Gorgias replies, "The definition seems to me very fair, Socrates; for persuasion is the chief end of rhetoric."[31]

Aristotle shares the idea that rhetoric seeks persuasion as its primary end. In the *Rhetoric*, he declares, "Rhetoric may be defined as the faculty of observing in any given case the available means of persuasion."[32] Finally, consider Cicero's definition of rhetoric. A vital part of politics, he declares, arises from "that form of artistic eloquence which is generally known as rhetoric, the function of which is that of speaking in a manner calculated to persuade, and the goal of which is that of persuading by speech."[33]

These ancient definitions highlight two primary qualities of rhetorical speech. The first concerns the end of rhetoric: its orientation toward persuasion. According to such ancient conceptions, rhetoric seeks to persuade—to induce the agreement of listeners. The second quality concerns the specific means used by rhetoric: the "calculated" use of linguistic techniques that induce persuasion through "eloquence" and other "artistic" uses of language. On these views, the end of persuasion is reached through the conscious use of linguistic techniques that elicit emotion, redescribe perceived virtues or vices, or appeal to the values and beliefs particular to each audience.

The conception of rhetoric I propose in this book shares the ancients' view of the *means* of rhetoric but argues for a slightly more expansive view of rhetoric's *end*. I define rhetoric by stipulation as *speech that seeks to influence the choices, beliefs, or actions of others through "artistic" uses of language.* While similar to most traditional definitions, this conception of rhetoric presumes that although political rhetoric is often "designed to persuade,"[34] it can also be designed to exert other forms of influence, such as coercion or manipulation. This definition adopts Kenneth Burke's insight that rhetoric is not inherently persuasive—that it simply consists in "the use of words by human agents to form attitudes or to induce actions in other human agents."[35]

So on this more expansive view, rhetoric is not confined to situations in which the speaker seeks to persuade listeners by inducing genuine agreement. In some instances, rhetoric may also be used to manipulate—to reshape the actions or beliefs of listeners in ways that diminish their capacity to choose for themselves. As discussed in chapter 2, persuasive speech seeks to induce agreement and entails a capacity on the part of listeners to choose whether to accept the proposed agreement. Manipulation, by contrast, uses covert or irrational forms of force to interfere with this capacity.

While the ancients cite persuasion as the explicit end of rhetoric, their accounts often implicitly endorse this more expansive definition. These accounts hint at the idea that rhetoric is not inherently persuasive—that it can turn manipulative. In Cicero's *De Oratore*, for instance, Antonius declares that in addressing an audience, "you must try to shift or impel them so that they become ruled not by deliberation and judgment but rather by sheer impetus and perturbation of the mind."[36] In my terms, Antonius's words involve speech quite different from persuasion. He calls for a rhetoric seeking not to induce agreement but to override the rational capacities of listeners to choose for themselves. In short, his appeals to emotion seek manipulation, not persuasion. On this more expansive view, therefore, the end of rhetoric is more than mere persuasion. Rhetorical speech affects the choices, beliefs, or actions of others by persuasive or manipulative forms of influence.

While I call for a more expansive view of rhetoric's end, I share the second half of the ancient conception of rhetoric: the idea that rhetoric involves "eloquence" and "artistic" uses of language as its means. Iris Marion Young's definition of rhetoric highlights this quality of rhetorical speech. As she puts it, rhetoric concerns "the way content is conveyed as distinct from the assertive value of the content."[37] Unlike "purely rational argumentation," rhetoric appeals to emotion, metaphor, eloquence, and other linguistic techniques that enhance the way content is conveyed. Rhetorical speakers often present substantive arguments, but the additional use of such linguistic techniques typifies this mode of speaking.

In this book, I explore the moral implications of three primary rhetorical techniques, as discussed in Quentin Skinner's *Reason and Rhetoric in the Philosophy of Hobbes*. This list is not exhaustive, but it highlights the most powerful rhetorical techniques that ancient and modern speakers use to exert influence.

The first is the doctrine of *loci communes*: the doctrine of common places.[38] This doctrine suggests that speakers reframe rhetorical appeals to accommodate the various beliefs, dispositions, and values of specific listeners.[39] Put differently, speakers should navigate the pathways of rationality and emotion that vary from audience to audience by reworking their rhetorical appeals. On Quintilian's view, the doctrine of common places has three primary qualities. First, successful orators must relate their views to the opinions and beliefs shared by the audience. Second, orators must base their arguments on assumptions shared throughout the audience. Finally, Quintilian advises orators to appeal to the prejudices of particular audiences.[40] Used effectively, these features of *loci communes* encourage speakers to use a dynamic message—one that shifts with context.

The insight behind this doctrine is that the arguments and emotional appeals that successfully influence one audience may be different from the rhetorical appeals that persuade another. In *De Oratore*, Antonius states, "I take the orator to be a man capable of using language acceptable to his hearers and of using such arguments as are best accommodated to the establishment of his case."[41]

The doctrine of *loci communes* pervades modern political speech. Candidates, lawmakers, and interest groups often shift their rhetoric to appeal to the values and beliefs of particular audiences. Chapter 3 presents an in-depth case study of the contemporary Christian right's use of this rhetorical tactic. The Christian right's "two-tiered rhetoric"—its use of explicitly religious reasons internally to mobilize fellow believers and more publicly accessible reasons externally to persuade outsiders—is a paradigm case of *loci communes*. To appeal to non-Christians and other citizens who do not share their values, groups like Focus on the Family reframe their arguments in a more publicly accessible moral vocabulary that all citizens could accept. In this sense, the rhetoric of Christian right leaders like James Dobson embodies Cicero's maxim that "no single kind of oratory suits every cause or audience or speaker or occasion."[42]

The second rhetorical technique used in ancient and contemporary politics is what the Greeks called *paradiastole*: the practice of "redescription."[43] Unlike the doctrine of common places, where rhetoric shifts to accommodate various audiences, this technique seeks to transform the meaning of words and values. It enables speakers to redescribe the virtues of the opposition as vices or to redescribe their own vices as virtues. The colloquial use of the word "spin" often implies this rhetorical technique. To spin an argument or a phrase is to turn it around—to shift its meaning to put one's own position in the most favorable light. As Quentin Skinner explains, when engaging in "paradiastolic redescription,"

> we simply replace whatever descriptions our opponents may have offered with a different set of terms that serve to describe the action with no less plausibility, but place it at the same time in a different moral light. We seek to persuade our hearers to accept our redescription, and hence to adopt a new emotional attitude towards the action involved—either one of increased sympathy or acquired moral outrage.[44]

The rhetorical technique of redescription gives speakers a way to shift the meaning of words or the moral complexion of actions or states of affairs. *Paradiastole* enables speakers to transform their opponent's virtues into vices, while transforming their own vices into virtues.

As Skinner points out, this technique takes two primary forms. First, *paradiastole* redescribes the received definition of words or phrases to put the speaker's position in its best possible light. Perhaps the most infamous contemporary example of this form of redescription arose during the Clinton impeachment hearings. Responding to charges of perjury, President Clinton defended himself by contesting the meaning of a single word. He argued that his guilt or innocence "depends on what the meaning of the word 'is' is."[45] Clinton's attempt to redescribe the meaning of "is" was an attempt to cover up his vices by recasting the meaning of a single word. Thucydides also offers examples of this mode of speech. In describing revolution, he states, "Words had to change their ordinary meaning and to take that which was now given them. Reckless audacity came to be considered the courage of a loyal supporter; prudent hesitation, specious cowardice; moderation was held to be a cloak for unmanliness."[46]

The second form of paradiastolic redescription also arises in ancient and modern political discourse. Using this alternative form of redescription, explains Skinner, "We can argue . . . that a given action has been wrongly assessed not because the terms used to describe it have been misdefined, but rather because the action itself has a different moral complexion from that which the terms used to describe it suggest."[47] Rather than redefining the meaning of words, this second form of redescription redefines the moral quality of specific situations, events, and states of affairs. In criticizing modern political language, George Orwell bemoans the pervasiveness of this mode of redescription. Orwell's worry is that political speech relies on redescription to speak in "defense of the indefensible"—to transform immoral states of affairs into seemingly moral ones.[48] "People are imprisoned for years without trial," declares Orwell, "or shot in the back of the neck or sent to die of scurvy in Arctic lumber camps: this is called *elimination of unreliable elements*."[49]

Finally, a third rhetorical technique used in ancient and modern political rhetoric is the arousal of emotion. In *Rhetoric*, Aristotle emphasizes the powerful role of emotion in persuasive speech. To debate effectively, he declares, "You must make use of emotions."[50] While Aristotle viewed emotion as a persuasive tool for guiding listeners toward reflection on rational arguments, Roman rhetoricians often employed emotion to achieve a more manipulative end: to direct listeners away from arguments and exploit the irrational side of human nature.[51] As Cicero declares, "It is inflaming the feelings of our listeners by our speech, or else in quieting them down after they have been inflamed, that the power of oratory and its greatness can above all be discerned."[52]

Modern politicians also use emotional appeals to exert influence over citizens. Consider, for example, Condoleezza Rice's argument for invading Iraq: "There will always be some uncertainty about how quickly he [Saddam Hussein] can acquire nuclear weapons. But we don't want the smoking gun to be a mushroom cloud."[53] Her point rests on a reasonable argument for national security, but also appeals to the vivid imagery of a "mushroom cloud" to incite fear and alarm. Like most rhetoric, it appeals to emotion to bring to life more substantive claims about national security.

Rhetorical appeals to emotion reinforce Plato's point that rhetoric may be more than mere speech. It creates "an experience" inciting "delight and gratification."[54] While emotional rhetoric may present audiences with reasons, it also seeks to create an experiential atmosphere where the passions and emotions of listeners maximize the likelihood of persuasion.[55]

In this book, I argue that rhetorical techniques like *loci communes*, *paradiastole*, and appeals to emotion have no inherent moral quality. Each of these techniques can be used to persuade fellow citizens in ways that respect their capacity to choose. Likewise, each technique can be used to manipulate fellow citizens. As we will see, it is not the rhetorical technique but the holistic act of rhetoric—its content, intent, and context—that determines its moral quality.

So the question at the core of *The Morality of Spin* is not simply a question of rhetorical technique. This book focuses on a broader set of questions about rhetoric. It asks, What types of rhetorical acts and contexts enhance and what types diminish deliberative democracy?

Existing theories of deliberative democracy offer no clear response. Many of these ideal theories simply reject, or at least discount, the use of rhetoric in deliberative democracy. Habermas's emphasis on rational argumentation, for instance, leaves these three forms of rhetoric outside the scope of ideal deliberation. By defining discourse as excluding "all force . . . except for the force of the better argument," he seems to reject rhetorical techniques that seek persuasion by appealing to emotion or other forms of rhetorical persuasion that go beyond reasoned argument alone.[56] Similarly, Gutmann and Thompson's principle of "civic integrity," which calls for "consistency in speech," seems to reject rhetoric based on *loci communes*, in which speakers reframe arguments to appeal to the beliefs and values of particular audiences.

While neither Habermas nor Gutmann and Thompson argue explicitly against rhetoric, their accounts bring to light the atmosphere of ambivalence that surrounds its use in democratic politics. They point to the need for a theory of rhetoric that more directly addresses the moral status of political rhetoric in deliberative democracy. This is the central aim of *The Morality of Spin*. The goal is not to categorically reject or embrace the use of rhetoric in democratic politics. Instead, the goal is to look deeper into the moral ambiguities of this form of political speech. It is to clarify the features of speech and context that cause some forms of rhetoric to enhance and other forms to diminish the democratic process.

The Plan

Chapter 1 outlines the account of rhetoric implicit within two prominent deliberative theories: John Rawls's theory of "public reason" and Jurgen Habermas's theory of "communicative action." Both theories further our understanding of manipulative and strategic speech, but neither provides a fully satisfactory account. Rawls's conception of public reason lacks a fully developed account of manipulation. Habermas offers a more robust account of manipulation but with an overly narrow definition that excludes many apparently manipulative acts. This account of Habermas plays an important role in setting up the theoretical framework of chapter 2. If you are a more casual reader with no interest in diving deep into Habermas, however, you should feel free to skip ahead to chapter 2.

Chapters 2 and 3 draw upon the shortcomings of these existing accounts to outline a constructive theory of the moral dimensions of political rhetoric. Chapter 2 seeks to disentangle the various moral qualities of rhetoric by distinguishing persuasion and manipulation. Persuasive rhetoric exerts influence transparently and respects the choices of others. It takes two forms: "deliberative persuasion," which induces agreement with an orientation toward understanding; and "strategic persuasion," which induces agreement with an orientation toward winning. Manipulative rhetoric, by contrast, arises when (1) agent A uses hidden or irrational force to affect agent B's choices, and (2) agent A acts intentionally. In democratic politics, manipulation takes three forms: lying, concealment, and distraction. Unlike persuasion, manipulation often works covertly. It diminishes individual autonomy and democratic self-rule by interfering with other citizens' capacity to choose. Two contextual conditions intensify the dangers of manipulative rhetoric: invisibility and asymmetrical relations of power. Given its potential dangers, manipulation ought to be viewed with a presumption of immorality and subject to robust contestation.

Chapter 3 uses a case study of the rhetoric of Christian right activists to identify instances of deliberative persuasion, strategic persuasion, and manipulation in American politics. Throughout the last thirty years, Christian right activists have used a "two-tiered rhetoric": they typically use religious reasons to mobilize fellow Christians and more publicly accessible reasons to influence broader audiences. By taking into account the agent's context, self-reflections, and the consistency between past and present speech acts, I argue that this two-tiered approach has, at various moments in the history of the Christian right, represented all three forms of speech. In its "stealth" campaign of the early 1990s, the Christian Coalition used two-tiered rhetoric to manipulate. In its rhetoric of "No Special Rights," the Colorado Christian right of the early 1990s used the two tiers to persuade strategically. Finally, in appeals to social science and "humanism" made by contemporary activists of Focus on the Family, two-tiered rhetoric more closely approximates the deliberative ideal of persuasion.

Chapters 4 and 5 turn from the moral qualities of rhetorical speech to the moral qualities of rhetorical context. Chapter 4 explores the interaction between deliberative, strategic, and manipulative rhetoric and the broader deliberative context. I argue that the discursive environment within which rhetoric emerges plays a powerful role in determining its moral quality. In "contestatory spaces"—where a diversity of views is debated under conditions of fair competition—the exchange of rhetoric tends to enhance democracy. Such contexts enhance the moral quality of persuasive speech and may allow for the emergence of morally legitimate forms of strategic and even manipulative speech. By contrast, in "one-sided information spaces"—where a single political, religious, or ethical perspective is insulated from oppositional views—the exchange of rhetoric undermines democracy. Such contexts have corrosive effects on even ideal forms of deliberative persuasion and deepen the dangers posed by manipulative rhetoric.

In chapter 5, I apply this theoretical framework for assessing the moral quality of rhetorical context to the practices of America's most powerful Christian right organization, Focus on the Family. I argue that the conservative Christian "counterculture" promoted by Focus and other groups has created an "enclave infrastructure"—an insulated cultural space that minimizes direct engagement with oppositional views. This one-sided information space poses two threats to contestatory democratic conditions. First, it cultivates anti-contestatory attitudes of polarization and intolerance. Second, it cultivates anti-contestatory practices, such as "info-blasting," which diminish the openness and competitive nature of public political debate. Finally, I explore an important tension that emerges when assessing groups like Focus between deliberative and participatory ideals of democracy. While this enclave infrastructure undermines the deliberative ideal of robust contestation, it also fosters an important participatory virtue: active political engagement. To account for this tension, I argue that we ought to aspire toward a balance between the values of participation and deliberation—one that promotes the participatory virtues of enclave spaces but discourages their anti-contestatory democratic vices.

Notes

1. Dennis Hastert, "It's Time We Let the Death Tax Die," April 13, 2005, http://speaker.house.gov/library/health/050413deathtax.shtml.

2. Plato, "Gorgias," in *The Essential Dialogues of Plato* (New York: Barnes and Noble Classics, 2005), 134, 462c.

3. Plato, "Gorgias," 134–35, 463a.

4. Plato, "Gorgias," 131, 459c. For more in-depth accounts of Plato's conception of rhetoric, see Robert Wardy, *The Birth of Rhetoric* (New York: Routledge, 1998); George A. Kennedy, *A New History of Classical Rhetoric* (Princeton: Princeton University Press, 1994); and James L. Kastely, "In Defense of Plato's *Gorgias*," *PMLA* 106, no. 1 (1991).

5. Aristotle, "Rhetoric," in *The Complete Works of Aristotle*, ed. Jonathan Barnes (Princeton: Princeton University Press, 1984), 2263, bk. 3: 1417a38.

6. Aristotle, "Rhetoric," 2268, bk. 3: 1419b10.

7. Simone Chambers, "Rhetoric, Public Opinion, and the Ideal of a Deliberative Democracy," *2006 Princeton Conference on Deliberative Democracy.*

8. Bruce Ackerman and James S. Fishkin, "Deliberation Day," *Journal of Political Philosophy* 10, no. 2 (2002): 132.

9. Jurgen Habermas, *The Theory of Communicative Action*, trans. Thomas McCarthy (Boston: Beacon Press, 1984), 25.

10. Not all deliberative theories share this rationalist emphasis. In recent years, many deliberative democrats shifted from this implicit rejection of emotion toward rhetorical appeals to emotion. Gutmann and Thompson, for example, assert that "in the political arena passionate rhetoric can be as justifiable as logical demonstration." See Amy Gutmann and Dennis Thompson, *Why Deliberative Democracy?* (Princeton: Princeton University Press, 2004), 51. See also John Dryzek, *Deliberative Democracy and Beyond* (New York: Oxford University Press, 2002); Jane Mansbridge, "Everyday Talk in the Deliberative System," in *Deliberative Politics*, ed. Stephen Macedo (New York: Oxford University Press, 1999); Amy Gutmann and Dennis Thompson, *Democracy and Disagreement* (Cambridge: Belknap Press, 1996); and Sharon Krause, *Civil Passions* (Princeton: Princeton University Press, 2008).

11. Gutmann and Thompson, *Democracy and Disagreement*, 135.

12. Bryan Garsten, "The Rhetoric Revival in Political Theory," *Annual Review of Political Science* 14 (2011).

13. Quentin Skinner, *Reason and Rhetoric in the Philosophy of Hobbes* (Cambridge: Cambridge University Press, 1996), 2.

14. Habermas, *The Theory of Communicative Action*, 25.

15. Gutmann and Thompson, *Democracy and Disagreement*, 81.

16. Gutmann and Thompson, *Democracy and Disagreement*.

17. Bryan Garsten, *Saving Persuasion* (Cambridge: Harvard University Press, 2006), 198.

18. Joshua Cohen, "Deliberation and Democratic Legitimacy," in *Democracy*, ed. David Estlund (New York: Blackwell Publishers, 2002), 101.

19. Cohen, "Deliberation and Democratic Legitimacy."

20. Iris Marion Young, *Inclusion and Democracy* (New York: Oxford University Press, 2000), 66.

21. Iris Marion Young, "Communication and the Other: Beyond Deliberative Democracy," in *Democracy and Difference*, ed. Seyla Benhabib (Princeton: Princeton University Press, 1996), 132.

22. Garsten, *Saving Persuasion*, 3. For other defenses of the use of rhetoric in democratic deliberation, see Bernard Manin, "On Legitimacy and Political Deliberation," *Political Theory* 15, no. 3 (1987); and Gutmann and Thompson, *Why Deliberative Democracy?*, 50–51.

23. Garsten, *Saving Persuasion*.

24. I define "moral" as "relating to the distinction between right and wrong . . . in relation to the actions, desires, or character of . . . human beings." Thus what I call the "moral quality of speech" refers to whether speech embodies ideal or problematic moral qualities. "Moral," *Oxford English Dictionary*, 2008.

25. Sissela Bok, *Lying* (New York: Vintage Books, 1999), 18–20.

26. Jane Mansbridge, *Beyond Adversary Democracy* (Chicago: University of Chicago Press, 1983), xiii.

27. This method *resembles* Rawls's notion of reflective equilibrium but is not the same.

28. John Rawls, *A Theory of Justice*, rev. ed. (Cambridge: Harvard University Press, 1999), 18.

29. "Spin," *Oxford English Dictionary*.

30. "Spin," *Oxford English Dictionary*.

31. Plato, "Gorgias," 125, 453a.

32. Aristotle, "Rhetoric," 2155.

33. Skinner, *Reason and Rhetoric*, 2.

34. Garsten, *Saving Persuasion*, 5.

35. Kenneth Burke, *A Rhetoric of Motives* (Berkeley: University of California Press, 1969), 41.

36. I am grateful to Skinner for this quote; see Skinner, *Reason and Rhetoric*, 121.

37. Young, *Inclusion and Democracy*, 65.

38. For a discussion of this doctrine and rhetoric generally, see Skinner, *Reason and Rhetoric*.

39. Garsten, *Saving Persuasion*.

40. Skinner, *Reason and Rhetoric*, 117.

41. Skinner, *Reason and Rhetoric*, 117–18.

42. Cicero, *De Oratore* (Cambridge: Harvard University Press, 1942), 167–69, bk. 3, 211.

43. Skinner, *Reason and Rhetoric*, 151.

44. Skinner, *Reason and Rhetoric*, 145.

45. Timothy Noah, "Bill Clinton and the Meaning of 'Is,'" *Slate Magazine*, September 13, 1998.

46. Thucydides, *The Peloponnesian War* (New York: Free Press, 1996), 199–200, 3.82.

47. Skinner, *Reason and Rhetoric*, 142.

48. George Orwell, "Politics and the English Language," in *Collected Essays* (London: Secker and Warburg, 1961), 363.

49. Orwell, "Politics and the English Language." Emphasis in original.

50. Aristotle, "Rhetoric," 2263, bk. 3: 1417a38.

51. Skinner, *Reason and Rhetoric*, 123.

52. Skinner, *Reason and Rhetoric*, 122.

53. Wolf Blitzer, "Search for the 'Smoking Gun,'" *CNN*, January 10, 2003, http://edition.cnn.com/2003/US/01/10/wbr.smoking.gun/.

54. Plato, "Gorgias," 134, 462c.

55. Geoffrey Nunberg, *Talking Right* (New York: PublicAffairs, 2006). The experiential quality of spin resembles corporate marketing strategies and branding techniques. When an auto company markets its latest car, its message is often not that their car has a more sophisticated transmission than the rivals. Instead of promoting the car's technical superiority, they are more likely to present you with an experience—images of a young, affluent, and attractive couple cruising through the wine country in Napa. Such images have great persuasive force because they connect the product with a set of unconscious desires, emotional associations, and ideals of self.

In politics, just as in marketing, spin appeals to a broad spectrum of considerations. Political spin does not simply outline the details of an individual or group's policy proposals; it grounds these arguments in an experiential narrative connecting with the emotions of potential voters.

56. Habermas, *The Theory of Communicative Action*, 25.

PART I

EXISTING ACCOUNTS

CHAPTER ONE

~

Deliberative Democracy and Political Rhetoric

Rawls and Habermas on Rhetoric's Moral Status

The American pragmatist philosopher John Dewey feared democracy was in decline. He worried that the vast and complex modern democratic state had outgrown many of its founding ideas and practices. As he puts it, "We have inherited . . . local town-meeting practices and ideas. But we live and act and have our being in a continental national state."[1] The problem of the democratic public, Dewey argues in *The Public and Its Problems*, is that as it has grown in size and complexity, it has become increasingly "amorphous and unarticulated."[2] "It is not that there is no public," Dewey insists. "There is too much public, a public too diffused and scattered and too intricate in composition."[3]

While Dewey expresses concern about the decline of citizen competence and the incoherence of the modern public will, he argues that this "eclipse of the public"[4] should not lead us to establish an intellectual aristocracy where experts and elites rule a confused and docile public.[5] Instead, he argues that discussion, rhetoric, and communication can be refined in certain circumstances to realize the classical ideal of democracy as rule of the people. Thus Dewey departs from the views of elite theorists like Joseph Schumpeter who argue that rhetorical conditions of "secrecy, prejudice, bias, misrepresentation, and propaganda as well as sheer ignorance" are inevitable.[6] To realize a more ideal democracy, Dewey argues that such impoverished conditions of public debate must be improved. "The essential need," he declares, "is the improvement of the methods and conditions of debate, discussion and persuasion. That is *the* problem of the public."[7]

Dewey's turn toward debate and discussion is reflected as a central theme in contemporary theories of deliberative democracy.[8] Like Dewey, most deliberative democrats argue for a return to the traditional ideal of democracy as rule of the people as a whole. They reject Schumpeter's pessimistic view that public political debate is inherently manipulative and his embrace of asymmetrical power relationships that place ultimate authority in the hands of political elites. By contrast, deliberative democracy, as Cohen describes it, is "an association whose affairs are governed by the public deliberation of its members."[9] It is a form of collective self-rule, in which debate and discussion play a central role in conferring legitimacy on the democratic process. The essence of this view is not competitive struggles between elites but what Gutmann and Thompson call the *"reason-giving* requirement": the notion that "in a democracy, leaders should . . . give reasons for their decisions, and respond to the reasons that citizens give in return."[10]

This chapter examines the accounts of the moral status of rhetoric implicit in several prominent deliberative theories of democracy. While these accounts offer important insights, I claim that they fail to provide a comprehensive framework for evaluating the moral dimensions of rhetoric. I begin by outlining several arguments for deliberative democracy. I then assess the accounts of the moral dimensions of rhetoric implicit in two prominent deliberative theories: John Rawls's theory of *public reason*, and Jurgen Habermas's theory of *communicative action*. Both theories further our understanding of manipulative and strategic speech, but I argue that neither theory provides a fully satisfactory account. Rawls's conception of public reason offers important insights into the nature of manipulation but lacks a fully developed account. Habermas's account comes closer but lacks a fully developed conception of manipulative speech.

Deliberative Democracy

For deliberative democrats, the exchange of arguments and reasons is central to the democratic process. While deliberative theorists offer somewhat different views on the purpose, justification, and ideal context of public deliberation, most argue that when citizens encounter disagreements over moral or political matters, such disagreements ought to be resolved, insofar as possible, through the exchange of reasons.

Amy Gutmann and Dennis Thompson offer one such ideal of deliberative democracy, arguing that a complete definition of deliberative democracy arises from four characteristics. First, deliberation is characterized by appeals to moral reasons and arguments.[11] Laws may be enacted through assertions of power, interest group bargaining, or voting, but they must be justified by moral arguments and reasons. As Gutmann and Thompson put it, "In deliberative democracy an important way . . . agents take part [in the governance of their own society] is by presenting and responding to reasons, or demanding that their representatives do so, with the aim of justifying the laws under which they must live together."[12] Second, deliberation occurs when these principles and arguments are accessible to all citizens. Like Rawls, Gutmann and Thompson assert that our basic commitments to reciprocity and mutual respect demand that we use reasons others could accept.[13] As Gutmann and Thompson explain, "A public justification does not ever get started if those to whom it is addressed cannot understand its essential content."[14]

Third, they argue that deliberations should be directed toward decisions binding for some period of time.[15] Deliberations are the prelude to a decision that has lasting consequences. Finally, Gutmann and Thompson argue that deliberation is dynamic and provisional. Even after binding decisions, citizens ought to debate and challenge the structure of laws, policies, and institutions. As they put it, deliberative democracy "keeps open the possibility of a continuing dialogue, one in which citizens can criticize previous decisions and move ahead on the basis of that criticism."[16]

This provisional nature of deliberation extends to deliberative theories themselves. There is, for instance, no consensus on the justification for deliberation. Traditionally, deliberation has been justified on the grounds that it cultivates citizen virtues—enhancing the happiness, public-spiritedness, and autonomy of citizens. One way to justify deliberation is to take up Aristotle's claim that politics promotes human flourishing. If "man is by nature a political animal,"[17] we can assume that political deliberation allows citizens to realize their essential nature. A less controversial, but related, justification claims that political deliberation enables citizens to see beyond selfish interests and take up a more publicly oriented perspective. As John Stuart Mill puts it, "The private citizen . . . is called upon, while so engaged, to weigh interests not his own; to be guided, in case of conflicting claims, by another rule than his private partialities; to apply, at every turn, principles and maxims which have for their reason of existence the common good."[18]

While these justifications are important, two other arguments constitute the primary case for deliberation in contemporary discussions. The first—*the legitimacy argument*—is perhaps the most powerful justification for deliberation. This argument emphasizes deliberation's unique role in conferring legitimacy on the democratic process. On this view, the practice of deliberation plays an essential role in justifying the coercive exercise of state power.

The term "legitimacy" arises in myriad contexts. For our purposes, think of legitimacy as arising from a free and equal process of justification for coercive power.[19] As I will discuss in chapter 2, coercion is a particular form of power—one that arises through the use of an openly communicated threat of sanction.[20] While unjustified coercive power can undermine democratic conditions, justified coercion plays an essential role in democratic life. Taxation, laws against murder, and environmental regulations—all of these practices depend upon an openly communicated threat of sanction. To ensure that corporate CEOs pay their fair share of taxes, for instance, the state must threaten those who seek to evade taxation with fines and jail time.

So on my use of the term, legitimacy arises when the coercive power of the state emerges from a free and equal process of public justification. As Mansbridge points out, such an ideal of legitimacy is likely to be beyond full realization. Yet legitimacy need not be an on/off concept. Instead, we can think of it as existing on a spectrum.[21] Democratic procedures may rarely reach full legitimacy, but some come closer than others.

Even if the full realization of legitimacy remains elusive, deliberation plays a unique role in moving democratic procedures closer to this end. First, unlike other, more aggregative, procedures, deliberation enables all citizens to have their perspectives considered seriously in the decision-making process. In ideal deliberations, all citizens, not simply those in the numerical majority, have their interests considered. As Christopher Eisgruber points out, other decision-making procedures, such as pure majoritarianism, fail to meet the demands of "impartiality" implicit in the ideal of democracy as rule of the people. "To qualify as democratic," he explains, "a government must respond to the interests and opinions of all the people, rather than merely serving the majority, or some other fraction of the people."[22] Eisgruber's idea of impartiality might be better named inclusiveness. It is the idea that the interests of "all the people" should be considered and that this is achieved only when decision-making accounts for each person's voice, not simply the voice of the majority.

While pure majoritarianism fails to achieve inclusiveness, the public deliberation of citizens on roughly equal terms comes closer to realizing this ideal. As Bernard Manin points out, even when aggregative majority rule is employed, it is deliberation that plays the vital role in conferring legitimacy:

> Because it [the decision] comes at the close of a deliberative process in which everyone was able to take part, choose among several solutions, and remain free to approve or refuse the conclusions developed from the argument, the result carries legitimacy. The decision results from a process in which the mi-

nority point of view was also taken into consideration. Although the decision does not conform to all points of view, it is the result of the confrontation between them.[23]

Like Eisgruber, Manin argues that the primary virtue of deliberation is that it enables all citizens to have their interests considered during decision making. Not all citizens can be assured their views will prevail. But even for the losers, deliberation provides a more compelling reason to accept the final decision—namely, that (1) the decision emerged from the confrontation of all interests, not just those of the numerical majority; and (2) the winning side was forced to justify its position using moral reasons and arguments.

In addition to this procedural claim, the legitimacy-conferring value of deliberation also flows from a second, more substantive, claim that the reasons and arguments used in deliberation should be accessible to all citizens. John Rawls's conception of public reason is the most prominent articulation of this argument. As noted in the next section, Rawls claims that legitimacy arises from deliberations where citizens and lawmakers use the right kinds of reasons—publicly accessible reasons—that others can reasonably be expected to endorse.[24] On this view, the essence of legitimacy goes beyond the equal consideration of interests to an adherence to the norm of public reason. Political legitimacy requires that citizens engage each other on a shared basis that all could reasonably accept. This means that in justifying coercive state policies such as mandatory income taxes or securities regulations, lawmakers must not invoke esoteric economic principles or the word of God. Instead, they must appeal to reasons that all citizens could endorse—only then can the coercive power of the state be deemed legitimate.

The second justification for deliberation—*the epistemic argument*—emphasizes the positive effects of deliberation on collective knowledge. Since ancient Greek reflections on democracy, theorists have noted the epistemic benefits of collective reasoning: the fact that deliberation can correct mistakes in our collective understanding and improve the quality of information in the public marketplace of ideas. For instance, Aristotle views the benefits of collective wisdom through the metaphor of a potluck dinner: "The many, of whom none is individually an excellent man, nevertheless can when joined together be better—not as individuals but all together—than those [who are best], just as dinners contributed [by many] can be better than those equipped from a single expenditure."[25] When combined, Aristotle thinks, the intelligence of the many can surpass the intelligence of the gifted few.[26]

Modern deliberative democrats make this epistemic claim for deliberation on two levels. On the one side, deliberation has important benefits at the individual level. "Through the give and take of argument," explain Gutmann and Thompson, "participants can learn from each other, come to recognize their individual and collective misapprehensions, and develop new views and policies that can more successfully withstand critical scrutiny."[27] By exposing citizens to the interests of others, deliberation clarifies the interests and values at stake for various parties, while also helping transform and shift poorly informed preferences and correct epistemic errors. On the other side, deliberation corrects errors and improves the marketplace of ideas at the social level. When contestation and debate flourish, socially held beliefs are constantly reexamined, ineffective beliefs are uncovered, and new and better arguments often rise to the surface.[28] As noted in chapter 4, a growing empirical literature on group behavior indicates that these epistemic benefits of deliberation are largely contextual—that they fail to arise in polarized environments where only one side of the argument is expressed.[29]

Deliberative Tools for Understanding Political Rhetoric

Do deliberative theories of democracy give us the tools for understanding when rhetoric enhances and when it diminishes democracy? I address this question by considering two prominent deliberative theories: Rawls's *public reason* and Habermas's *communicative action*. Neither Rawls nor Habermas directly address this question, but their accounts provide important conceptual tools that set the stage for a more complete account of the moral dimension of rhetoric in chapter 2.

Rawls's Public Reason

Rawls's conception of public reason stipulates that political power is legitimate when justified by reasons that all citizens could reasonably accept. This conception employs "the liberal principle of legitimacy"—namely that, "our exercise of political power is proper and hence justifiable only when it is exercised in accordance with a constitution the essentials of which all citizens may reasonably be expected to endorse in the light of principles and ideals acceptable to them as reasonable and rational."[30] Applied to political discourse, this principle demands that basic laws and institutions be justified in terms "that others can reasonably be expected to endorse."[31] While this insight is not unique to Rawls,[32] his concept of public reason is the most prominent and robust articulation of this ideal.

Rawls tells us that modern conditions of pluralism create the need for some idea of public reason. Since modern states consist of citizens with diverse religious and philosophical conceptions of the good, no single com-prehensive doctrine can serve as the shared basis for justifying laws and institutions.[33] In conditions of reasonable pluralism, grounding laws and institutions on claims about the will of the Christian God would unfairly exclude many citizens from full membership in the political community. For those who believed in a different God or no God at all, the state would not be justified on grounds they could endorse. To treat all citizens with equal respect and accommodate reasonable pluralism, Rawls insists that we should justify matters of basic justice on terms that all citizens can accept.

Public reason does not sanction censorship or the systematic exclusion of religious citizens from public political debates. As Stephen Macedo explains,

> No liberal advocates censoring religious speech: no liberal seeks to deny First Amendment protection to those who advocate theocracy, or to those who would use the criminal law to punish heresy or apostasy. The liberal claim is that it is wrong to seek to coerce people on grounds that they cannot share without converting to one's faith.[34]

So public reason seeks not to banish religious citizens from modern politics but to encourage them to offer a public rationale for claims about basic justice.

Rawls's conception of public reason has inspired an array of criticism.[35] Jeffrey Stout, for example, worries that limiting public discussions erodes the honesty, passion, and zeal of democratic life. Stout argues against public reason and for a more unconstrained public political forum—one that he claims will allow for richer, more honest, debate. Instead of asking people of faith to rely upon public reasons, Stout envisions a political discourse that embraces and encourages religious arguments. Welcoming religious speech may bring "into reflective expression commitments that would otherwise remain implicit in the lives of the religious communities."[36]

This debate over public reason is important, but I am interested pri-marily in whether public reason helps explain when political rhetoric enhances or diminishes democracy. Public reason illuminates an impor-tant form of illegitimate and democracy-diminishing political rhetoric. Rawls's account makes a compelling case that in certain deliberative cir-cumstances—in the "public political forum"[37]—candidates, lawmakers, or judges using non-public rhetoric based on comprehensive doctrines erode the legitimacy of the democratic process. Such rhetoric fails to satisfy the demands of mutual respect and reciprocity that Rawls sees as implicit in the idea of democracy.

Rawls's account also implicitly addresses the question of when political speech turns manipulative. In "The Idea of Public Reason Revisited," Rawls's final articulation of public reason, he mentions the concept of manipulation several times.[38] Rawls most often cites manipulation as arising when political speech fails to adhere to the guiding principle behind public reason, what he calls the *criterion of reciprocity*. According to this criterion, citizens should address others as free and equal citizens using reasons that others could accept. As Rawls puts it,

> The criterion of reciprocity requires that when those terms are proposed as the most reasonable terms of fair cooperation, those proposing them must also think it at least reasonable for others to accept them, as free and equal citizens, and not as dominated or manipulated, or under the pressure of inferior political or social position.[39]

This criterion stipulates that speakers must address others in a particular way. The reasons and arguments they offer should not be oriented toward manipulating listeners or exploiting their weaknesses. Rather, speakers must exchange reasons with an implicit commitment to an egalitarian power relation and to engaging in the sincere exchange of reasons. This means that the argument for public reason is most explicit in discouraging the public expression of arguments based on comprehensive doctrines; it also discourages manipulative speech. For Rawls, both forms of speech fail to meet the demand of civic friendship because they do not treat others as free, equal, and reasonable.

Rawls also outlines a second, more specific, form of manipulation, which arises when speakers veil comprehensive doctrines beneath the façade of public reason. One essential feature of public reason is what Rawls calls the "completeness requirement." This requirement stipulates that each political conception "should express principles, standards, and ideals, along with guidelines of inquiry, such that the values specified by it can be suitably ordered or otherwise united so that those values alone give a reasonable answer to all, or nearly all, questions involving constitutional essentials and matters of basic justice."[40] Put differently, the reasons speakers express must arise from a free-standing political conception of justice, with an ordering of values based on the political conception itself, not on esoteric moral or religious comprehensive doctrines.

Rawls's completeness requirement aims to prevent a particular form of manipulation—namely, speakers masking comprehensive views with public reasons. As he puts it, this requirement stipulates that "public values

. . . are not puppets manipulated from behind the scenes by comprehensive doctrines."[41] Instead, public reasons must arise from public political values standing free from comprehensive doctrines. "What we cannot do in public reason," he declares, "is to proceed directly from our comprehensive doctrine, or a part thereof, to one or several political principles and values, and the particular institutions they support."[42]

Rawls's conception of public reason takes an important first step toward addressing questions of the moral dimensions of political rhetoric. He correctly insists that in the public political forum, candidates, lawmakers, and judges ought to base their support for laws and institutions on reasons that all citizens could accept. He also explores two forms of manipulative speech that arise in public political debates. Yet Rawls's moral framework provides only a thin and partial account of the strategic and manipulative side of political rhetoric. By addressing only the relation of manipulation to comprehensive doctrines, he leaves unexplored the possible distinction between manipulative and strategic speech as well as the risks that manipulation poses to democracy. To address these questions, we must turn from Rawls to Habermas's theory of communicative action.

Habermas's Communicative Action

While Rawls's theory lacks a robust analysis of strategic and manipulative speech, Habermas's theory of communicative action offers a three-fold distinction between various ideal speech types: communicative, open strategic, and manipulative speech acts. These distinctions, although incomplete in some respects, play a vital role in setting up my constructive theory of when political rhetoric enhances or diminishes democracy.

Think of Habermas's overarching theoretical project in *The Theory of Communicative Action* as an attempt to redescribe modern rationality in a social or interactive vocabulary. His theory of communicative action emerges against the backdrop of critiques of modern rationality. Habermas's Frankfurt School predecessors, such as Adorno, Horkheimer, and Heidegger, believed that the instrumental and technical nature of many modern understandings of rationality caused immeasurable social harms. Far from improving the human condition, such rationality trivializes human experience, debases social relations, and leads us to treat fellow humans as mere "resources" for maximizing selfish ambitions.

Habermas's project maintains this suspicion of modern rationality as "instrumental mastery." Yet he moves beyond mere critique by proposing a more socially embedded and constructive account of rationality called "communicative action."[43] On this view, rationality is no longer constituted solely

by the means/end calculations of agents seeking to maximize self-serving outcomes. Though there is still room for instrumental rationality in Habermas's
account, his view of rationality extends to the social practices of communication. To be rational comes to mean more than maximizing goods. It becomes
tightly intertwined with the norms of conversation, debate, and deliberation.

Habermas illuminates this socially informed account of rationality by
juxtaposing strategic and communicative action. The orientation of speech
distinguishes these two forms of action. He defines strategic action as action
that "*rests content* with an explication of the features of action oriented directly to success."[44] The purely strategic actor "is oriented to his own success
and behaves cooperatively only to the degree that this fits with his egocentric calculus of utility."[45] This form of action corresponds to the instrumental conception of rationality so often assailed by Frankfurt School critics.
Strategic action is akin to an "egocentric" form of utility maximization: a
purely instrumental attempt to secure self-serving ends. Another distinctive
feature of strategic action is that it seeks to influence others through external considerations that have little to do with the argument. When acting
strategically, explains Simone Chambers, "participants often attempt to sway
each other by introducing influences unrelated to the merits of an argument,
for example, threats, bribes, or coercion."[46] Rational strategic actors do not
engage in argument for the sake of communication and understanding but to
ensure the success of their own projects and ends.

Communicative action, by contrast, represents Habermas's attempt to
craft an account of rationality that arises from the norms of communication.
Communicative action is oriented toward understanding. It arises "whenever
the actions of the agents involved are coordinated not through egocentric
calculations but through acts of reaching understanding."[47] On this model, it
is not enough to simply seek influence. We must also open ourselves to the
possibility that others could influence us. Unlike strategic action, communicative action "excludes all force . . . except for the force of the better argument."[48] Communicative action does not involve bribes or manipulation, but
only reasons and concerns that directly affect the argument.

In communicative action, the relation between speaker and listener has
a reciprocal, two-way, character.[49] The speaker's words invite the listener to
respond in a dialogue that aspires to understanding and agreement. Strategic
action, on the other hand, arises when the listener is spoken *to* rather than
spoken *with*. In this way, strategic action is uncommunicative; it encourages
practices that seek simply to influence the actions of others, not to achieve
mutual understanding.

Behind the concepts of communicative and strategic action is a basic claim about the pluralism of rationality: rationality is a three-dimensional idea. In contrast to most modern accounts of rationality, where rational action is akin to utility maximization, Habermas argues that there is no single form of *rationality*, but rather three interconnected *rationalities* whose combination determines whether a particular action is strategic or communicative.

For Habermas, rationality is a world-dependent phenomenon; its content hangs on the three "modes of being" that constitute human experience. Inspired by Popper, he argues that three worlds constitute human experience.[50] The first is the objective world, defined as the "correlate of the totality of true propositions." This world is largely asocial, composed of objective concepts, ideas, and abstractions.[51] The second is the social world, which encompasses the intersubjective relations of humans. The third is the subjective world, which consists of individual states and experiences.[52] Unlike Popper, who views the three worlds as part of a larger interconnected world, Habermas sees these worlds as distinct (see figure 1.1).[53]

Objective World   Social World   Subjective World

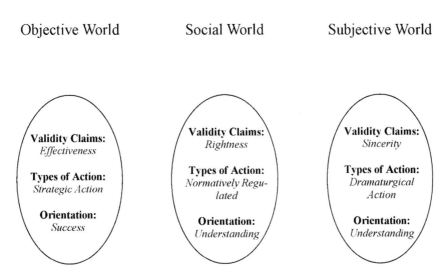

Validity Claims: **Validity Claims:**   **Validity Claims:**
Effectiveness   *Rightness*   *Sincerity*

Types of Action: **Types of Action:**   **Types of Action:**
Strategic Action   *Normatively Regu-*   *Dramaturgical*
                             lated   *Action*

Orientation: **Orientation:**   **Orientation:**
Success   *Understanding*   *Understanding*

Figure 1.1. This figure is a modified version of Habermas's diagram illustrating the distinctions between the three worlds. The types of actions, validity claims for evaluating actions, and the orientation of actions shift in relation to the world. The objective world is the realm of strategic action, while the other two worlds allow actions to seek understanding. For a more complete representation of these distinctions, see Habermas, *The Theory of Communicative Action*, 329.

Habermas defines a world "as the totality of what is the case; and what is the case can be stated in the form of true propositions."[54] When Habermas says a world counts as the "totality of what is the case," he means that each world constitutes a distinctive "mode of being." Each world has different objects and events, each uses a different language of communication, and, most important, each has its own form of rationality, that is, has its own criteria for evaluating reasons. To call a claim or action rational is, as Chambers suggests, to say "that it could be defended with reasons."[55] So what we call rational depends on the distinctive "validity claims" in each of these worlds. Such validity claims are, in their most basic form, "yes/no" statements about the truth, rightness, or sincerity of particular actions. These claims provide criteria for evaluating rational action and are open to criticism.

In the objective world, validity claims are based on "truth" or "efficacy." They address the question of whether "the statement made is true." In the social world, the criterion for validity claims is "rightness." Such claims evaluate whether actions fit within the intersubjectively negotiated context of interpersonal relations. In the subjective world, the criterion for validity is "sincerity" or "truthfulness." To be rationally valid in this world, the speaker must meet the standards of sincerity—he must mean what he says.[56]

Because each world has its own form of rationality, each has its own distinctive form of rational action. In the objective world—the asocial world of "true propositions"—the primary form of action is what Habermas calls "teleological." Such actions follow a straightforward rationale: "The actor," explains Habermas, "is supposed to choose and calculate means and ends from the standpoint of maximizing utility."[57] In the social world, the primary form of action is "normatively regulated action." This social form of action arises when individuals coordinate their actions through interpersonal communication and orient their actions toward "common values."[58] In the subjective world, the primary mode of action is "dramaturgical action." Dramaturgical action is guided by the desire of participants to put forth a stylized presentation of self before others.[59] There are thus three separate worlds of experience, each with its own rationality and its own modes of action.

How does the distinction between communicative and strategic action map onto this theoretical framework? Habermas urges us to think of strategic action as a *"one-world* concept."[60] Given their lack of interaction and their emphasis on means/end calculations oriented to success, strategic acts in his account occur solely within the objective world of true propositions. This means that strategic actions can be regarded as a subclass of teleological acts: ones in which actors maximize utility by seeking to influence the actions of others. Strategic acts are asocial because they use others as a mere means to success. They occur in an ontological space distinct from the social space where communication and mutual understanding flourish.

The placement of communicative action in this conceptual framework is more complex. Unlike strategic action, which exists within one world, communicative action floats between all three worlds. It is a multi-world concept. In Habermas's words, communicative action "presupposes language as a medium of uncurtailed communication whereby speakers and hearers, out of the context of their preinterpreted lifeworld, refer simultaneously to things in the objective, social, and subjective worlds in order to negotiate common definitions of the situation."[61] So communicative action is neither wholly objective, wholly social, nor wholly subjective. Instead, it embodies a three-dimensional form of rationality where communication is oriented toward a single goal: understanding. This is why Habermas sees strategic action as a derivative of communicative action. Strategic actions correspond to one part of communicative action (the means/end calculations of the objective world), but are also "parasitic" on communicative action because they sit on the periphery of the social and subjective worlds and because they are oriented toward success, not understanding.[62]

Habermas's final move is to suggest that the distinction between communicative and strategic action appears in the structure of speech itself. Following Austin, he argues that there are three primary forms of speech acts: locutionary, illocutionary, and perlocutionary acts. For our purposes, illocutionary and perlocutionary acts are of primary importance, for these two forms indicate moments of strategic and communicative action. Communicative action arises from illocutionary acts. These are acts where the "speaker performs an action in saying something."[63] They are statements of command or confession where the speaker seeks to convey meaning to the listener. Perlocutionary acts, by contrast, signal strategic action. They arise when "the speaker produces an effect upon the hearer. By carrying out a speech act he brings about something in the world."[64]

Whereas communicative speech acts "act in saying something," strategic speech acts "bring about something through acting in saying something."[65] As a result, strategic action is less concerned with the meaning of speech than the intention of the agent. The strategic speaker does not convey meaning to reach an understanding but uses speech only as a tool for achieving success. Habermas argues that this speech act distinction shows that the kind of communicative action that arises from illocutionary acts is the "*original mode* of language use."[66] In other words, conveying meaning to achieve understanding is the inherent end of language. Thus strategic attempts to use language as a tool of influence are "parasitic" on this original mode of language use.

The final step in this analysis is to outline the various forms of strategic action. Habermas sees strategic action as having several distinct forms (see figure 1.2).

As we have seen, strategic action arises when actions are oriented toward success alone rather than understanding. Within this larger umbrella of strategic action lie two subsets: open strategic action and concealed strategic action. Open strategic action occurs when participants in discourse understand

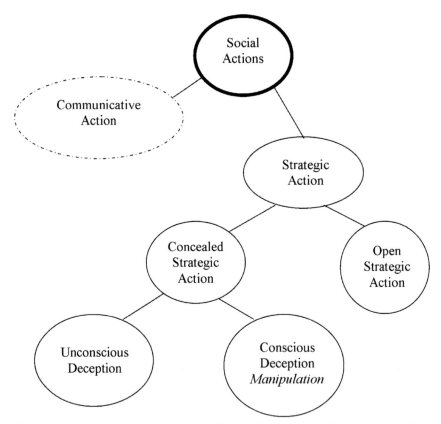

Figure 1.2. This figure reproduces in a slightly altered form Habermas's map of the relations between the many forms of strategic action. Habermas's conception of manipulation demands that the strategic orientation of action be concealed and that the attempt to mask the strategic orientation be a conscious act. For Habermas's chart, see Habermas, *The Theory of Communicative Action*, 333.

that the speaker's actions are oriented toward success, not understanding. It arises when strategic aims are transparent to all parties in the conversation. Concealed strategic action, by contrast, occurs when the speaker's orientation to success is masked by a façade of communicative action. In "these interactions," Habermas remarks, "at least one of the participants is acting strategically, while he deceives other participants regarding the fact that he is *not* satisfying the presuppositions under which illocutionary aims can normally be achieved."[67] When the speaker pretends to be guided by understanding but withholds information, motivations, and interests, his actions take on this more concealed form.

Habermas tells us that this kind of deception is sometimes unconscious: speakers at times unknowingly deceive their audiences about the orientation of their speech. A more insidious form of concealed strategic action, what Habermas calls "conscious deception" or "manipulation," arises when speakers knowingly veil strategic actions behind the façade of an action oriented toward understanding. Habermas explains that an actor is engaged in manipulation when

> he deceives his partner concerning the fact that he is acting strategically—when, for example, he gives the command to attack in order to get his troops to rush into a trap, or when he proposes a bet of $3,000 in order to embarrass others, or when he tells a story late in the evening in order to delay a guest's departure.[68]

So on Habermas's account, manipulation is a particular form of deception. It occurs when speakers seek to deceive listeners as to their orientation of speech—when they cover up the strategic orientation of their actions by pretending to act communicatively.

There is more to Habermas's theory of discourse than these three ideal speech types. In works like *The Structural Transformation of the Public Sphere* and *Between Facts and Norms*, Habermas addresses how communicative action fits within the broader "public sphere," which he describes as "the *social space* generated in communicative action."[69] This more political and contextual account is important and touches on many of the same issues I discuss in chapters 4 and 5. Yet the task of this chapter and the next is to explore the moral qualities of the speech act itself—to outline a three-fold distinction between morally ideal, morally decent, and morally problematic forms of rhetoric. As a result, I have limited this chapter to a focused examination of Habermas's distinctions between communicative and strategic action. These three ideal types of action—communicative, open strategic, and manipulation—set the stage for my constructive account of rhetoric in chapter 2. Here, I maintain the rough framework of this three-part distinction. Yet to understand the moral dimensions of rhetoric more fully, I argue for an alternative interpretation of the three forms of speech and action.

First, I argue for a more expansive and slightly different account of what constitutes each of these three forms of speech. With respect to manipulation, for instance, Habermas tells us that manipulative acts arise from "conscious deception." They result from *intentional* efforts to conceal and confuse others about the orientation of one's actions. "In situations of concealed strategic action," he explains, "at least one of the parties behaves with an orientation to success, but leaves others to believe that all the presuppositions of communicative action are satisfied."[70] So manipulation is a particular form of concealment, arising when the actor's strategic orientation is masked behind a façade of communicative action.

I share Habermas's view that manipulation is a "conscious" form of action and thus distinct from "unconscious deception." Yet I argue that while manipulation includes acts of "deception," it also includes more overtly irrational forms of power. For instance, some speakers may be open about their strategic orientation and thus not engage in any form of deception. If, however, they seek to disrupt others' capacity to choose by eliciting "dark urges" and "extra-rational" impulses, then I shall argue that they are still engaged in manipulation.

Second, I argue for a slightly different set of moral relationships between these three forms of speech. What I call "deliberative persuasion" and "strategic persuasion" map roughly onto Habermas's categories of communicative action and open strategic action. Yet Habermas takes a darker view than I of the moral status of open strategic action.[71] Simone Chambers interprets his view as asserting that communicative action treats listeners as ends, while strategic actions treat them as a mere means.[72] Although Habermas does not use this means/ends language, his descriptions of strategic action have a similarly pejorative bent. In *The Theory of Communicative Action*, Habermas tells us that strategic acts are oriented toward "instrumental mastery,"[73] constitute an impoverished form of communication with "parasitic" effects on communicative action,[74] and operate in an "asocial" manner.[75] In other works, Habermas occasionally hints at a partial endorsement of strategic action, although he never describes such actions as "legitimate."[76] Instead, he appears to accept strategic speech and action as a politically inevitable but somewhat illegitimate form of action.

My conception of strategic persuasion, by contrast, views openly strategic speech as a conditionally acceptable and morally decent part of public political debate. When a speaker engages in open strategic persuasion, listeners have adequate awareness of the speaker's strategic orientation. Understanding that the speaker has this orientation, they can choose whether or not to accept the speaker's persuasive appeals. So while openly strategic speakers aim to win, they do not seek to bypass or control the rational faculties of fellow citizens. In this sense, their listeners are neither instrumentalized nor treated as a mere means.

In what lies ahead, I will outline this alternative account of the three-part distinction between deliberative, strategic, and manipulative rhetoric. Drawing on the conceptual insights of Rawls and Habermas, the next chapter provides a detailed discussion of the moral distinctions between ideal forms of deliberation and more non-ideal forms of strategic and manipulative speech. With this conceptual framework in place, chapter 3 turns to an empirical analysis of three moments when these forms of speech surfaced in the rhetoric of the contemporary Christian right.

Notes

1. John Dewey, *The Public and Its Problems* (Chicago: Gateway Books, 1946), 133.

2. Dewey, *The Public and Its Problems*, 131.

3. Dewey, *The Public and Its Problems*, 137.

4. Dewey's *The Public and Its Problems* was written in reaction to Lippmann's *Public Opinion*. Dewey, *The Public and Its Problems*, 110–42. Dewey also expressed his concerns about Lippmann's view of democracy in "Public Opinion," *New Republic*, December 2, 1924, 52–54.

5. Dewey thinks that such elite theories problematically confuse the ideal of democracy with the kinds of antiquated institutional machinery found in the democracies of ancient Greece. In other words, Dewey worries that such theories reject the traditional ideal of democracy on the grounds that traditional institutional machinery used to realize this ideal breaks down in mass democracy. The Greek assembly and the New England town meeting break down in modern settings. Yet Dewey argues that this focus on the traditional institutional machinery of democracy obscures the *ideal* of democracy. It obscures the possibility of imagining new institutions and practices to achieve the democratic ideal under modern conditions. For a discussion of Dewey's critique of political realists, see Robert B. Westbrook, *John Dewey and American Democracy* (Ithaca, NY: Cornell University Press, 1991), 309.

6. Dewey, *The Public and Its Problems*, 209. For Schumpeter's account of elite democracy, see Joseph A. Schumpeter, *Capitalism, Socialism, and Democracy* (New York: HarperPerennial, 1976).

7. Dewey, *The Public and Its Problems*, 208.

8. For discussions of deliberative democracy, see Benjamin R. Barber, *Strong Democracy* (Berkeley: University of California Press, 2003); Joshua Cohen,

"Deliberation and Democratic Legitimacy," in *Democracy*, ed. David Estlund (New York: Blackwell Publishers, 2002); John Dryzek, *Deliberative Democracy and Beyond* (New York: Oxford University Press, 2002); Jon Elster, "The Market and the Forum: Three Varieties of Political Theory," in *Deliberative Democracy*, ed. James Bohman and William Rehg (Cambridge: MIT Press, 1997); David Estlund, "Beyond Fairness and Deliberation," in *Deliberative Democracy*, ed. James Bohman and William Rehg (Cambridge: MIT Press, 1997); Bruce Fishkin and James S. Ackerman, "Deliberation Day," *Journal of Political Philosophy* 10, no. 2 (2002); Jurgen Habermas, *The Theory of Communicative Action*, trans. Thomas McCarthy (Boston: Beacon Press, 1984); Jurgen Habermas, *Between Facts and Norms*, trans. William Rehg (Cambridge: MIT Press, 1998); Bernard Manin, "On Legitimacy and Political Deliberation," *Political Theory* 15, no. 3 (1987); Jane Mansbridge, *Beyond Adversary Democracy* (Chicago: University of Chicago Press, 1983); Philip Pettit, "Democracy, Electoral and Contestatory," in *Designing Democratic Institutions*, ed. Ian Shapiro and Stephen Macedo (New York: NYU Press, 2000); John Rawls, *Political Liberalism* (New York: Columbia University Press, 1993); John Rawls, "The Idea of Public Reason Revisited," in *The Law of Peoples with "The Idea of Public Reason Revisited"* (Cambridge: Harvard University Press, 1999); Cass Sunstein, "Beyond the Republican Revival," *Yale Law Journal* 97, no. 8 (1988); Amy Gutmann and Dennis Thompson, *Democracy and Disagreement* (Cambridge: Belknap Press, 1996). For critical accounts of deliberative democracy, see Bryan Garsten, *Saving Persuasion* (Cambridge: Harvard University Press, 2006); Lynn M. Sanders, "Against Deliberation," *Political Theory* 25, no. 3 (1997); Ian Shapiro, *The State of Democratic Theory* (Princeton: Princeton University Press, 2003); Michael Walzer, "Deliberation and What Else?" in *Deliberative Politics*, ed. Stephen Macedo (New York: Oxford University Press, 1999).

9. Cohen, "Deliberation and Democratic Legitimacy," 87.

10. Amy Gutmann and Dennis Thompson, *Why Deliberative Democracy?* (Princeton: Princeton University Press, 2004), 3.

11. Gutmann and Thompson, *Why Deliberative Democracy?*, 3–7.

12. Gutmann and Thompson, *Why Deliberative Democracy?*, 4.

13. This claim is similar to Rawls's conception of public reason, see Rawls, *Political Liberalism*; Rawls, "The Idea of Public Reason Revisited."

14. Gutmann and Thompson, *Why Deliberative Democracy?*, 4.

15. Gutmann and Thompson, *Why Deliberative Democracy?*, 5.

16. Gutmann and Thompson, *Why Deliberative Democracy?*, 6.

17. Aristotle, *The Politics*, trans. Carnes Lord (Chicago: University of Chicago Press, 1984), 37.

18. John Stuart Mill, "On Representative Government," in *John Stuart Mill On Liberty and Other Essays* (New York: Oxford University Press, 1998), 255.

19. For an overview of authority and legitimacy, see Tom Christiano, "Authority," *Stanford Encyclopedia of Philosophy*, 2004.

20. Robert Nozick, "Coercion," in *Philosophy, Science, and Method*, ed. Sidney Morgenbesser, Patrick Suppes, and Morton White (New York: St. Martin's Press, 1969).

21. Jane Mansbridge, "Deliberative Neo-Pluralism," unpublished manuscript (2007). Jane Mansbridge, "Using Power/Fighting Power: The Polity," in *Democracy and Difference*, ed. Seyla Benhabib (Princeton: Princeton University Press, 1996).

22. Christopher Eisgruber, *Constitutional Self-Government* (Cambridge: Harvard University Press, 2001), 19.

23. Manin, "On Legitimacy and Political Deliberation," 359.

24. Rawls, "The Idea of Public Reason Revisited."

25. Aristotle's argument is not limited to deliberation, but presents a claim similar to those of modern epistemic theories of deliberation. See Aristotle, *The Politics*, 101, 1281b1.

26. A different historical argument for the proposition that collective wisdom increases along with the size of the collectivity arises from Condorcet's Jury Theorem. Condorcet argues that majority rule tends to track the truth when the following conditions hold: (1) the voters' choice of propositions is better than random, (2) their votes are independent of one another, and (3) there are "true" propositions in political contexts. Condorcet's claim is that under these conditions as the number of voters increases, the probability of the majority arriving at the right decision increases. For a defense of Condorcet's Jury Theorem against its critics and a review of other arguments for collective wisdom, see Helene Landemore, *Democratic Reason*, PhD thesis, Harvard University, 2008.

27. Gutmann and Thompson, *Why Deliberative Democracy?* 12. See also Mansbridge, "Using Power/Fighting Power," 47; Manin, "On Legitimacy and Political Deliberation."

28. Gutmann and Thompson, *Democracy and Disagreement*, 43.

29. For more on the effect of context on epistemic outcomes of deliberation, see Allen Buchanan, "Political Liberalism and Social Epistemology," *Philosophy and Public Affairs* 32, no. 2 (2004); David Estlund, "Beyond Fairness and Deliberation," in *Deliberative Democracy*, ed. James Bohman and William Rehg (Cambridge: MIT Press, 1997); Tali Mendelberg, "The Deliberative Citizen: Theory and Evidence," in *Political Decision Making, Deliberation and Participation* (New York: Elsevier Science, 2002); Diana Mutz, *Hearing the Other Side* (New York: Cambridge University Press, 2006); Cass Sunstein, "Deliberative Trouble? Why Groups Go to Extremes," *Yale Law Journal* 110, no. 1 (2000); and Cass Sunstein, *Infotopia* (New York: Oxford University Press, 2006).

30. For Rawls's early articulation of public reason, see Rawls, *Political Liberalism*, 217. For his later articulation of public reason, see Rawls, "The Idea of Public Reason Revisited." For an overview of public reason spanning early and later Rawls, see Charles Larmore, "Public Reason," in *The Cambridge Companion to Rawls*, ed. Samuel Freeman (New York: Cambridge University Press, 2003), 368–93.

31. Rawls, *Political Liberalism*, 226.

32. See, for example, Gutmann and Thompson's principle of "reciprocity" in Gutmann and Thompson, *Democracy and Disagreement*, 55. For slightly different versions of public reason, see Charles Larmore, *Patterns of Moral Complexity* (Cambridge:

Cambridge University Press, 1987); Robert Audi, *Religious Commitment and Secular Reason* (Cambridge: Cambridge University Press, 2001); Jurgen Habermas, "Religion in the Public Sphere," *European Journal of Philosophy* 14, no. 1 (2006).

33. It is important to emphasize that the constraints of public reason do not single out religious doctrines, but apply to all religious, moral, and ethical "comprehensive doctrines." See Samuel Freeman, "Deliberative Democracy: A Sympathetic Comment," *Philosophy and Public Affairs* 29, no. 4 (2000): 396–411.

34. Macedo makes this claim in the context of his discussion of the transformative effects of liberal institutions. See Stephen Macedo, "Transformative Constitutionalism and the Case of Religion: Defending the Moderate Hegemony of Liberalism," in *Constitutional Politics: Essays on Constitution Making, Maintenance, and Change*, ed. Sortirios A. Barber and Robert P. George (Princeton: Princeton University Press, 2001), 182.

35. For criticisms of Rawls's conception of public reason, see Nicholas Wolterstorff, *Religion in the Public Square* (New York: Rowman & Littlefield, 1997); Jeffrey Stout, *Democracy and Tradition* (Princeton: Princeton University Press, 2004); Kent Greenawalt, *Private Consciences and Public Reasons* (New York: Oxford University Press, 1995).

36. Stout, *Democracy and Tradition*, 112. Rogers Smith offers a similar argument against "public reason," stressing the ideal of engaging seriously with the most deeply held political convictions of religious citizens. See Rogers Smith, *Stories of Peoplehood* (New York: Cambridge University Press, 2003), 179–86.

37. As Rawls defines it, the public political forum consists of three parts: "the discourse of judges in their decisions, and especially of the judges of a supreme court; the discourse of government officials, especially chief executives and legislators; and finally, the discourse of candidates for public office and their campaign managers, especially in their public oratory, party platforms, and political statements." Rawls, "The Idea of Public Reason Revisited," 133–34.

38. For his two primary passages on the idea of manipulation, see Rawls, "The Idea of Public Reason Revisited," 137, 145.

39. Rawls, "The Idea of Public Reason Revisited," 137.

40. Rawls, "The Idea of Public Reason Revisited," 145.

41. Rawls, "The Idea of Public Reason Revisited," 145.

42. Rawls, "The Idea of Public Reason Revisited," 146.

43. Habermas, *The Theory of Communicative Action*, 11.

44. Habermas, *The Theory of Communicative Action*, 101.

45. Habermas, *The Theory of Communicative Action*, 88.

46. For a detailed explanation of Habermas's conception of rationality, see Simone Chambers, *Reasonable Democracy* (Ithaca, NY: Cornell University Press, 1996), 9.

47. Habermas, *The Theory of Communicative Action*, 286.

48. Habermas, *The Theory of Communicative Action*, 25.

49. For more on this point, see Frederick A. Olafson, "Habermas as a Philosopher," *Ethics* 100, no. 3 (1990).

50. Karl Popper, *Objective Knowledge* (New York: Oxford University Press, 1972).

51. Habermas, *The Theory of Communicative Action*, 84.

52. I am indebted to Schiemann for the precise terminology in these definitions of the three worlds. See John W. Schiemann, "Meeting Halfway between Rochester and Frankfurt," *American Journal of Political Science* 44, no. 1 (2000): 84.

53. Habermas, *The Theory of Communicative Action*, 84.

54. Habermas, *The Theory of Communicative Action*, 77.

55. Chambers, *Reasonable Democracy*, 90.

56. Habermas, *The Theory of Communicative Action*, 99.

57. Habermas, *The Theory of Communicative Action*, 85.

58. Habermas, *The Theory of Communicative Action*.

59. Habermas, *The Theory of Communicative Action*, 86.

60. Habermas, *The Theory of Communicative Action*, 88.

61. Habermas, *The Theory of Communicative Action*, 95.

62. Habermas, *The Theory of Communicative Action*, 288.

63. Habermas, *The Theory of Communicative Action*, 289.

64. Habermas, *The Theory of Communicative Action*.

65. Habermas, *The Theory of Communicative Action*.

66. Habermas, *The Theory of Communicative Action*, 288.

67. Habermas, *The Theory of Communicative Action*, 294.

68. Habermas, *The Theory of Communicative Action*.

69. Habermas, *Between Facts and Norms*, 360. Jurgen Habermas, *The Structural Transformation of the Public Sphere* (Cambridge: MIT Press, 1991). A full account of Habermas's vast theory of discourse is beyond the scope of this chapter. This chapter also does not touch upon his principles of discourse ethics as articulated in *Moral Consciousness and Communicative Action* and *Justification and Application*. Jurgen Habermas, *Moral Consciousness and Communicative Action*, trans. Christian Lenhardt and Shierry Weber Nicholsen (Cambridge: Polity Press, 1990); Jurgen Habermas, *Justification and Application*, trans. Ciaran Cronin (Cambridge: Polity Press, 1993).

70. Habermas, *The Theory of Communicative Action*, 332.

71. Olafson, "Habermas as a Philosopher."

72. Simone Chambers, "Discourse and Democratic Practices," in *The Cambridge Companion to Habermas*, ed. Stephen K. White (New York: Cambridge University Press, 1995), 238.

73. Habermas, *The Theory of Communicative Action*, 11.

74. Habermas, *The Theory of Communicative Action*, 288.

75. For Habermas, this form of influence is "objective" and "asocial" because it operates solely within the instrumental or "objective" world. Unlike communicative action, strategic action does not occur in the "subjective" or the "social" world. Habermas, *The Theory of Communicative Action*, 329.

76. Jane Mansbridge points out that in a 1976 article on Hannah Arendt, Habermas "lightly" criticized her for failing to account for strategic action. As Habermas puts it, "We cannot exclude the element of strategic action from the concept of the political." Jurgen Habermas, "Hannah Arendt: On the Concept of Power," in *Philosophical-Political Profiles*, ed. Jurgen Habermas (Cambridge: MIT Press, 1985), 183. For Mansbridge's discussion, see Mansbridge, "Using Power/Fighting Power."

PART II

THE MORAL QUALITIES
OF RHETORICAL SPEECH

CHAPTER TWO

~

When Rhetoric Turns Manipulative

Disentangling Persuasion and Manipulation

For Rawls and Habermas, manipulation is an important and yet largely unexplored concept. Both regard manipulation as a dangerous deliberative vice—as the antithesis of public reason and communicative action. While important, the idea of manipulation sits at the periphery of each of these theories. By focusing primarily on ideal forms of public reason and communicative action, Rawls and Habermas overlook many of the conceptual complexities of manipulation and other strategic forms of speech.

This chapter seeks to bring manipulation out from underneath the shadows of ideal theory. Using Habermas's three-part distinction as a jumping-off point, I outline a conceptual distinction between manipulation and persuasion. This distinction differentiates between rhetoric that undermines and rhetoric that promotes individual autonomy and democratic self-rule. On my account of this distinction, manipulation works either covertly or overtly. It arises when (1) agent A uses hidden or irrational force to affect agent B's choices, and (2) agent A acts intentionally. Among its many varieties, I outline three primary ways in which both overtly and covertly manipulative speech arises: lying, concealment, and distraction.

Persuasion, by contrast, respects the choices of others and takes two forms. *Deliberative persuasion* arises when rhetoric is used openly to induce agreement with an orientation toward mutual understanding, while *strategic persuasion* arises when agreement is induced openly with an orientation toward winning. While persuasion respects individual autonomy and democratic legitimacy, manipulation threatens these values. Moreover, the dangers of manipulative speech intensify in the presence of two contextual conditions: invisibility and asymmetrical relations of power. Given these dangers, I shall argue that manipulation ought to be viewed with a presumption of immorality and subject to robust public contestation.

Conceptual Limits

My account of persuasion and manipulation has important limits. It will not attempt to reveal the essence of these concepts. Instead, I take a more Wittgensteinian approach. On this view, the meaning of concepts arises not from essences but from the social practices of everyday life. The task of understanding concepts like manipulation becomes a task of clustering similarities and "family resemblances" that arise in practical occurrences of the phenomena to which ordinary speakers give that name.[1] Wittgenstein claims that we are unlikely to find a single common thread uniting all such cases.[2] Yet we can examine the "complicated network of similarities overlapping and crisscrossing" to develop rough conceptions based on "family resemblance."[3]

In this chapter, I aim to examine the "family resemblances" that arise in ordinary speech to create analytic categories that enhance our understanding of persuasive and manipulative rhetoric. In this sense, I aim not to provide a definitive account of the ordinary language usage of persuasion and manipulation but to offer conceptual distinctions that will be analytically useful in enhancing our understanding of politics.[4]

I should also note that the three primary categories I outline—deliberative persuasion, strategic persuasion, and manipulation—should be regarded as abstract "ideal types."[5] I do not claim that all real-world political rhetoric fits neatly into these three conceptual boxes. Rather, these categories illuminate the different moral qualities of purely deliberative, purely strategic, and purely manipulative speech. In practice, each act of political rhetoric will fall somewhere along the spectrum from purely deliberative to purely manipulative speech.

Toward a Conception of Manipulation

What is the nature of manipulative rhetoric? One response argues that persuasion offers listeners the choice as to whether or not to be influenced, whereas manipulation effectively coerces them. As Bryan Garsten puts it, "The speaker who manipulates his audience so as to bring them to a belief or action without their consent, as Kant thought orators moved men 'like machines,' has not persuaded but coerced them."[6]

Manipulation does indeed bring actors "to a belief or action without their consent." Yet this response conflates manipulation and coercion. As Nozick reminds us, the essential feature of coercion is that it operates as a known threat.[7] Coercion arises when A "threatens to do something" if B does not comply with A's desires and B knows about this threat.[8] Thus transparency and the use of explicitly communicated threats are central features of coercion. If someone jumps out of a dark alley and shouts, "Give me your money or I'll kill you!" and you produce the money, then you have been coerced.

Manipulation alters the beliefs, actions, and choices of others in a different way. Consider an example. Suppose that I try to manipulate you to vote Democratic. Rather than influencing you by presenting arguments, I affect your choices and actions by working behind the scenes to restructure your informational environment. Imagine that you are a newcomer to the details of party politics but a fervent opponent of abortion. If I can for a short time shield you from learning that most Democrats support abortion rights, I may be able to get you to vote Democratic at least once. Without telling you, I filter the political information you receive. I provide selected news and information, change the subject when the issue of abortion arises, and tell your colleagues and friends to do the same.[9] In this case, I have interfered with your choice of candidates using covert tactics that you do not fully understand. This is a paradigm case of manipulation.

A combination of two conditions distinguishes manipulation. The first stipulates that in manipulation, A uses hidden or irrational force to affect B's choices. This condition specifies two of manipulation's essential features. First, it stipulates that manipulation is a form of force. Unlike other forms of power, which offer other agents a choice between compliance and noncompliance, the force in manipulation diminishes the capacity of others to comply. Like other forms of force, manipulation changes others' actions, beliefs, or choices, whether or not they choose to comply. In Bachrach and Baratz's words, when forced, "the intended victim is stripped of the choice between compliance and noncompliance."[10] In the Democratic voting example, when I get you to vote Democratic by depriving you of information, I take away your choice as to whether to comply with my wishes. Instead, I, the manipulator, choose for you. I never threaten you with sanctions or deprivations. I simply change your actions invisibly, without your knowledge, choice, or consent.

In contrast to Bachrach and Baratz, I understand the kind of force used in manipulation as a form of power. On their view, power arises only when (1) A and B have conflicting interests, (b) B complies with A's wishes, and (c) "B does so because he is fearful that A will deprive him of a value or values which he regards more highly than those which would have been achieved by noncompliance."[11] According to this conception, power is limited to coercion—to actions where agents use explicit threats to affect the choices of others.

Following Steven Lukes, I think of power more expansively. As Lukes puts it, the central idea of power is that "A in some way affects B . . . in a non-trivial or significant manner."[12] Manipulation satisfies this broader criterion, for it arises in situations where A and B have a conflict of interest, latent or otherwise, and A uses an indirect form of force to change B's choices, beliefs, or actions. On Lukes's more expansive concept of power, manipulation is indeed a form of power that affects others using hidden or irrational force. As he argues, "*Manipulation* is . . . an 'aspect' or sub-concept of *force* (and distinct from coercion, power, influence, and authority), since here 'compliance is forthcoming in the absence of recognition on the complier's part either of the source or the exact nature of the demand upon him.'"[13]

This first condition also stipulates a second essential feature of manipulation. It asserts that manipulation is a particular kind of force—one exercised in hidden or irrational ways. While I define manipulation as a form of force, it is important to point out that many other forms of force operate in non-manipulative ways. For instance, if I get you to vote Democratic by carrying you over my shoulder to the voting booth, selecting the Democratic candidate, wrapping your hand around the voting lever, and pulling your arm down, I have forced but not manipulated you to vote Democratic.

What makes the form of force used in manipulation distinctive is that it is either hidden or irrational. Consider first manipulation based on hidden force. *Covert manipulation* occurs when A affects B's choices using hidden forms of force. In such instances, the victim of manipulation does not fully understand the nature of the manipulator's wishes. As Alan Ware puts it, in such cases, "B either has no knowledge of, or does not understand, the ways in which A affects his choices."[14] Most forms of manipulation consist of such hidden forms of force. In fact, many theoretical accounts limit manipulation solely to such hidden or invisible actions.[15]

Now consider manipulation based on overtly irrational force. *Overt manipulation* arises when agents openly interfere with the rational capacities of others by exploiting the victim's irrational tendencies. As Gutmann and Thompson point out, "Not all manipulation is deceptive. A politician can manipulate potential supporters by openly exploiting their weaknesses."[16] As I will discuss later on, not all appeals to emotion or other non-rational considerations constitute an irrational form of force. Far from exerting irrational force on the choices of others, many appeals to emotion serve as a pointer to reason. They encourage, rather than diminish, the capacity of other agents to weigh the costs and benefits involved in choosing between various options. When, however, emotional appeals overwhelm or bypass the listener's capacity to choose, they exert a manipulative form of irrational force. Such appeals overwhelm and distract others in ways that disrupt their capacity to choose freely.

To illuminate this possibility, consider a variant on the Democratic voting example. This time imagine that I use a variation on Lyndon Johnson's 1964 "daisy commercial" to induce you to vote Democratic. I show you the image of an innocent little girl counting daisies. Next, you hear the menacing voice of a military commander counting down to a nuclear explosion. As the countdown reaches zero, you see the graphic imagery of a mushroom cloud. Next, you hear the chilling voice-over: "These are the stakes. We must either love each other or we must die. Vote for the Democrats on November 3rd. The stakes are too high for you to stay home."[17] My intent here is to use fear to overwhelm your rational capacities—to get you to vote Democratic on the basis of the irrational thought that you might die if you vote Republican. If my efforts are successful, if my appeals to fear significantly distort your capacity to choose, I will have overtly manipulated you.

The second condition stipulates that in every instance of what I call manipulation, A's use of hidden or irrational force is intentional. The absence of such intention changes the moral quality of actions. Returning to the first example, suppose that I keep you from knowing the Democrats' position on abortion simply because the issue makes me feel uncomfortable and, as a result, I change the subject whenever it comes up in conversation. The effects might be the same. You might still end up voting for Democrats on the basis of incomplete information. Nevertheless, under the conception I propose, we would not say I manipulated you. Manipulation requires intent. It demands that interference in the choices of others be intentional.[18]

In addition to these two conditions, manipulation shares with coercion and persuasion the requirement that B's actions or beliefs change to meet A's wishes. A citizen has not been *persuaded* unless the speaker convinces that citizen to change his or her mind. Similarly, a citizen has not been *manipulated* unless the speaker's covert tactics or appeals to irrational impulses successfully override the citizen's rational capacity to choose. This prerequisite specifies that changing B's beliefs or actions is not enough. To persuade, coerce, or manipulate, A must induce a change in B that aligns with the change A intended to induce. In the Democratic voting example, I only manipulate you if I get you to vote Democratic. If my efforts to change your actions result in your voting for the Communist Party, I have not manipulated you.

Three Forms of Manipulation

To understand how manipulation arises, we must also examine the specific forms it takes in political discussions. Of these, I outline three varieties. *Lying* and *concealment* represent manipulation's invisible forms. *Distraction* is manipulation's most ambidextrous form; it can exercise force covertly or overtly. For each form of manipulation, I provide a political example. These examples are not meant to provide a comprehensive empirical case for manipulation but only to illuminate the distinctive qualities of the three forms.

The first form of manipulation is lying. When speakers lie, they affect the choices of others by intentionally disseminating information they know to be false. Lies enable manipulators to surreptitiously reshape the beliefs, actions, and choices of others. As Sissela Bok points out, by distracting agents or affecting their assessments of certainty, lies interfere with their capacity to choose.[19] If one of your objectives were to run a marathon and I tell you that long-distance running has been found to cause cancer, I have covertly altered the nature of your choice to run the marathon.

One of the most famous recent political lies occurred in January 1998. When confronted with allegations that he had an affair with former White House intern Monica Lewinsky, President Clinton insisted, "I did not have sexual relations with Monica Lewinsky. I have never had an affair with her." Four days later, Clinton declared, "There is not a sexual relationship, an improper sexual relationship, or any other kind of improper relationship."[20]

This case illuminates the complexities in identifying a lie. It appears that in Clinton's mind, he did not have "sexual relations with Monica Lewinsky" because he never had sexual intercourse with her. In this sense, Clinton's initial statement may not have been a lie, for he may have actually believed that he never had "sexual relations." Yet Clinton's later statements represent a paradigm case of lying. While Clinton might have believed he never had "sexual relations" with Lewinsky, he could not have believed that this was a "proper" relationship. By claiming to have had no "improper relationship," therefore, Clinton lied. He sought to manipulate citizens and the grand jury—to influence them by intentionally disseminating information he knew to be false.

The second form of manipulation is concealment. Concealment arises when speakers intentionally withhold relevant information from other agents.[21] When politicians intentionally withhold information that might undermine their case for going to war, for instance, we say that they "manipulated" fellow citizens. Yet the simple act of withholding information is not inherently manipulative. When voicing arguments, lawmakers and citizens often legitimately withhold information that might undermine their character or the merits of their proposal. As Bok points out, the complexity of even the most mundane human actions makes full disclosure of the truth nearly impossible.[22] No matter how complete, our descriptions are likely to omit some relevant facts or motivations.

Concealment, however, is a distinctive form of omission. While other forms of omission may be purely incidental or motivated by concerns over propriety, in concealment, speakers omit information with the intent to hide. It is this intent that makes concealments manipulative. When speakers intentionally conceal facts and information that would influence the choices of others, they exert a hidden form of force. They intentionally affect the choices of others in ways that cannot be fully understood.

Consider an example of manipulative concealment, which I explore in greater detail in chapter 3. In the early 1990s, the Christian Coalition adopted a strategy that its own leaders described as "stealth" campaigning.[23] Christian right activists sought to take control of school boards, city councils, and local-level Republican Party committees by running political campaigns based on a two-tiered message. Within friendly churches, candidates described in detail their plans to legislate according to divine principle. In more public settings, candidates dropped references to God, pretending to be "ordinary" Republicans concerned primarily with economic issues. Christian Coalition leaders instructed activists "Hide your strength," "Don't flaunt your Christianity," and "Give the impression that you are there to work for the Party, not to push an ideology."[24]

The Christian Coalition's concealment of its religious convictions was manipulative. "Stealth" candidates hid their religious convictions to win over citizens who would ordinarily oppose their religious agenda. These tactics were also intentional. As Ralph Reed, former head of the Christian Coalition, remarked when describing these tactics, "I want to be invisible. I do guerrilla warfare. I paint my face and travel at night. You don't know it's over until you're in a body bag. You don't know until election night."[25] Reed's words illustrate that during this period, the concealments of the Christian right were not accidental. They were part of a carefully orchestrated plan to influence fellow citizens in ways these citizens could not fully understand.

The third form of manipulation is distraction. Manipulative distraction takes on two forms. The first arises from *informational distraction*. This tactic covertly alters the choices of others by flooding the information space with so much information that listeners become confused and overwhelmed. As Goodin points out, "The opportunity it [this tactic] sees for manipulation lies not at the level of fudging facts but rather at the level of interpreting them.

Once you have overloaded people with information, all of it both pertinent and accurate, they will be desperate for a scheme for integrating and making sense of it. Politicians can then step in with an interpretive framework which caters to their own policy preferences."[26] In this form of manipulation, politicians exploit their disproportionate power to shape and control the content of public political debate. They rig discursive conditions by flooding fellow citizens with irrelevant information to ensure that their view prevails.

A second form of distraction—*emotional distraction*—also arises in political settings. Tactics of emotional distraction have a long history in the rhetorical tradition. As Cicero puts it, "You must try to shift or impel them [listeners] so that they become ruled not by deliberation and judgment but rather by sheer impetus and perturbation of mind."[27]

Rhetorical appeals to emotion turn manipulative in two circumstances. The first arises when speakers covertly appeal to listeners' irrational tendencies. When the speaker intentionally triggers the emotional responses of others in ways that fall beneath the awareness of listeners, such appeals become manipulative. This covert form of emotional distraction arose during the 1988 presidential election. To undermine the credibility of his Democratic opponent Michael Dukakis, George H. W. Bush and his aides communicated an implicit racial message by invoking the case of Willie Horton, an African-American man convicted of murder in Massachusetts and sentenced to life in prison. During Dukakis's term as governor of Massachusetts, Horton escaped while on furlough, assaulting a white family and raping the woman.

As Tali Mendelberg points out, throughout the campaign, neither Bush nor his aides ever made any explicit mention of Horton's race.[28] Instead, they relied on the media to communicate an implicitly racial message. Whenever the Horton story surfaced in media accounts, the visual imagery of Horton's mug shot lurked in the background, offering voters a subtle reminder that Dukakis allowed a *black* man to rape a *white* woman. With this implicit message, the Bush campaign was able to appeal to the racial prejudices of voters without ever making the appeal explicit. It was able to prime the predispositions of voters in a silent and invisible way that interfered with their capacity to choose. There is also evidence to suggest this strategy was intentional—that the Bush campaign intentionally sought to sway the public on the basis of this implicit racial message.[29]

The second form of emotional distraction is more overt. Rather than appeal to the emotions of listeners in implicit ways beneath their awareness, it makes appeals to emotion explicit. Overt forms of emotional distraction arise when speakers intentionally seek to override the listener's rational capacity to choose through direct appeals to irrational tendencies, prejudices, or fears. Consider, for instance, Lyndon Johnson's 1964 daisy commercial, which portrayed Barry Goldwater as a radical extremist by appealing to deep-seated fears of American citizens. Unlike the implicitly racial message of the Horton ads, the daisy commercial sought to alter the choices of voters by using explicit and overt appeals to emotion. Its horrific imagery and messages may have affected the choices of others by inciting a sense of terror designed to turn them toward Johnson—the candidate who stood for love.

Emotion and Manipulation

Willie Horton and the daisy commercial illustrate the manipulative potential of distracting rhetorical appeals to emotion. Yet is all emotional rhetoric manipulative? On some accounts of deliberative democracy, this conclusion seems plausible. These accounts define deliberation as a process of discussion based on reason alone, free from appeals to passion and emotion. For instance, as Joshua Cohen defines it, "Deliberation is *reasoned* in that parties to it are required to state their reasons for advancing proposals."[30] Habermas also insists upon the primacy of reason. "Participants in argumentation," he argues, "have to presuppose in general that the structure of their communication . . . excludes all force . . . except the force of the better argument."[31] Such passages do not directly argue that all emotional rhetoric is manipulative. Yet by placing reason at the center of deliberation, they imply that emotion has corrosive effects on the deliberative process, for it introduces into discussions a form of force other than "the force of the better argument."[32]

Recently, many deliberative democrats have shifted away from this implicit rejection of emotion toward ideals that more explicitly embrace rhetorical appeals to emotion.[33] Gutmann and Thompson, for example, assert that "in the political arena passionate rhetoric can be as justifiable as logical demonstration."[34] Underlying this shift is the notion that reason and emotion are not inherently at odds. John Dryzek, for instance, tells us "emotions themselves can be subjected to rational justification, because emotions often rest on beliefs."[35] On this view, emotions are not inherently irrational.[36] While they may override reason in some cases, they may serve as an important "pointer to ethical judgment" in others.[37]

To illuminate the possibility of emotion working with, rather than against, reason, Dryzek points to Martin Luther King's rhetoric. During the civil rights movement, King frequently invoked rational arguments based upon the Declaration of Independence and the Constitution when speaking to white audiences. Yet, as Dryzek suggests, these arguments were not purely rational:

> It was the place of the Declaration of Independence and the Constitution in the *hearts* of white Americans that King could reach. The attachment to these documents and the processes that created them is largely, though not exclusively, emotional, rather than a matter of prudent calculation. . . . Certainly there was rational argumentation here too, but the transmission was aided, perhaps even made possible, by the accompanying rhetoric.[38]

Such examples complicate the simple dichotomy between emotion and reason. They show that, more often than not, persuasive political arguments appeal to a mixture of reason and emotion. They also show that no necessary antagonism exists between these two human capacities.

What distinguishes emotional manipulation from fully legitimate forms of persuasion that appeal to the emotions? The two conditions of manipulation help draw this distinction. The first concerns the effect of emotional rhetoric on listeners. It stipulates that manipulation occurs when emotional rhetoric overwhelms, distracts, or bypasses listeners' rational capacities. When appeals to emotion no longer incite or aid rational reflection but, rather, interfere with the agent's capacity to reason, rhetoric turns manipulative. Such forms of rhetoric depart from legitimate forms of persuasion because, as Dryzek puts it, they create psychological conditions where emotion no longer "answer[s] to reason."[39]

The second condition concerns the speaker's intention. In persuasion, the speaker's appeals to emotion arise with the intent to induce agreement openly. Emotion is used, not to override listeners' rational capacities, but to enhance the prospect of achieving understanding or success. In manipulation, the speaker's appeals to emotion arise with the intent to interfere with the other agent's rational capacity to choose. In such cases, emotion is not used with an intent to prompt rational reflection but to distract others or bypass rational reflection altogether.

Two Forms of Persuasion

Now consider the distinction between manipulation and persuasion. I define persuasion broadly as the free and open exchange of reasons, arguments, or appeals "in order to induce . . . agreement."[40] By limiting persuasion to free and open exchanges, this definition distinguishes persuasion and manipulation as two separate forms of speech.

Such persuasive attempts to induce agreement often include more than merely rational arguments. On Aristotle's definition, for instance, persuasion arises from both the quality of the argument and the quality of the rhetorical context. He tells us that "persuasion is a sort of demonstration . . . furnished by the spoken word"[41] that succeeds or fails based upon three qualities. First, it depends on the suitability of the arguments to the context. In Aristotle's words, "Persuasion is effected through the speech itself when we have proved a truth or an apparent truth by means of the persuasive arguments suitable to the case in question."[42] Second, it depends on the speaker's character. Character can be persuasive, Aristotle argues, because "we believe good men more fully and more readily than others."[43] Finally, it depends on the audience's emotional state. Friendly audiences are more likely to be influenced than hostile audiences. Aristotle tells us that by understanding these three qualities of the speech situation, speakers increase their chances of inducing listeners to cooperation or agreement.

As seen in chapter 1, theorists of deliberation point to an important distinction between two primary ways agents use speech within such contexts of persuasion to induce agreement. Benjamin Barber, for instance, distinguishes between "talk" and "speech." He argues that talk has a reciprocal quality. It "involves receiving as well as expressing, hearing as well as speaking."[44] Speech, on the other hand, works unilaterally. It arises when the speaker seeks to induce agreement without full consideration of the arguments and concerns expressed by others. Barber describes talk as involving listening:

"I will listen" means . . . not that [1] I will scan my adversary's position for weaknesses and potential trade-offs. . . . It means, rather, [2] "I will put myself in his place, I will try to understand, I will strain to hear what makes us alike, I will listen for a common rhetoric evocative of a common purpose or a common good."[45]

In my terms, scanning "the adversary's position for weaknesses" would be a form of strategic persuasion; putting myself in his place and listening would be a form of deliberative persuasion. Similarly, Habermas's communicative action maps roughly onto my concept of deliberative persuasion, while his open strategic action maps onto my concept of strategic persuasion.

In deliberative persuasion, the speaker seeks to induce agreement with an orientation toward mutual understanding.[46] Consider an example. Suppose I seek to persuade you to vote for the Democratic Party's candidates in the upcoming election. If I am engaged in deliberative persuasion, I will provide arguments and reasons that I genuinely believe. I will also *listen* to your reactions and counter-arguments. I will try to find common ground between your views and mine, and I will be open to the possibility that your responses might prompt me to reconsider my support for the Democrats. In this sense, my efforts at persuasion are oriented toward reaching understanding—toward arriving at a fuller appreciation of the relative advantages of the Democratic and Republican platforms.

This orientation toward understanding arises from three primary qualities of deliberative persuasion. The first is *openness to revision*. In deliberative persuasion, speakers engage in debate with a willingness to revise their preexisting beliefs and preferences. As Bernard Manin points out, the word "deliberation" itself embodies this spirit of openness. According to Hobbes's definition, for instance, "Deliberation is nothing else but a weighing, as it were in scales, the conveniences, and inconveniences of the fact we are attempting."[47] Such definitions illustrate the two-tiered structure of deliberation. They remind us that deliberation occurs externally, when parties exchange reasons, and also occurs internally, when individuals balance reasons for and against their own beliefs and plans of action.

When engaged in deliberative persuasion, parties talk in a *deliberative* way. As Manin puts it,

> [Participants when deliberating] know what they want in part: they have certain preferences and some information, but these are unsure, incomplete, often confused and opposed to one another. The process of deliberation, the confrontation of various points of view, helps to clarify information and to sharpen their own preferences. They may even modify their initial objectives, should that prove necessary.[48]

This deliberative spirit of openness does not, however, mean that speakers are no longer engaged in persuasion. It simply means that in their efforts to persuade, speakers offer arguments and information with an openness to the possibility that the agreement they originally sought to induce might need alteration or revision. For instance, I might initially try to convince you to vote Democratic but during our conversation realize that both our interests and ideals would be better served by voting for a third party. My openness to revision would thus result in a shift in the agreement I originally sought to induce, from voting for the Democrats to voting for a third party.

The second quality of deliberative persuasion is *sincerity*. In deliberative persuasion, speakers offer arguments and reasons they genuinely believe. If I am truly interested in understanding, I will refrain from using purely strategic reasons that I do not accept but that put my position in its best possible light.

While such arguments may increase my chances of persuading you, they do so at the expense of the deliberative commitment to understanding.

The third quality is a *focus on the merits*. In deliberative persuasion, speakers refrain from strategic efforts to use facts and arguments selectively to bolster their case. Instead, deliberative speakers engage in what Joseph Bessette calls "reasoning on the merits."[49] They seriously examine and consider all relevant facts and arguments. They seek not to distract others from important considerations but to engage in a good faith exploration of the substantive issues at stake.

In *strategic persuasion*, by contrast, the speaker's efforts to induce agreement are oriented toward winning rather than understanding. Strategic speakers seek not to achieve mutual understanding but to successfully convince others to adopt *their* view or to agree with *their* proposed course of action. In the Democratic voting example, rather than presenting my best arguments in the hopes of achieving a better understanding of the relative advantages of the two parties, suppose I offer arguments crafted solely for the purpose of winning the debate. I scan your arguments and beliefs for potential vulnerabilities, and I find that while you support the Republicans on most issues, you reject the party's opposition to abortion. Despite my own reservations about legalizing abortion, I build my case for voting Democratic on the abortion issue. I convince you that abortion is a crucial issue and that the Democrats are the only party that will support your convictions. Throughout our discussion, I do not hide my strategic intentions. Both you and I know I am acting strategically, with the intent to successfully induce you to vote Democratic. In this example, I use rhetoric to win—to successfully induce your agreement—and not to achieve understanding, but I do so openly.

It is important to note that strategic persuasion is not defined by the mere existence of an orientation toward winning. In all forms of persuasion, even deliberative persuasion, some orientation toward winning exists, for all forms of persuasion seek to win over the listener by successfully inducing agreement. The defining characteristic of strategic persuasion is that this intent to win trumps the intent to achieve mutual understanding. In strategic persuasion, the speaker's primary intent is to win—to induce others to adopt their positions. In deliberative persuasion, by contrast, the speaker's primary intent is to understand. They seek to successfully induce agreement but act with a provisional commitment to their own point of view. They are open to clarifying and revising their view in light of the reactions of others.

Strategic persuasion's orientation toward winning over understanding arises from three primary qualities. The first feature of strategic persuasion is that speakers engage in discussion with an *unwillingness to revise* existing preferences and beliefs. Unlike deliberative persuasion, in strategic persuasion the agreement that speakers wish to induce remains static throughout the discussion. Strategic speakers seek not to explore the merits of issues to achieve mutual understanding but simply to win over the listener. When I seek strategically to persuade you to vote Democratic, for instance, I am not open to changing my own position based upon your reactions. Instead, I use arguments and rhetoric carefully crafted to induce you to agree with my preference for the Democrats.

The second is *insincerity*. Speakers engaged in deliberative persuasion appeal to sincere reasons and arguments, but speakers who persuade strategically need not express genuine beliefs. They might express sincere arguments when it proves expedient. Yet they will often abandon sincerity, opting for arguments crafted solely for the purpose of convincing the audience at hand. Thus strategic speech is not inherently insincere. There may be instances when strategic speakers rely on sincere arguments and reasons. Unlike in deliberative persuasion, however, in strategic persuasion speakers may appeal to insincere arguments and reasons crafted to win the debate.

The third feature of strategic persuasion is the *selective use of facts and arguments*. In the *Oxford English Dictionary*, the words "strategy" and "strategic" often refer to the direction of military campaigns. "Strategy" is defined generally as "a plan for successful action based on the rationality and interdependence of the moves of the opposing participants."[50] In the realm of political discourse, strategic action thus entails using facts and arguments selectively to anticipate the moves of the opposition and out-maneuver them. So unlike deliberative persuasion, where the actor brings out as much relevant information as possible to achieve understanding, in strategic persuasion the actor uses facts and arguments selectively in an attempt to win.

While strategic forms of persuasion are often inauthentic and even insincere, they operate in a context of relative openness and transparency. Both the speaker and listener understand the strategic nature of the rhetoric employed. In rare instances, the strategic orientation of speech might be communicated explicitly. The speaker might say, "I plan to convince you to accept my view" or "Say what you like, but I will not waver on my position." Such speakers indicate an orientation toward winning by expressing an unwillingness to revise existing beliefs.

Most often, however, the strategic orientation of speech is inferred from the context and role of the speaker. As Erving Goffman notes, we define most situations not through explicit "expressions given" but through "impressions given off."[51] This second, more implicit, form of communication consists of non-verbal contextual cues such as the speaker's occupation, social status, and past and present actions.

The strategic orientation of speech most often arises through such cues. When two presidential candidates debate, for instance, most listeners will arrive at a strategic definition of the situation. While neither candidate explicitly communicates an intent to win, listeners can infer that intent from their role as candidates competing against one another. In rare instances, exceptions might arise. During the course of debate, a noble Democrat might concede that the Republican's policies offer a more effective solution to the nation's problems. When such exceptions arise, the definition of the situation is likely to change from a strategic to a more deliberative speech situation.

Disentangling Manipulation from Persuasion

These three categories of rhetoric provide the theoretical tools for disentangling manipulation from other forms of power and influence. Consider the difference between manipulation and persuasion. If I were to persuade you to vote Democratic, instead of hiding information from you, I would use arguments, stories, or talking-points to convince you that Democrats offer a better set of policies than Republicans. Such persuasive actions differ from manipulation in three primary ways. First, unlike manipulation, persuasion is always transparent. Both deliberative and strategic persuasion change others' beliefs or actions in ways that both parties understand. In persuading B, A does not hide her wishes but communicates these wishes to B.

Second, in contrast to manipulation, persuasive actions allow other actors to choose whether to comply with the persuader's demands. Unlike manipulation, persuasive actions offer choice and respect the other agent's capacity to choose. As Bachrach and Baratz point out, in persuasion, agents seek compliance not by exerting force but by exerting influence. In their definition, one person has *influence* over another "to the extent that the first without resorting to either a tactic or an overt threat of severe deprivations, causes the second to change his course of action."[52] Unlike manipulation or coercion, influence affects others without resorting to threats or taking away others' choice to comply. Such acts respect other agents' capacity to choose. In Kant's words, they treat others not as mere means but as ends in themselves.[53] In my efforts to persuade you to vote Democratic, for instance, you have the ultimate choice over whether to comply with my wishes. In my efforts to manipulate you, by contrast, I take away this choice.

While not the central focus of this inquiry, it is also worth distinguishing manipulation and coercion. If I were to coerce you to vote Democratic, rather than hiding information or offering you reasons, I would threaten you. I might tell you that if you do not vote Democratic, I will torch your front lawn. Coercive actions differ from manipulation in two ways. First, unlike manipulation but like persuasion, coercion works transparently. It occurs only when I threaten you and you understand the nature of this threat. Second, in contrast to manipulation, coercion resembles persuasion because it allows other agents to choose whether to comply with the coercer's demands. Even if I threaten to kill you if you don't hand over your money, you still have a choice. You may choose to give up your life rather than comply with my demands, but this is a decision that you have the ultimate capacity to make.

Despite these differences, manipulation and coercion share one important characteristic: both fail to respect the choices of others. Manipulation fails to respect others' choices by using hidden or irrational tactics to interfere forcefully with others' capacity to choose. Coercion does so by invoking threats and sanctions. In both cases, other agents lose their capacity for rational self-determination. They are treated not as ends but as mere means, as instruments whose capacity to choose can be worked using threats or force.

In addition to these general distinctions between persuasion, coercion, and manipulation, consider the more particular distinctions between our three primary speech types: deliberative persuasion, strategic persuasion, and manipulation. To illuminate the various qualities of these three forms of speech, I outline below how these three forms of rhetoric vary with respect to four primary qualities of speech: (1) the speaker's openness to revise existing beliefs, (2) the speaker's sincerity, (3) the speaker's rhetorical emphasis, and (4) the speaker's general orientation (see table 2.2).

Manipulation shares many of the qualities of strategic speech but departs from purely strategic speech in three ways. First, manipulation always involves some level of insincerity. In fact, manipulative actions are the an-

Table 2.1. Features of Persuasion, Coercion, and Manipulation

	Type of relation?	Transparent?	Others given a choice?	Choices of others respected?	Use of sanctions or threats?
Persuasion	Influence	Yes	Yes	Yes	No
Manipulation	Power by Force	Sometimes*	No	No	No
Coercion	Power by Threat	Yes	Yes	No	Yes

*"Manipulation" is sometimes "transparent" because while most manipulation is covert, arising from hidden force, it can also occur overtly, arising from openly irrational force.

Table 2.2. Features of Deliberative, Strategic, and Manipulative Speech

	Speaker's Openness to Revising Existing Beliefs	Speaker's Sincerity	Speaker's Rhetorical Emphasis	Speaker's General Orientation
Deliberative Persuasion	Openness to Revision	Sincere	Focus on the Merits	Understanding
Strategic Persuasion	Unwillingness to Revise	Sincere or Insincere	Selective Use of Facts and Arguments	Winning
Manipulation	Unwillingness to Revise	Insincere	Use of Hidden or Irrational Force	Winning at All Costs

tithesis of sincere ones. When speakers lie, conceal relevant information, or distract listeners by appealing to irrational tendencies, they act with a lack of genuineness and with hidden ulterior motives. Such actions are in direct opposition to the "honesty," "genuineness," and "straightforwardness" that define sincerity.[54]

Second, unlike deliberative speakers who focus on the merits, and strategic speakers who selectively use facts and arguments, manipulative speakers use hidden or irrational force to influence others. In manipulation, speakers use these forms of force to achieve their ends in ways that interfere with other citizens' capacities to choose. Finally, unlike strategic speakers who act with an intent to win, manipulative speakers act with an intent to win *at all costs*. Manipulative speakers are so intent on winning—on controlling others' actions and beliefs—that they are willing to resort to immoral tactics that diminish the listener's autonomy. They win by acting outside the norms of good-faith political discussion.

Figure 2.1 illuminates the three primary moral dimensions of political rhetoric. The three categories of speech mark out the contours of a moral spectrum running from morally ideal forms of deliberative persuasion to morally problematic forms of manipulation. Between these polarities lie morally decent forms of strategic persuasion. While the contextual conditions I discuss in chapter 4 influence our moral evaluations of particular forms of speech, my task in the remainder of this chapter will be one of disentangling the various moral dimensions of these three ideal types.

What makes the third dimension—the dimension of manipulation—a greater threat to individuals and democracies than the others? When it emerges in everyday life, manipulation produces a psychological loss of trust and feelings of betrayal. Yet I argue that these feelings also have a moral core. While not all manipulation is immoral, I argue that it ought to be viewed

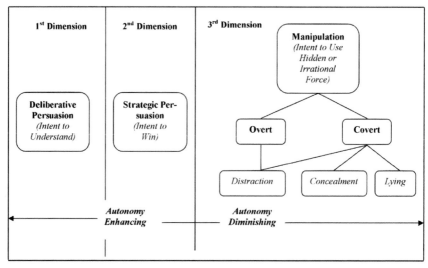

Figure 2.1.

with the presumption of immorality. Put differently, it ought to be viewed *prima facie* as a moral wrong.[55] This means that the burden of proof ought to rest on those who manipulate. Their use of lies, concealments, or distractions should be considered immoral unless and until they provide a compelling justification.

This presumption of immorality rests on two primary sets of arguments. The first is non-consequentialist in nature. It contends that manipulation undermines individual autonomy—that it strips away our capacity to engage in free, informed, and reflective choice. By enabling other agents to interfere with our beliefs, actions, and choices, manipulation creates conditions that diminish our capacity to choose our own ends. Kant's moral philosophy illuminates the threat manipulation poses to our capacity for rational self-determination.[56] For Kant, freedom arises from the capacity to choose one's own ends and to reason for one's self. To ensure that we respect the freedom of others in our actions, Kant asserts the Formula of Humanity: "Act so that you treat humanity, whether in your own person or in that of another, always as an end and never as a means only."[57] Acting in accord with this formula demands that we act toward others in ways they could assent to.

As I present it, deliberative and strategic persuasion cohere with Kant's Formula of Humanity. In persuasion, listeners have the capacity to choose for themselves whether to comply with the speaker's wishes. Even when my efforts to convince you to vote Democratic are oriented toward winning, I still treat you as a rational being. I respect your capacity to choose by being open about my efforts to induce agreement.

Manipulation, by contrast, treats listeners as a means. Although Kant never directly addresses the morality of manipulation, he does address deception, which plays an essential role in many forms of covert manipulation. Kant considers deception an immoral, even evil, practice because it undermines the Formula of Humanity. Instead of treating others in ways they could assent to, deception deprives others of the ability to assent altogether. In Korsgaard's words, "People cannot *assent* to a way of acting when they are given no chance to do so . . . the victim of a false promise cannot assent to it because he doesn't know it is what is being offered."[58] Manipulation more generally has similarly corrosive effects on an agent's capacity to choose freely. Intentionally depriving listeners of crucial information, telling them falsehoods, or overriding their rational capacities demeans individual autonomy. By covertly or overtly removing the individual's ability to assent to the other agent's actions, manipulation treats its victims as mere means, not as ends in themselves.

Yet the dangers of manipulation extend beyond such non-consequentialist concerns over individual autonomy. Manipulation also produces damaging consequences both at the individual and social level. It distorts informed decision-making, while also undermining the legitimacy of the democratic process. Thus the danger of manipulative rhetoric is not simply that it treats others as a means but that it creates conditions of choice that distort sound decision-making and erode the democratic ideal of popular sovereignty.

At the individual level, manipulation erodes the conditions of choice in two primary ways. First, it undermines the accuracy and reliability of the information that citizens use in making political decisions. As Bok explains, "All our choices depend on our estimates of what is the case; these estimates must in turn often rely on information from others. Lies distort this information and therefore our situation as we perceive it, as well as our choices."[59] Bok's reflections on lying can be extended to manipulation more generally. Manipulative lying, concealment, and distraction all have similar effects on the individual: they diminish significantly the capacity to choose on the basis of sound facts and information.

Second, manipulation creates asymmetrical power relations in favor of the manipulator. As Bok puts it, "To the extent that knowledge gives power, to that extent do lies affect the distribution of power; they add to that of the liar, and diminish that of the deceived, altering his choices at different levels."[60] In the language of Philip Pettit, the asymmetries in power that arise from manipulation constitute a relationship of domination. Such conditions enable manipulators to interfere with the choices of other agents on an arbitrary basis or, as Pettit puts it, "at their pleasure."[61] By exerting either hidden or irrational force, in other words, manipulation takes away the capacity of others to challenge or contest the influence of the manipulator.

Manipulation is even more dangerous in the social or political realm. When political actors withhold crucial information, lie about the possible costs and benefits of policies, or distract citizens from important considerations, they erode the capacity of large numbers of citizens to engage in collective decision-making. By broadening the scope of manipulation to a collective scale, political manipulation poses two additional dangers. First, it erodes the epistemic quality of political debate.[62] Rather than enabling citizens to challenge relevant facts, assumptions, and arguments, manipulation silently conceals, distorts, and perverts these considerations. It obscures implicit assumptions, distracts listeners from important reasons, or disseminates outright lies. As a result, manipulation diminishes the likelihood that public deliberations will result in sound epistemic outcomes.

Second, and more fundamentally, political manipulation threatens the ideal of democracy as rule of the people. The word "democracy" embodies this ideal of rule of the people; it is a fusion of two Greek roots: *demos* (the people) and *kratos* (rule). Implicit within this ideal is the notion that ultimate political authority resides with the people themselves, not with a monarch or group of elites. As Madison expresses it, "The people are the only legitimate fountain of power, and it is from them that the constitutional character, under which the several branches of government hold their power, is derived."[63]

Political manipulation undermines this democratic ideal. If the principle underlying democracy is rule of the people, the principle underlying manipulation is rule of the rhetorically devious few.[64] Lies, concealments, and distractions enable skillful manipulators to wield unchecked and often invisible control over the actions and beliefs of others. These tactics erode publicity and transparency. More important, they create dangerously asymmetrical relationships of power. When manipulated, citizens are denied what Pettit calls the "power of challenge": the power to scrutinize publicly the actions of other citizens and representatives to ensure that these actions represent the people's common interests.[65] The people can no longer exercise this power because, when done covertly, political manipulation removes this capacity without anyone ever being the wiser.

Now consider the moral qualities of deliberative persuasion, which I deem morally ideal, and strategic persuasion, which I deem morally decent. Despite their differences, I argue that both forms of persuasion steer clear of the moral dangers of manipulation by respecting the capacity of listeners to choose. When speakers employ either mode of persuasion, their intent to induce agreement is transparent to listeners. All parties understand that the speaker's words are oriented toward convincing listeners to accept the agreement that the speaker hopes to induce. As a result, both forms of persuasion allow listeners to choose whether or not to be persuaded by the speaker's rhetorical appeals. Listeners have full awareness of the speaker's intent to influence them and retain ultimate choice over whether to accept or reject the speaker's appeals.

While both forms of speech respect others' choices, deliberative persuasion is a more normatively desirable form of speech. Rather than using rhetoric simply to promote their own views and interests, deliberative speakers use rhetoric to achieve mutual understanding and solidarity. In democratic politics, the sense of respect and civility expressed by this deliberative kind of "talk" is preferable to the adversarial and confrontational forms of "speech" used in strategic political contests. Deliberative forms of persuasion are more likely to cultivate what John Rawls calls "civic friendship." As Rawls puts it, such relationships arise from deliberations where citizens

> exchange views and debate their supporting reasons concerning public political questions. They suppose that their political opinions may be revised by discussion with other citizens; and therefore these opinions are not simply a fixed outcome of their existing private or nonpolitical interests.[66]

Purely strategic speakers lack this openness to revise existing beliefs and thus engage with fellow citizens in a more adversarial manner. As a result, their orientation toward winning runs a greater risk of cultivating polarization and intolerance between groups, parties, and individuals.

The moral preference for deliberative persuasion does not, however, mean that strategic persuasion is wholly immoral or illegitimate. On my view, strategic persuasion occupies an important middle ground between deliberative persuasion and manipulation. It is a form of speech that is often morally decent. The morally decent status of strategic persuasion means that it neither diminishes nor enhances democracy in significant ways. It plays a legitimate role in politics but is less desirable than deliberative persuasion.

Why should we regard strategic persuasion as morally decent? Consider three primary reasons. First, strategic persuasion lacks the morally ideal qualities of deliberative persuasion. As mentioned previously, strategic forms of persuasion often lack the virtues of mutual respect and civic friendship. They cultivate a more adversarial discourse—one based less on understanding than on winning.

Second, strategic persuasion lacks the morally problematic qualities of manipulative rhetoric. While less desirable than deliberative persuasion, strategic persuasion shares two vital democratic virtues. Strategic persuasion embodies the virtue of transparency and the virtue of respect for the choices of others. Like more deliberative forms of persuasion, it involves the open exchange of reasons and leaves listeners free to decide for themselves whether to be persuaded. This means that in contrast to manipulative forms of speech, which distort choice, strategic forms of persuasion offer others the capacity to choose for themselves.

Third, strategic persuasion pervades modern democratic politics. To reject all forms of strategic speech would be to reject many core practices of democratic politics such as campaigning, debating, and advocacy. Within electoral competition between parties and interest groups, strategic action is inevitable. Given that democratic institutions create significant incentives to political success, rival parties and interest groups can be expected to use language to promote their own interests and out-maneuver opponents. Denying the legitimacy of all forms of strategic persuasion would deny the legitimacy of many strategic practices that play an essential role in real-world democratic politics.

Exceptions to the Immorality of Manipulation

Is manipulation always immoral? Considering the dangers that both personal and political manipulation pose, it is tempting to answer yes—to take an absolute stance against the practice. This categorical rejection of manipulation, however, is too strong. Moral evaluations of manipulation, I argue, depend on context. In most circumstances, we are likely to reject manipulation—to argue that it is an immoral and undesirable form of political speech. Yet the circumstances of politics are complex, and situations will arise where manipulation is morally permissible.

In game situations, for instance, where all players consent, manipulation is often morally permissible. In some forms of gambling and sports, the rules of the game permit manipulative acts that would otherwise be morally impermissible. In football, deceiving opponents, using trick plays, concealing strategies, and engaging in other kinds of manipulative action are permitted and encouraged. Certain forms of manipulation are also permitted in poker and more informal game situations like deceptive bargaining in a bazaar.[67] In each of these instances, manipulation is permissible because agents autonomously choose to enter the game.

There are, however, important limits to the moral permissibility of manipulation in such game situations. First, the consent of players must be informed and voluntary. They must freely decide to enter the game and fully understand the manipulative practices that its rules permit.[68] Second, the game's manipulative practices must not have detrimental effects on non-players.[69] Manipulation, deception, or violence cannot be justified if they negatively affect non-players. Although manipulation may be permissible in poker or football, it is not in public debates between candidates. In public political debates, manipulation may misinform and mislead non-players who do not fully understand the manipulative nature of the game.

Finally, players must not face barriers to exit.[70] If players cannot easily exit the game, or if circumstances of poverty or deprivation force them to play, the game's manipulative practices lose their moral permissibility. In such instances, players no longer make an autonomous choice to play but are forced into the game as a result of bad fortune.

Such game situations extend beyond formal games such as poker or football. They also arise in ordinary conversation. As anthropologist Harvey Sachs points out, the decorum of polite conversation often requires a certain degree of manipulation. When someone says, "How are you?" Sachs observes that we tend not to say, "Rotten!" even though that may be true. To prevent our conversational partner from having to say, "Really, what happened?" and engage in the long conversation that would surely ensue, we tend to just say, "Fine, how are you?"[71] Sachs's study illuminates the inevitability of certain forms of manipulation. It also shows that in our everyday interactions we often accept and readily deploy manipulative half-truths as a way of avoiding awkward or uncomfortable disclosures. When greeting an acquaintance on the street, we often tacitly agree to participate in a game that requires us to deceive others of our true condition.

Such cases show that context plays a profound role in determining the moral status of specific acts of manipulation. Consider two contextual conditions that magnify the potential harms of manipulative speech: *invisibility* and *asymmetries of power*. Both conditions limit the capacity of victims of manipulation to contest, challenge, or even understand the ways manipulators use force to affect their choices. Put differently, these conditions intensify the extent to which manipulative speech interferes with the capacity of other agents to choose, while also diminishing the possibilities for publicly contesting and challenging manipulation.

The first contextual condition concerns the visibility of manipulation. As manipulative acts become increasingly covert, victims of manipulation become increasingly unaware that their choices have been interfered with. Invisibility leads to a loss of awareness that diminishes the capacity of citizens to contest and challenge manipulative actions. In conditions of transparency, manipulation still poses dangers to individual autonomy and democratic decision-making. Yet the openness of overt manipulation diminishes these dangers. When manipulation is visible, citizens gain the awareness that their choices have been shaped by manipulative force. Transparency may not always enable them to resist manipulation, but it creates awareness and opens the possibility that citizens might contest and challenge the actions of those who manipulated them.

Second, manipulation is increasingly dangerous as power relations become more unequal in favor of the manipulator. Within symmetrical power relationships, manipulation may often be relatively harmless. When a lawmaker seeks to override the rational capacities of other similarly powerful lawmakers in the course of negotiations over a bill, manipulation appears almost harmless, for it arises in a symmetrical context of power. Other lawmakers have roughly equal political skills, knowledge, and resources. They have equal capacities to expose and challenge these tactics or to counter them through the use of similar tactics.

As power relationships grow more asymmetrical, however, the immorality of manipulation increases. When a lawmaker seeks to emotionally manipulate members of a disadvantaged minority group, these tactics become increasingly problematic, for members of the disadvantaged group lack sufficient political and financial resources to fight back. They may be unable to expose or counter the lawmaker's tactics of manipulation. By diminishing the victim's capacity to challenge and contest manipulative acts, asymmetrical power relations intensify the force of manipulation, diminishing the possibilities for curtailing manipulative speech. They increase the extent to which manipulators can successfully interfere with others' capacity to choose for themselves.

Given its dangers, manipulation should also be subject to robust public scrutiny and contestation. The force exerted by manipulative speech is most often covert. Manipulation works in the shadows to reshape the choices of others. As a result, the most effective antidote to manipulation is public scrutiny and exposure. When manipulative acts are brought out from the shadows, when the "private assumptions" and "hasty calculations" of would-be manipulators are contested, the force of manipulative actions is diminished.[72] In *Between Facts and Norms*, Habermas also emphasizes the role of exposure. As he puts it, "Public opinions that can acquire visibility only because of an undeclared infusion of money or organizational power lose their credibility as soon as these sources of social power are made public."[73] Once exposed, those who resort to manipulative forms of speech and action often pay a high price. Public exposure of their manipulative actions not only reduces the force that their actions exert on the choices of others. It also results in the loss of credibility, esteem, and the trust of other citizens. This is a point I explore in greater detail in chapter 4.

Unintentionally Invisible Forms of Influence

This chapter focuses primarily on the axis of political rhetoric running from persuasion to manipulation. In the realm of political discourse, my contention is that these categories of discourse have the most profound moral implications for democracy. It is, however, worth mentioning another form of speech that arises in democratic politics: *unintentionally invisible influence.* Those who exert unintentionally invisible forms of influence may exert covert forms of influence and erode democracy, but from the moral and democratic perspective, the lack of conscious intent makes these actions less troubling.

Such unintentionally invisible forms of influence share manipulation's quality of influencing others using hidden forms of force but lack its intent. As an example, consider the use of male pronouns and nouns such as "he," "man," and "mankind."[74] When used to refer to generic subjects, such pronouns may exert an invisible form of influence. As feminist theorists of language point out, such categories exert a subtle and often covert form of male domination.[75] As Dale Spender declares, "There *is* sexism in the language. It *does* enhance the position of males, and males *have* had control over the production of cultural forms."[76]

The use of male pronouns in ordinary language does not, however, generally constitute manipulation because it does not derive from conscious intent. When Neil Armstrong took his first steps on the moon and uttered his famous line, "That's one small step for man, one giant leap for mankind," he was not manipulating women. Although his use of masculine language may have subtly helped further the domination of women, we have no evidence that he intended this outcome.

Understanding the hidden power of language and discourse is an important task. As Foucault observes, discourses on sexuality, criminal justice, race, and mental illness all exert an invisible form of power—one largely unnoticed—that shapes our actions and beliefs.[77] This task of unmasking unintentionally invisible forms of power, however, lies outside the bounds of this analysis.

This distinction between intentional and unintentional forms of influence plays a central role in moral and political thinking. As Pettit remarks, to lose this distinction "would be to lose the distinction between securing people against the natural effects of chance and incapacity and scarcity and securing them against the things that they may try to do to one another. This distinction is of the first importance in political philosophy, and almost all traditions have marked it by associating a person's freedom with constraints only on more or less intentional interventions by others."[78] This moral distinction explains the primacy of manipulation in our discussion of the moral qualities of rhetorical speech. Unlike unintentionally invisible influence, manipulation is a conscious effort to sway fellow citizens in hidden ways and a direct affront to the legitimacy of the democratic process.

This chapter has outlined three moral dimensions of political rhetoric. Deliberative persuasion arises with the intent to understand; strategic persuasion with the intent to win; and manipulation with the intent to interfere using hidden or irrational force. This three-fold distinction helps disentangle morally decent persuasive rhetoric from morally problematic manipulation. It provides a conceptual framework for understanding when rhetoric respects the values of individual autonomy and democracy and when it diminishes these values.

The proposed concept of manipulation foreshadows the argument of chapter 4—that the quality of deliberative environments profoundly affects the moral qualities of these three forms of speech. As we shall see, the moral dangers of manipulation tend to diminish when exchanged in contestatory spaces. Such spaces provide incentives to expose hidden forms of manipulation and combat asymmetries of power.

Before turning to this structural analysis of the moral qualities of discursive context, I address in chapter 3 the empirical task of identifying various forms of rhetoric in concrete political settings. Using the rhetoric of one of America's most influential social movements, the modern Christian right, I identify several real-world instances of deliberative persuasion, strategic persuasion, and manipulation.

Notes

1. Anet Biletzki, "Ludwig Wittgenstein," *Stanford Encyclopedia of Philosophy*, 2006.

2. Ludwig Wittgenstein, *Philosophical Investigations* (New York: Prentice Hall, 1999), 65.

3. Wittgenstein, *Philosophical Investigations*, 66.

4. In drawing these distinctions, I appeal to the definitional structure commonplace in discussions of power relations. For simplicity, assume two agents—agent A and agent B—are involved in an interaction. Although this structure ignores

many of the complex interactions that arises in real-world scenarios of persuasion and manipulation, the simplification helps illuminate the distinctive features of the different forms of rhetorical influence. Robert Dahl, *Modern Political Analysis* (Englewood Cliffs: Prentice-Hall, 1984). William Connolly, *The Terms of Political Discourse* (Princeton: Princeton University Press, 1993). Steven Lukes, *Power: A Radical View* (New York: Palgrave Macmillian, 2004).

5. For Weber's original account of the concept of "ideal types," see Max Weber, "Objectivity in Social Science and Social Policy," in *The Methodology of the Social Sciences*, ed. E. A. Shils and H. A. Finch (New York: Free Press, 1949).

6. Bryan Garsten, *Saving Persuasion* (Cambridge: Harvard University Press, 2006), 7. Bok draws a similar analogy between manipulation and coercion, see Sissela Bok, *Lying* (New York: Vintage Books, 1999). For a popular account of manipulation as a form of coercion, see Douglas Rushkoff, *Coercion: Why We Listen to What "They" Say* (New York: Riverhead Trade, 2000).

7. For more on coercion, see Robert Nozick, "Coercion," in *Philosophy, Science, and Method*, ed. Sidney Morgenbesser, Patrick Suppes, and Morton White (New York: St. Martin's Press, 1969); and Scott Anderson, "Coercion," *Stanford Encyclopedia of Philosophy*, 2006.

8. Nozick, "Coercion," 441.

9. I am indebted to William Connolly, who uses a similar set of examples to illuminate conceptions of power. See William Connolly, *The Terms of Political Discourse* (Princeton: Princeton University Press, 1993).

10. Peter Bachrach and Morton S. Baratz, *Power and Poverty* (New York: Oxford University Press, 1970), 28.

11. Bachrach and Baratz, *Power and Poverty*, 24.

12. Lukes, *Power*, 26.

13. Lukes, *Power*, 18. Emphasis in original.

14. Alan Ware, "The Concept of Manipulation," *British Journal of Political Science* 11, no. 2 (1981): 165.

15. As Bachrach and Baratz put it, in manipulation, "A seeks to disguise the nature and source of his demands upon B and, if A is successful, B is totally unaware that something is being demanded of him." See also Bachrach and Baratz, *Power and Poverty*, 31; Robert Goodin, *Manipulatory Politics* (New Haven, CT: Yale University Press, 1980); and Ware, "The Concept of Manipulation." For an account of manipulation that leaves open the possibility of overt manipulation, see Joel Rudinow, "Manipulation," *Ethics* 88, no. 4 (1978).

16. For empirical cases of manipulation, see Amy Gutmann and Dennis Thompson, *Ethics and Politics: Cases and Comments* (New York: Wadsworth Publishing, 2005), 160.

17. Gutmann and Thompson also refer to this ad as a case of manipulation, see Gutmann and Thompson, *Ethics and Politics*, 162.

18. In some cases, manipulation may also arise from intentional negligence. In these cases, actors intentionally neglect to assess whether their actions might exert indirect control over others. Imagine that my town is debating an ordinance

prohibiting smoking in restaurants and bars. I oppose this ordinance. After a few minutes of Internet research, I find a study showing that secondhand smoke benefits health. While I realize this study may be flawed, I accept its conclusions because it strengthens my argument. I use this study to influence my fellow townspeople to oppose the proposed ordinance. Is this a case of manipulation? I do not consciously intend to deceive. I have evidence, however questionable, that secondhand smoke has important health benefits. Yet my actions could be manipulative on the basis of their intentionally negligent character. I have "manipulated" fellow citizens because I intentionally neglected to scrutinize information that I knew to be questionable in order to strengthen my arguments. Thus agents also satisfy the third condition of manipulation if they intentionally avoid scrutinizing information that they have good reason to believe is unreliable. This qualification to the intentionality condition is similar to Ware's point that manipulation can occur when "a rational person would have expected" that his or her actions would result in a covert form of influence. This condition does not implicate agents who are ignorant. If I were ignorant of the general scientific consensus that smoking has harmful effects and had no reason to doubt the Internet study, my actions would not constitute manipulation. The intentionality condition is satisfied only when negligence is intentional—that is, when agents know their information is questionable or that their actions may influence others covertly but intentionally avoid any critical inquiry. See Ware, "The Concept of Manipulation," 173.

19. Bok, *Lying*, 19.

20. Peter Baker and John F. Harris, "Clinton Admits to Lewinsky Relationship; Challenges Star to End Personal 'Prying,'" *Washington Post*, August 18, 1998, A1.

21. While concealment is often viewed as a lesser evil than lying, these two forms of manipulation have the potential to be equally deceptive. In fraud and securities law in the United States, for instance, deliberate efforts to conceal material facts are punished with the same severity as deliberate efforts to propagate falsehoods. "Fraud," *American Jurisprudence* 37 (2001): 32–56.

22. Bok, *Lying*, 4.

23. Sara Diamond, *Not By Politics Alone* (New York: Guilford Press, 1998); Matthew Freeman, *The San Diego Model: A Community Battles the Religious Right* (Washington, DC: People for the American Way, 1993); Jean Hardisty, "Constructing Homophobia: Colorado's Right-Wing Attack on Homosexuals," in *Eyes Right!*, ed. Chip Berlet (Boston: South End Press, 1995); Clyde Wilcox and Carin Larson, *Onward Christian Soldiers?* (Boulder, CO: Westview Press, 2006); James Penning, "Pat Robertson and the GOP: 1988 and Beyond," *Sociology of Religion* 55, no. 3 (1994).

24. "How to Participate in a Political Party," internal memo obtained by People for the American Way and used at the Iowa Republican County Caucus, March 1986. On file with author.

25. Jean Hardisty, *Mobilizing Resentment* (Boston: Beacon Press, 1999), 110.

26. Goodin, *Manipulatory Politics*, 58.

27. Cicero, quoted in Quentin Skinner, *Reason and Rhetoric in the Philosophy of Hobbes* (Cambridge: Cambridge University Press, 1996), 121.

28. Tali Mendelberg, *The Race Card* (Princeton: Princeton University Press, 2001), 3.

29. Mendelberg offers extensive evidence suggesting that the Bush campaign intentionally sought to appeal to the latent racial prejudices of white voters. First, she notes that in the original news stories about the Massachusetts furlough program, Horton's case was discussed along with the cases of other white criminals. The Bush campaign, however, disregarded these other cases and only mentioned Horton. Second, she notes that the Bush campaign sought to create a sense of informality and familiarity by using the name "Willie Horton," even though he went by the name "William Horton." Finally, she notes that the Bush campaign displayed a clear understanding that the image would effectively terrify white voters, particularly women. As one campaign strategist remarked, "Every woman in the country will know what Willie Horton looks like before this election is over." Mendelberg, *Race Card*, 134–68.

30. Joshua Cohen, "Deliberation and Democratic Legitimacy," in *Democracy*, ed. David Estlund (New York: Blackwell Publishers, 2002), 93.

31. Jurgen Habermas, *The Theory of Communicative Action*, trans. Thomas McCarthy (Boston: Beacon Press, 1984), 25.

32. For criticisms of this rational emphasis of deliberative democrats, see Nancy Fraser, "Rethinking the Public Sphere: A Contribution to the Critique of Actually Existing Democracy," in *Habermas and the Public Sphere*, ed. Craig Calhoun (Cambridge: MIT Press, 1992); Jane Mansbridge, "Practice-Thought-Practice," in *Deepening Democracy*, ed. Archon Fung and Erik Olin Wright (New York: Verso, 2003); Lynn M. Sanders, "Against Deliberation," *Political Theory* 25, no. 3 (1997); Iris Marion Young, "Communication and the Other: Beyond Deliberative Democracy," in *Democracy and Difference*, ed. Seyla Benhabib (Princeton: Princeton University Press, 1996); Iris Marion Young, *Inclusion and Democracy* (New York: Oxford University Press, 2000); Sharon Krause, *Civil Passions* (Princeton: Princeton University Press, 2008); Martha Nussbaum, *Upheavals of Thought: The Intelligence of Emotions* (Cambridge: Cambridge University Press, 2001); Amelie Rorty, "Explaining Emotions," in *Explaining Emotions*, ed. Amelie Rorty (Los Angeles: University of California Press, 1980).

33. See for instance John Dryzek, *Deliberative Democracy and Beyond* (New York: Oxford University Press, 2002); Jane Mansbridge, "Everyday Talk in the Deliberative System," in *Deliberative Politics*, ed. Stephen Macedo (New York: Oxford University Press, 1999); Amy Gutmann and Dennis Thompson, *Democracy and Disagreement* (Cambridge: Belknap Press, 1996); Amy Gutmann and Dennis Thompson, *Why Deliberative Democracy?* (Princeton: Princeton University Press, 2004).

34. Gutmann and Thompson, *Why Deliberative Democracy?*, 51.

35. Dryzek, *Deliberative Democracy and Beyond*, 53.

36. For more on this insight, see Cheryl Hall, "Recognizing the Passion in Deliberation: Toward a More Democratic Theory of Deliberative Democracy," *Hypatia* 22, no. 4 (2007). See also Cheryl Hall, "Where Is the Passion in Deliberative Democracy?" presentation at the annual meeting of the American Political Science Association, Washington, D.C. (September 2005).

37. Dryzek, *Deliberative Democracy and Beyond*, 53.

38. Dryzek, *Deliberative Democracy and Beyond*, 52.

39. Dryzek, *Deliberative Democracy and Beyond*, 53.

40. "Persuasion," *Oxford English Dictionary*, 2007.

41. Aristotle, "Rhetoric," in *The Complete Works of Aristotle*, ed. Jonathan Barnes (Princeton: Princeton University Press, 1984), 2153, 1355a5.

42. Aristotle, "Rhetoric," 2155, 1358b18–21.

43. Aristotle, "Rhetoric," 2155, 1358b6–7.

44. Benjamin R. Barber, *Strong Democracy* (Berkeley: University of California Press, 2003), 174.

45. Barber, *Strong Democracy*, 175.

46. My formulation of deliberative and strategic persuasion is indebted to Habermas's distinction between communicative actions oriented toward understanding and open strategic actions oriented toward success, although my categories differ from Habermas's in important ways (see my discussion of Habermas at the end of chapter 1). For Habermas's discussions of these categories, see Habermas, *The Theory of Communicative Action*.

47. I am grateful to Bernard Manin's paper on promoting debate as a form of deliberation for this definition. See Bernard Manin, "Democratic Deliberation: Why We Should Promote Debate Rather Than Discussion," working paper (2005): 15. For the original citation in Hobbes, see *De Cive*, XIII, 16.

48. Bernard Manin, "On Legitimacy and Political Deliberation," *Political Theory* 15, no. 3 (1987): 351.

49. Joseph M. Bessette, *The Mild Voice of Reason* (Chicago: University of Chicago Press, 1994), 46.

50. "Strategy," *Oxford English Dictionary*, 2007.

51. Erving Goffman, *The Presentation of Self in Everyday Life* (New York: Doubleday, 1959), 4.

52. Bachrach and Baratz, *Power and Poverty*, 30.

53. For Kant's discussion of treating others as ends, see Immanuel Kant, *Grounding for the Metaphysics of Morals* (Indianapolis: Hackett Publishing, 1993).

54. "Sincerity," *Oxford English Dictionary*, 2008.

55. Bok and Goodin make similar claims on this point. See Bok, *Lying*, 30; and Goodin, *Manipulatory Politics*, 26.

56. Kant, *Grounding for the Metaphysics of Morals*. Immanuel Kant, "What Is Enlightenment?" in *Kant: Political Writings*, ed. H. S. Reiss (New York: Cambridge University Press, 1991).

57. Kant, *Grounding for the Metaphysics of Morals*.

58. Christine M. Korsgaard, "The Right to Lie: Kant on Dealing with Evil," *Philosophy and Public Affairs* 15, no. 4 (1986): 332.

59. Bok, *Lying*, 19.

60. Bok, *Lying*, 19.

61. Philip Pettit, *Republicanism* (New York: Oxford University Press, 1997), 55.

62. For more on the epistemic effects of deliberation, see David Estlund, "Beyond Fairness and Deliberation," in *Deliberative Democracy*, ed. James Bohman and William Rehg (Cambridge: MIT Press, 1997); Samuel Freeman, "Deliberative Democracy: A Sympathetic Comment," *Philosophy and Public Affairs* 29, no. 4 (2000); Cass Sunstein, *Infotopia* (New York: Oxford University Press, 2006); Gutmann and Thompson, *Democracy and Disagreement*.

63. James Madison, *The Federalist Papers* (New York: Penguin Books, 1987), 313.

64. This worry is similar to Hobbes's concern that the use of rhetoric in democracy results in a *de facto* oligarchy, where skillful orators rule. As he puts it, "In a multitude of speakers therefore, where always, either one is eminent alone, or a few being equal amongst themselves, are eminent above the rest, that one or few must of necessity sway the whole; insomuch, that a democracy, in effect, is no more than an aristocracy of orators, interrupted sometimes with the temporary monarchy of one orator." See Thomas Hobbes, *The Elements of Law*, Part II, Ch. 2.5.

65. Philip Pettit, "Democracy, Electoral and Contestatory," in *Designing Democratic Institutions*, ed. Ian Shapiro and Stephen Macedo (New York: NYU Press, 2000), 117–19.

66. John Rawls, "The Idea of Public Reason Revisited," in *The Law of Peoples with "The Idea of Public Reason Revisited"* (Cambridge: Harvard University Press, 1999), 138.

67. Bok, *Lying*, 103–4.

68. Bok, *Lying*, 103–4.

69. Arthur Isak Applbaum, *Ethics for Adversaries* (Princeton: Princeton University Press, 1999), 116–17.

70. Applbaum, *Ethics for Adversaries*, 117; Bok, *Lying*, 104.

71. Harvey Sacks, "Everyone Has to Lie," in *Sociocultural Dimensions of Language Use*, ed. Mary Sanches and Ben G. Blount (New York: Academic Press, 1975), 69–71.

72. Bok, *Lying*, 92.

73. Jurgen Habermas, *Between Facts and Norms*, trans. William Rehg (Cambridge: MIT Press, 1998), 364.

74. I am grateful to Jane Mansbridge for pointing me toward this example.

75. Catherine MacKinnon, *Toward a Feminist Theory of the State* (Cambridge: Harvard University Press, 1989). Dale Spender, *Man Made Language* (Boston: Pandora, 1980).

76. Spender, *Man Made Language*, 144.

77. Michel Foucault, *The History of Sexuality* (New York: Random House, 1990). Michel Foucault, *Discipline and Punish: The Birth of the Prison* (New York: Random House, 1995).

78. Pettit, *Republicanism*, 52–53.

CHAPTER THREE

~

From Theoretical to Actual Manipulation

The Christian Right's Two-Tiered Rhetoric

Think of Glenn Stanton as the Christian right's ambassador to the American mainstream. Author of *Why Marriage Matters* and *Marriage on Trial*, he is James Dobson's point man on same-sex marriage in America's most powerful Christian right organization, Focus on the Family.[1]

I first met Stanton on a crisp Colorado morning in June 2004. As I approached the outskirts of Colorado Springs, it was impossible to miss Focus's eighty-one-acre campus. Perched upon a hill, Focus's four sprawling buildings, adorned with tinted green windows, made Dobson's ministry look less like a church and more like the corporate headquarters for IBM or Walmart.

After a quick lunch in the "Chapelteria," Focus's multipurpose cafeteria and chapel, my guide, a young female intern, escorted me past a sign reading Restricted Access to Stanton's office in the public policy division. We weaved through a vast expanse of cubicles until we reached Stanton's executive-sized cube in the far corner.

Stanton is nothing like the classic caricature of a right-wing religious fundamentalist. Avoiding bombast and arrogance, he speaks about politics with a rarified mixture of compassion and moral outrage. His polished speaking style makes even his most abrasive arguments seem soothing.

On same-sex marriage, Stanton effortlessly translates the religious claims of Sunday-morning sermons into publicly accessible reasons. In a 2003 document titled "Talking Points: Same-Sex Marriage," for example, he encourages fellow Christians to rely on arguments like the following:

1. Same-sex families always deny children either their mother or father.
2. The same-sex family is a vast, untested social experiment with children.
3. Where does it stop? How do we say no to group marriage?
4. Schools will be forced to teach that the homosexual family is normal.[2]

Underlying Stanton's talking points is the notion that same-sex marriage is wrong because it undermines the institution of marriage and hurts kids, not because it opposes scripture or religious convictions.

In one of our interviews, I asked Stanton why he advocates this kind of translation from religious to more publicly accessible reasons. He replied,

> People realize that "Thus saith the Lord" kinds of statements, while they're true, are just not persuasive. For those who put their confidence in the Lord, for those who wake up every morning seeking the Lord, it works. But for those people who don't care what the Lord says, you kind of come at it a different way and you help them. It's recognizing what their master is. If their master is common sense, then you try to make your point through common sense. If their master is humanitarianism and concern for others, you make your argument through that.[3]

Stanton is not unique in this approach. When I interviewed Alan Wisdom, vice-president of the conservative Christian Institute on Religion and Democracy, he also emphasized the necessity of publicly accessible arguments. As he told me, "For democratic decisions to be legitimate, there must be a perception of principles higher than self-interest. This means that Christians will have to use arguments in the public square that go beyond what we alone recognize. You have to appeal to things that people who don't accept your view of scriptural authority accept."[4]

Daniel Weiss, Focus's leading expert on pornography policy, spoke of this practice in almost Rawlsian terms: "We are speaking a language that the culture more clearly understands as a way of getting our message through," he told me. "I think it's respectful to the culture and I don't think that it's a betrayal of our beliefs either. It's a more effective way of communicating."[5] Weiss's statements echo Rawls's conception of public reason: the idea that when justifying matters of basic justice and constitutional essentials, candidates and lawmakers should rely on reasons "that others can reasonably be expected to endorse."[6]

Stanton, Wisdom, and Weiss all embrace a *two-tiered rhetoric*.[7] When speaking inside the religious community, such activists often appeal to scripture and religious conviction. When speaking to outsiders, they convey their concerns over political matters in a more publicly accessible vocabulary that appeals to a broader cross-section of citizens.[8]

Since the Christian right's initial period of mobilization in the late 1970s and early 1980s, its leaders have learned that, while Biblical reasons mobilize the faithful, a second tier of more publicly accessible reasons is necessary to persuade those who do not accept their religious commitments. As Dobson explains in a 2003 newsletter,

> As Christians, we believe that the Bible's admonitions against homosexual behavior, along with the design for marriage put forth in Genesis and affirmed by Paul, are reasons enough to oppose gay marriage. However, it is often said that God speaks to us through two books: the Bible and the "book of nature." Even for those who do not know Christ, the book of nature provides numerous reasons why homosexual behavior is harmful to individuals and to society as a whole.[9]

To encourage the use of "natural" reasons when talking to outsiders, Dobson's group trains members to use public arguments. As Stanton explained, "It is our desire to bring people up to a different level and argue more intelligently and more persuasively. You've got to do re-education. You've got to retrain people in that way."[10]

Applying Theory to Practice

This chapter applies chapter 2's theoretical framework to the rhetorical practices of the modern Christian right. It proposes an empirical methodology for identifying deliberative, strategic, and manipulative speech. In contrast to critics who portray the Christian right's two-tiered approach as purely manipulative,[11] I argue that this rhetoric has, at various moments in the history of the Christian right, represented all three qualities of political speech: at some points embodying the qualities of manipulation, at others strategic persuasion, and at others partially realizing the ideal of deliberative persuasion.

My aim in using the Christian right's two-tiered rhetoric to illuminate these categories is twofold. On one side, this analysis aims to bring the abstractions of the previous chapter to life. The case at hand is a vehicle for understanding the moral dimensions of spin and rhetoric not simply as a normative theory, but as a concrete framework for evaluating political speech. On the other, this case enriches and complicates this theoretical framework.

It reveals the empirical problems that arise in identifying these forms of speech and, ultimately, points toward the central argument of chapter 4: that manipulation ought to be addressed politically through structural conditions of robust contestation and understood philosophically in context.

Why study the Christian right over other interest groups? I argue that the Christian right offers an ideal lens through which to understand the moral implications of rhetoric because of both its similarities and differences from other interest groups. On the one hand, the Christian right is structurally similar to most other interest groups in American politics. It consists of a mixture of elite-level activists and grass-roots supporters who use rhetoric to both mobilize adherents and persuade outsiders. By understanding the Christian right's use of rhetoric, we get a window into the moral dimensions of interest group rhetoric more generally.

In spite of these structural similarities, the Christian right's use of rhetoric differs from other groups in one crucial respect: unlike non-religious groups, its internal rhetoric appeals to explicitly religious reasons. Other interest groups also employ two-tiered rhetoric, using one set of appeals to motivate their base and another to persuade the larger public. Yet the Christian right's two-tiered rhetoric is built around the use of explicitly religious reasons on the inside and more publicly accessible reasons on the outside. As a result, the Christian right's rhetorical approach helps shed light on the moral complexities that arise when religious groups attempt to appeal to fellow citizens using publicly accessible reasons.

As we have seen in chapter 1, many deliberative theories, such as Rawls's public reason, call for a more idealized form of this practice. They encourage those whose political beliefs rest on religious foundations to offer public reasons that other citizens could reasonably endorse.[12] The case of the Christian right helps inform and complicate the debate over public reason. It shows that the moral quality of such publicly accessible appeals rests on more than simply the degree to which they are based on publicly accessible reasons. As we will see, the Christian Coalition's "stealth" rhetoric offered publicly accessible reasons to fellow citizens but did so as part of a manipulative strategy to hide their core religious political ambitions. To a degree, Rawls and other deliberative theorists take this into account by emphasizing that such reasons should arise from mutual respect and civic friendship.[13] The case of the Christian right, however, shows just how radically the speaker's intent can alter the moral quality of speech. It can turn an otherwise good faith expression of public reasons into a manipulative attempt to conceal information crucial to the process of democratic decision-making. In this sense, the case of Christian right rhetoric helps supplement existing debates over public reason and religious discourse by offering a more in-depth account of the ways in which various deliberative, strategic, and manipulative intentions impact the moral status of rhetoric.

A Note on Method

Like Habermas's notions of communicative and strategic action, my theoretical distinctions between deliberative, strategic, and manipulative rhetoric rest largely on the intentional orientation of speech. In deliberative persuasion, speakers seek openly to induce agreement with an orientation toward understanding; in strategic persuasion, they seek openly to induce agreement with an orientation toward winning; and in manipulation, they seek to affect the choices of others by using hidden or irrational force. As a result, the empirical task of disentangling these forms of speech requires more than simply examining the objective content of what is said. It calls for a more complex investigation into the details of context and the speaker's motivation.

Although Habermas bases his distinctions on the orientation of the speaking actor, he offers little methodological guidance for measuring or observing that orientation in concrete political situations.[14] Instead, he suggests the speaker's orientation can be detected intuitively:

> Social actions can be distinguished according to whether the participants adopt either a success-oriented attitude or one oriented to reaching understanding. And, under suitable conditions, these attitudes should be identifiable on the basis of the intuitive knowledge of the participants themselves.[15]

He goes on to say that these distinctions are based not on the "predicates an observer uses when describing the processes of reaching understanding" but on "the pretheoretical knowledge of competent speakers, who can themselves distinguish situations in which they are causally exerting an influence *upon* others from those in which they are coming to an understanding *with* them."[16]

Habermas's remarks fail to provide concrete tools for identifying the orientation of speech. Outside observers with no direct access to the "intuitive" and "pretheoretical" understandings of speakers have no easy way of determining whether speech is deliberative, strategic, or manipulative. It is tempting to rely exclusively on interviews and direct questioning to penetrate this world of inner thought. Yet politically savvy actors often conceal their motivations, interpreting strategic and manipulative speech acts as efforts to persuade deliberatively.

If the orientation of speech cannot, as Habermas suggests, be determined "intuitively," how can we distinguish these forms of speech? Although the orientation of a speaker cannot be measured directly, I argue it can be inferred through a contextual analysis that accounts for the agent's surroundings, self-reflections, and consistency between past and present speech acts. As Kenneth Burke puts it in *A Grammar of Motives*, "Any complete statement about motives will offer *some kind of* answers to these five questions: what was done (act), when or where it was done (scene), who did it (agent), how he did it (agency), and why (purpose)."[17] Burke rightly suggests that a robust analysis of the orientation of speech should consider the qualities of context that give us a window into the speaker's purpose or intention. While contextual accounts inevitably lack precision, they may be our only means of identifying manipulative forms of speech that diminish autonomy.

I rely on three primary empirical indicators to identify the orientation of speech. The first concerns the speaker's impact on the choices of listeners. This indicator is particularly important in distinguishing manipulation from persuasive forms of speech. While persuasion works within conditions of transparency and respects the choices of listeners, manipulation often works covertly and interferes with the listener's autonomy. To identify manipulation, we must assess the speaker's effect on listeners. Were they unaware of the speaker's tactics? Do we have indications that their autonomy was undermined by the speaker's actions? If we answer yes to these questions and find that the speaker acted intentionally, it is likely manipulation occurred.

The second indicator addresses the speaker's intent. Manipulation requires not simply that speakers use hidden or irrational tactics to interfere with the choices of others but that they do so intentionally. The speaker's intent is also important in distinguishing deliberative persuasion, where speakers act with the intent to understand, from strategic persuasion, where speakers act with the intent to win. Accordingly, I use the speaker's self-reflections as a second indicator of their orientation of speech.

In my analysis of these self-reflections, I rely on a mixture of my own semi-structured interviews and the interviews of other researchers with Christian right activists. My interviews were conducted with six Christian right leaders,[18] three Colorado Springs lawmakers,[19] and sixteen liberal opponents of the Christian right.[20] I sought to diminish the numerical imbalance in favor of liberal activists by soliciting interviews with a wide range of activists and policy analysts at Focus on the Family, the Family Research Council, and other Christian right organizations. However, while liberal opponents of the Christian right were eager to grant interviews, Christian right activists were much more hesitant. More often than not, they turned down interview requests or simply never responded. Despite this imbalance, I have structured this chapter's analysis to ensure that the reflections of Christian right leaders are considered equally alongside the reflections of liberal opponents. In many cases, my analysis concerns the political rhetoric of activists in the late 1980s and early 1990s. To evaluate the self-reflections of activists during this period, I rely on historical accounts of the Christian right.[21]

Evaluating these self-reflections plays an important role in identifying the intent behind political rhetoric. Yet it is not enough simply to ask political elites about their rhetorical intentions, for skilled political activists often conceal their strategic and manipulative intentions. The third empirical indicator—*discursive consistency*—offers a more objective check on self-descriptions. This indicator measures the level of consistency between the rhetoric a single speaker uses across different discursive contexts. Discursive consistency enables us to assess the sincerity of political speech. When speakers use similar arguments before a wide array of audiences, we usually can infer that these are sincere statements of what they genuinely believe. When speakers employ arguments departing radically from their statements or beliefs expressed in other contexts, we may begin to doubt the sincerity of their rhetoric.

Evaluating discursive consistency is particularly helpful in differentiating deliberative persuasion from other forms of rhetoric. Recall that sincerity is one primary quality of deliberative persuasion's orientation toward understanding. Insincerity, by contrast, arises in both strategic persuasion and manipulation. When engaged in strategic persuasion, speakers appeal to the reasons most likely to successfully induce agreement, reasons that often depart from their genuine beliefs. When engaged in manipulation, speakers use concealment, lying, and other forms of insincerity to covertly affect the choices of listeners. Thus discursive inconsistency—disjunctures between what agents say in various contexts—often indicates a departure from deliberative persuasion. When the rhetoric used in what Goffman calls the "front-stage" (public settings) departs radically from the rhetoric used in the "back-stage" (internal discourse), we are likely to find strategic or manipulative orientations of speech.[22]

It should be noted that there is a crucial distinction between discursive inconsistency and discursive difference. Discursive inconsistency entails some level of "incompatibility, contrariety, or opposition."[23] Discursive difference, by contrast, may arise from arguments that are different in form and substance but fully compatible with one another. Imagine a minister using two different arguments to oppose a war. Inside his church, he bases his opposition on the Bible. Outside his church, he bases his opposition on the loss of American lives that would result. These arguments are different but not inconsistent. There is no contrariety or opposition between them. For our purposes, this distinction helps narrow the scope of the indicator of discursive inconsistency. It illustrates that to qualify as inconsistent, the various rhetorical appeals of speakers must not simply be different: they must stand in tension with one another.

To assess the discursive consistency of the Christian right's two-tiered rhetoric, I juxtapose its internal and external political communications. As I define these, by stipulation in the present analysis, *internal communications* occur when Christian right leaders direct their messages toward like-minded Christians. Such communications generally arise in training memos, newsletters, direct-mailings, and Internet Action-Alerts. *External communications*, by contrast, occur when Christian right leaders direct their messages at broader, more pluralistic audiences. These communications arise in public speeches, media appearances, and debates with political opponents. As Wittgenstein might put it, the line dividing external and internal, public and private, communications is a line with "blurred edges."[24] Yet it provides an analytically useful distinction for distinguishing deliberative persuasion from strategic persuasion and manipulation.

This analysis of the intent behind political speech has important limits. The full picture of an agent's motivation is seldom one-dimensional. Political speech almost always arises from a complex tapestry of motivations.[25] Yet for normative purposes, it is still useful to identify broadly instances of deliberative, strategic, and manipulative speech. While agents often act on mixed motives, one motivation or orientation of speech often plays a primary role in guiding action. Thus the diversity and multiplicity of motives should not lead us to abandon the empirical evaluation of deliberative, strategic, and manipulative speech. Just as difficulties in identifying intention do not dissuade courts of law from prosecuting lies and concealments in fraud, securities, and perjury cases, they should not dissuade political scientists from attempting to identify intentions in the similarly complex circumstances of politics.

In analyzing the context, self-reflections, and consistency of Christian right rhetoric, a certain degree of bias may be inevitable. For the purposes of full disclosure, I should note that while I am a Christian, I disagree with much of the Christian right's political agenda. As a native of Boulder— Colorado's capital of left-wing politics—and someone who never listened to Dobson's daily radio program until 2004, my reaction the first day I traveled to Focus's headquarters was nothing short of culture shock. Over the years, however, as I have studied the Christian right, talked with Focus's public policy operatives, and had lunch with ordinary members in its Chapelteria, I have seen beyond the liberal caricature of Christian right activists as cynical fundamentalists seeking theocracy. In many ways, they are the mirror image of my activist friends on the left. Both groups believe deeply in moral or religious principles and seek to mobilize fellow citizens to realize these ideals politically. So although I still disagree with the Christian right's agenda, I have sought to provide a balanced account of the implications that their rhetorical practices hold for democracy.[26]

In what follows, I begin with a case where the Christian right's two-tiered rhetoric turned manipulative. I then discuss moments when this approach was used to persuade strategically and deliberatively. I discuss strategic persuasion between manipulation and deliberative persuasion because this category of speech is the most difficult to identify and is best illuminated when contrasted with manipulation. This ordering also corresponds to the temporal sequence of these moments in the Christian right's two-tiered rhetoric.

Manipulative Lying and Concealment: "We're Flying below the Radar"

Pat Robertson's futile bid to become the Republican presidential candidate in 1988 was a hugely successful failure.[27] Although George H. W. Bush handily defeated him, Robertson's strategy of creating a fifty-state grass-roots network of activists throughout the country soon became the institutional backbone for the Christian Coalition.[28] Robertson's political miscalculation helped to create one of the most powerful political interest groups in recent history. By 1993, the Christian Coalition had 350,000 members nationwide, its newsletter *Christian America* had an annual circulation of 200,000 subscribers, and it had 750 chapters covering all fifty states.[29]

The Christian Coalition's focus on grass-roots organizing marked an important tactical shift. It signified the emergence of a Christian right focused less on exerting direct influence on Congress and the president and more on transforming state and local politics. "We believe that the Christian community in many ways missed the boat in the 1980s by focusing almost entirely on the White House and Congress," declared its executive director in a 1990 interview. "We think the Lord is going to give us this nation back one precinct at a time, one neighborhood at a time, and one state at a time."[30]

By focusing on state and local politics, the Christian Coalition sought to accomplish two goals. First, it sought to take control of the Republican Party apparatus at local levels.[31] Christian right activists understood that once they controlled Republican Party committees in each precinct, they would effectively control candidate recruitment and fundraising efforts.[32] Second, the Christian Coalition sought to elect conservative Christians to city and county offices in the hopes that they would promote the Christian right's agenda in school boards and city councils across America. They also viewed these local offices as a springboard to higher-level state and national positions. At a 1995 Christian Coalition training seminar, for instance, Charles Cunningham, the director of voter education for the Christian Coalition, declared, "Local candidates, particularly those for school board, are the farm teams for the future, for higher elected office."[33] The strategy was simple: flood local offices with conservative Christians and then take over Republican Party committees to ensure these candidates were given the resources to move up to higher office.

To realize these ambitions, the Christian Coalition of the late 1980s and early 1990s relied on a variant of the Christian right's two-tiered rhetoric, which critics and some of its own leaders dubbed the "stealth" strategy.[34] While religious arguments pervaded Sunday sermons and in-group discussions, Christian Coalition leaders trained rank-and-file activists to conceal their religious agenda when speaking in public settings. In contrast to other manifestations of the Christian right's two-tiered rhetoric, in which activists were trained to translate religious commitments into public reasons, in this case the leadership of the Christian Coalition advocated wholesale concealment. In 1986, for instance, Pat Robertson's presidential campaign, which laid the institutional groundwork for the Christian Coalition, distributed an internal memo advocating that volunteers at the Iowa Republican County Caucus conceal their religious convictions. Titled "How to Participate in a Political Party," this memo instructed activists to "hide your strength." "Don't flaunt your Christianity," the memo insists. "Give the impression that you are there to work for the Party, not to push an ideology." The memo encourages activists, rather than expressing the religious concerns motivating their participation, to "come across as being interested in economic issues."[35] Though this memo predates the founding of the Christian Coalition in 1989, it illuminates the genesis of the Christian Coalition's strategy of concealment. The strategy was not to translate Biblical arguments into the language of social science or civil rights but to hide religion altogether.

Concealment was to be only temporary. Once elected, stealth candidates came out of the shadows and pushed their overtly religious ambitions. In the aftermath of the 1990 school board elections in San Diego, for instance, Dean Szabo, a newly elected member, pulled out his Bible during a discussion of abortion counseling and declared, "There are the laws of the State of California and there are also the laws that are written in this book."[36] Another newly elected school board member with ties to the Christian Coalition announced during a meeting, "We want to have it like it was 100 years ago when God, the Ten Commandments, and prayer were the focus of schools."[37] Newly elected school board members also sought to implement a number of religiously motivated policy changes. They advocated teaching creationism, challenged the instruction of contraception, and sought to ban Roald Dahl's *The Witches* on the grounds that it "promoted the religious practice of witchcraft."[38]

The stealth strategy capitalized on two structural features of local-level politics. First, it capitalized on the lack of public scrutiny in local elections. At the city and county level, oppositional candidates and media outlets rarely challenge school board, city council, and party committee candidates, making it easy for Christian stealth candidates to "fly under the radar." Second, this strategy capitalized on political apathy and low voter turnout at the local level. During the 1990 school board elections in San Diego, Christian Coalition field director Guy Rodgers remarked, "We don't have to worry about convincing a majority of Americans to agree with us. Most of them are staying home and watching 'Falcon Crest.' They're not involved, they're not voting."[39] Because few Americans vote in local elections and few citizens investigate the positions of candidates for lower-level office, a well-organized and impassioned minority such as the Christian Coalition could effectively determine the outcome of these elections.

In what ways was this manifestation of the Christian right's two-tiered rhetoric manipulative? The Christian Coalition's stealth tactics relied upon two primary forms of manipulation. The first was simple lying. To conceal their religious commitments and ties to the Christian Coalition, some candidates fabricated their resumes and deceived others about the nature of their religious beliefs. In the 1992 San Diego school board elections, for instance, one stealth candidate cited his work as a volunteer for his church's youth group as a qualification for office. It was then revealed that this "youth group" was in fact the local chapter of the Christian Coalition.[40] Lies also arose in the efforts of Christian Coalition candidates to be perceived as non-fundamentalist, ordinary Republicans. The Iowa Caucus memo explicitly uses the word "pretend" in its instructions to members:

> Whenever possible, meeti [sic] people from the secular world of politics. Take time to socialize with them and always be friendly and polite. Convince them that you are interested in all the political issues, especially those related to economics. Pretend to be interested in and supportive of all the party candidates for office.[41]

The second form of manipulation used covert or indirect tactics to conceal all traces of its religious political ambitions. The Christian Coalition's tactics of concealment exerted a powerful influence on fellow citizens in two areas. First, these tactics enabled the Christian right to control many local Republican committees without the knowledge of non-Christian Republicans. Following the 1990 San Diego elections, for instance, Christian Coalition activists had effectively taken over the county Republican Central Committee.[42] Roger W. Burdette, a Republican Party member, made a similar observation about his party committee in Virginia. During party meetings, he noted, "The way [Pat Robertson Republicans] took effective control was just to send 10 to 12 people to each meeting. When they need a volunteer to be vice chairman or something, they just raise a hand."[43] The influence exerted in local Republican Party committees had national implications. By the 1992 presidential election, Christian Coalition members accounted for three hundred out of the two thousand total convention delegates at the Republican National Convention.[44] In Iowa, Christian Coalition activists dominated the delegation, holding forty-two out of forty-seven seats.[45]

Second, the stealth strategy allowed Christian Coalition candidates to exert power in local-level elections throughout the country. In some counties, these tactics were so successful that entire school boards fell under the control of Christian right activists. In the 1990 San Diego County elections, for instance, sixty of the Christian Coalition's eighty-eight candidates for local office were successfully elected.[46]

To evaluate whether these tactics were manipulative or merely strategic, recall the conception of manipulation outlined in chapter 2. Manipulation, I argued, arises when two conditions are met:

1. A uses hidden or irrational force to affect B's choices; and
2. A acts intentionally.

In what follows, I structure my analysis around these two conditions. We can only call these tactics manipulative, I argue, if the rhetorical practices of stealth candidates satisfy both conditions.

Condition 1—*Did the Christian Coalition use hidden force to interfere with the choices of fellow citizens?*

These campaigns were grounded explicitly on the idea of covertly influencing the political choices of mainstream voters and fellow Republicans in ways they could not fully understand. This clandestine form of influence took two forms. First, Christian Coalition candidates used targeted-marketing or narrowcasting to express their religious message. Rather than divulging these religious convictions in public, they directed their religious message solely to fellow Christians. To narrowcast their rhetoric, candidates conducted telephone surveys to identify Christian voters or limited their contacts to citizens listed in the directories of friendly churches.[47] They sought pulpit endorsements from sympathetic ministers and distributed campaign flyers on car windshields in church parking lots during Sunday services. These efforts to limit their religious message to this one segment of voters were so successful that one school board member, who was defeated by a Christian Coalition candidate, remarked of her opponent: "The first time anybody ever laid eyes on Cheryl Jones was the day she was sworn in as a board member."[48]

Most candidates were unable to evade all interactions in public settings. As a result, a second tactic resorted explicitly to covert influence. When speaking in diverse settings, candidates were counseled to hide their religious ambitions. As we have seen, the 1986 Iowa Caucus memo instructed activists, "Hide your strength" and "Don't flaunt your Christianity." It went on to say, "To a degree, keep your positions on issues to yourself. Jesus didn't overwhelm even his disciples with truth.—John 16:12."[49] Stealth candidates sought to interfere with citizens' autonomous capacity to choose by conveying the false impression that they were not Christian fundamentalists, that they cared equally about all Republican Party issues, and that they had no ulterior ideological agenda. In the closing lines of the Iowa Caucus memo, activists were instructed that secrecy is the key to political success: "The activities of the Church must not become public knowledge. There are those who seek to undermine our work."[50]

The covert nature of these tactics interfered with the capacity to choose of fellow Republican Party members and other citizens. These citizens were deprived of the opportunity to vote for the candidate whose platform best corresponded to their interests. By concealing their religious agenda, the Christian Coalition's candidates distorted voters' choice in ways that were invisible to these voters and thus impossible to understand, contest, or challenge.

Condition 2—*Was this hidden force exerted intentionally?*
The internal training memos and back-stage strategy discussions of Christian Coalition leaders leave little doubt that these tactics were intentional. Acting intentionally implies acting with conscious understanding. We say you intended to do something if your action was deliberate, if you did it "on purpose."[51]

Christian right activists speaking in the back-stage often expressed a conscious endorsement of stealth tactics. The most famous instance occurred when Ralph Reed, the executive director of the Christian Coalition, compared his group's tactics to guerrilla warfare. He declared,

> Stealth was a big factor in San Diego's success. But that's just good strategy. It's like guerrilla warfare. If you reveal your location, all it does is allow your opponent to improve his artillery bearings. It's better to move quietly, with stealth, under cover of night. You've got two choices: You can wear cammies and shimmy along on your belly, or you can put on a red coat and stand up for everyone to see. It comes down to whether you want to be the British army in the Revolutionary War or the Viet Cong. History tells us which tactic was more effective.[52]

Perhaps even more infamously, Reed later declared, "I want to be invisible. I do guerrilla warfare. I paint my face and travel at night. You don't know it's over until you're in a body bag. You don't know until election night."[53] Reed's words make his intention explicit, showing that he consciously understood the covert nature of these tactics.

Christian right training memos also reflect a conscious intent to conceal. Statements like "Hide your strength," "Don't flaunt your Christianity," and "Don't come across as a 'one-issue' person" in the 1986 Iowa Caucus memo show that religious concealment was far from incidental.[54] Instead, it was part of an orchestrated plan to control the Republican Party at local levels. Activists were directed by the leadership to mask their religious agenda and look out for vulnerabilities that might enable conservative Christians to extend their reach. The memo instructs, "Be ever aware of political changes and conflict within the county organization. Report any areas of vulnerability or lack of confidence in leaders to your Political Coordinator at once."[55]

The influence, invisibility, and intent of these stealth tactics represent a paradigm case of manipulation. They show that Christian Coalition candidates intentionally concealed their religious agenda to sway mainstream voters who did not share their religious aspirations. Beginning with Pat Robertson's presidential campaign and culminating in the local-level elections of the early 1990s, Christian Coalition candidates won elections for school boards, city councils, and Republican Party Committee posts by concealing their religious agenda.

Yet Christian Coalition activists at the time objected to such an interpretation. They argued that these candidates avoided religion so they could engage, not manipulate, fellow citizens. In the words of Jay Grimstead, a conservative Christian organizer during the 1990 San Diego election, "We went out and recruited a bunch of nice, intelligent people who all happened to be godly and praying people, but didn't announce it. They just put their names on the ballots and got elected."[56] Reed also objected to the portrayal of these tactics as manipulative. In a 1993 interview, he insisted, "The Left gets upset when our people do not run as theocrats, which is what they would like for them to do. That is a caricature of a person of faith. . . . We strongly discourage anybody from saying one thing, and doing another."[57]

These objections portray the concealments of Christian Coalition candidates as purely incidental. Yet these objections contradict the statements of Christian right leaders in organizing seminars and internal training memos, which indicate an intent to conceal.

Strategic Persuasion: "It's a Civil Rights Issue"

As the Christian right became more politically engaged in the late 1980s, its public political rhetoric increased in sophistication. Religious convictions continued to pervade internal communications, but the era ushered in new forms of two-tiered rhetoric. For audiences outside the community, public reasons based on the language of civil rights supplanted scriptural arguments and other forms of God-talk, with less emphasis on stealth campaigning.[58]

Examples of this rhetorical transformation abound. During this period, Jerry Falwell's Moral Majority changed its arguments in support of school prayer. Rather than emphasizing prayer's moral and religious benefits, the organization began to frame it as an issue of choice. As the Moral Majority's legislative director explained in an interview with Allen Hertzke, "We pushed school prayer three years in a row, but we framed the issue in terms of how prayer in schools is good. But some people feel that prayer in school is bad. So we learned to frame the issue in terms of 'student's [sic] rights,' so it became a constitutional issue. We are pro-choice for students having the right to pray in schools."[59] Allowing school prayer became no longer a religious issue but rather a question of respecting the rights of parents and students.

Arguments against abortion underwent a similar shift. Instead of discussing the religious reasons for opposing the practice, the Moral Majority recast abortion as a rights issue. It argued that abortion deprived the unborn of their right to life. As Jerry Falwell declared in a 1985 interview, "We are reframing the debate [on abortion]. This is no longer a religious issue, but a civil rights issue."[60]

The Christian right's appropriation of rights discourse appeared most prominently in discussions of gay rights. During the 1992 debate over Amendment 2, an amendment to the Colorado state constitution to strike down antidiscrimination ordinances based on sexual orientation, the Christian right relied heavily on rights claims. The campaign literature of Colorado for Family Values (CFV), the group that crafted the amendment, never mentions Christian scripture. Instead, its primary campaign slogan was "No Special Rights."[61] As Jean Dubofsky, who headed legal efforts to overturn Amendment 2 in *Romer v. Evans*, told me, "The 'No Special Rights' spin had a tremendous impact because at that point there was a lot of unhappiness about affirmative action for blacks and for women."[62] CFV argued that antidiscrimination ordinances based on sexual orientation extended "special rights" to an economically privileged social class of gays and lesbians. Gays and lesbians were in no need of such protections, it claimed, because they earn almost two times as much as average Americans and take four times as many overseas vacations.[63]

CFV's new rhetoric proved particularly successful because it also enabled them to reach racial minorities. Central to their argument was the notion that extending civil rights protections to gays and lesbians would devalue the legal and social status of existing minorities. Given the significant economic privileges homosexuals enjoy and the fact that being gay is a lifestyle choice, CFV argued, extending "special rights" to them would defile existing minority rights categories. In a fundraising letter, former Senator Bill Armstrong put it this way: "To equate the self-created personal miseries of pleasure-addicted gays—who sport average incomes of nearly $55,500 a year—with the innocent sufferings and crippling poverty of legitimate minority groups is an insult to those who've struggled to achieve true civil rights in America."[64]

In contrast to the Christian Coalition's manipulative stealth tactics, CFV's rhetoric of "No Special Rights" was a strategic form of persuasion. It occupied the rhetorical middle ground between manipulation and deliberative persuasion. It did not, like manipulation, interfere with citizens' capacity to choose using hidden or irrational tactics. Rather, the rhetoric of "No Special Rights" was an openly strategic attempt to persuade fellow citizens. This analysis, therefore, has three parts. First, I argue that the inconsistencies between the approach of "No Special Rights" and the Christian right's other discourses on politics and faith point to a strategic orientation. Second, I argue that the self-reflections of Christian right leaders during this period indicate strategic intent. Finally, I argue that contextual evidence concerning the effect of this message on other citizens and the intentions of Christian right activists who employed it suggest that the strategic orientation of the rhetoric of "No Special Rights" was openly understood. That is, it was strategic but not manipulative.

Rhetorical Inconsistency

During this period, rhetorical inconsistencies between the Christian right's rhetoric of "No Special Rights" and its other discourses occurred on three levels. The first level was theological. The public emphasis of this movement on civil rights failed to cohere with its private proclamations of the omniscient authority of God. On August 23, 1992, three months before the election, Kevin Tebedo, CFV's executive director, spoke to fellow Christians at the First Congregational Church in Colorado Springs about the importance of passing Amendment 2. As Jean Hardisty observed, Tebedo declared in his sermon that Amendment 2 is "*all* about authority. It's about whose authority takes precedence in the society in which we live . . . [I]s it the authority of God? The authority of the supreme King of Kings and Lord of Lords? You see, we say we should have the separation of church and state, but you see, Jesus Christ is the King of Kings and the Lord of Lords. That is politics; that is rule; that is authority."[65]

CFV's public campaign literature, by contrast, avoids any mention of divine authority. In fact, this literature portrays Amendment 2 as "*all* about" a very different form of authority: not the will of God but common sense principles of fairness and Supreme Court precedents. As CFV insists in its primary campaign tabloid,

> *All* Amendment 2 does is say "loud and clear" that special, protected civil rights are reserved for legitimate ethnic minorities who are truly disadvantaged. . . . Amendment 2 upholds America's common sense civil rights laws and Supreme Court decisions, which say that people who want a protected class status have to show they need it.[66]

In contrast to Tebedo's remarks that Amendment 2 is "*all* about [divine] authority," these public remarks claim that "*all* Amendment 2 does" is uphold U.S. civil rights laws.[67] Notice that the rhetorical inconsistency arises from the word "all." While one might reconcile the authority of God and civil rights laws, CFV's categorical suggestion that Amendment 2 is both *all* about divine authority and *all* about upholding U.S. civil rights law indicates a deep rhetorical inconsistency. When speaking to insiders, Christian right activists presented Amendment 2 simply as a religious mandate to restore divine authority. When speaking to the broader public, however, they presented Amendment 2 as having to do with upholding ideals of fairness and the civil rights precedents of the Supreme Court.

Second, the Christian right's "No Special Rights" message contradicted its more general rhetoric against civil rights protections for disadvantaged minorities. The argument that gays were a privileged group, undeserving of rights protections because they make more money, take more overseas vacations, go to college in greater numbers, and have better jobs than the average heterosexual had an important implication for the rights status of other minority groups.[68] By arguing that extending civil rights to gays would devalue the existing rights of "legitimate" minority groups, the Christian right implicitly expressed support for protecting the rights of blacks, women, and other disadvantaged minorities. As Didi Herman observes, "Paradoxically . . . the portrayal of the undeserving gays served to strengthen the legitimacy of laws for the deserving [minority groups], laws that many CR activists do not, at root, support at all."[69]

The Christian right opposed civil rights measures for "legitimate" minorities in a number of areas. First, activists like Will Perkins, who helped found CFV, openly expressed their disdain for policies that sought to protect the rights of women.[70] Second, the Christian right opposed multicultural education and other efforts to increase awareness of minority cultures, regarding such programs as efforts to indoctrinate children into the liberal ideology of "political correctness."[71] Finally, the Christian right vehemently opposed affirmative action programs for minorities. Like most early 1990s conservatives, these activists objected to the notion that blacks, Hispanics, or women should be given special consideration in educational and employment decisions.[72] These policy positions indicate that the Christian right's concern for the rights protections of "legitimate" minorities was insincere and strategic.

Third, the Christian right's rhetoric of "No Special Rights" contradicts its current arguments against same-sex marriage. In the wake of Amendment 2 and its repudiation by the Supreme Court in *Romer v. Evans* in 1996, the battleground over gay rights shifted from antidiscrimination ordinances to same-sex marriage. As we will see in the next section, once the battleground shifted, the Christian right quickly dropped its emphasis on civil rights. While the "No Special Rights" rhetoric worked in opposing antidiscrimination protections, this message lost its power when applied to marriage. To the contrary, a rights focus seems to actually strengthen the case *for* same-sex marriage. Same-sex marriage advocates take up the very same set of arguments that pervaded the early 1990s rhetoric of the Christian right. They argue that all citizens ought to have "equal rights," not "special rights," in marriage. In this new context, "No Special Rights" implies that heterosexuals should not enjoy an exclusive right to marriage that gays and lesbians do not also enjoy.

The hastiness with which the Christian right dropped its civil rights talk reinforces the strategic hypothesis. It suggests that these activists were not genuinely committed to the principle of "equal rights—not special rights." The fact that the Christian right quickly abandoned this principle once the battleground shifted and it was no longer expedient suggests that its commitment to "equal" civil rights was strategic, not deliberative. Its commitment to equal civil rights appeared not to arise from a genuine concern about the principle of equality but more from a strategic desire to win in debates over antidiscrimination ordinances.

Strategic Self-Reflections

Another source of evidence for the strategic nature of the rhetoric of "No Special Rights" arises from interviews with movement elites. As Gary Bauer, former director of the Family Research Council, declared in a 1989 interview with Michael Moen, the decision to adopt the more public language of rights was driven largely by concerns over political efficacy:

> Today the [Christian Right] movement realizes that it must employ the language that the American people feel comfortable with. If one does not use the words and phrases that people are used to, one runs the risk of alienating them. It is unfortunate that leaders cannot use the words and phrases that were once part of the national dialogue. In short, there is more sensitivity to language in the movement now. Religion may still motivate people, but there is no virtue in quoting Bible verses to policymakers with different value perspectives. The movement has come to see that fact, realizing that it must address policymakers with words and phrases to which they are attuned.[73]

Bauer indicates that this rhetorical shift is "unfortunate" but necessary for persuading those who do not share the movement's religious convictions.

Bauer's reflections leave open the possibility that this shift in rhetoric arose out of a desire to understand fellow citizens. Yet the reflections of CFV activists following the Amendment 2 campaign reflect a strong emphasis on winning rather than understanding. Tony Marco, CFV's leading political strategist, offered the following assessment of the movement's rhetoric in an internal memo:

> What gives gay militants their enormous power are money and the *operative presumption that gays represent some sort of "oppressed minority."* . . . If this is true, I conclude that (a) forcing gay activists to spend tons of money, and (b) demolishing the presumption that gays are an "oppressed minority" are the *only*

means by which gay militants' power can be destroyed *at its roots*. All other approaches to opposing "gay rights" are doomed to failure.[74]

Marco's words suggest that the rhetoric of "No Special Rights" was not oriented toward achieving greater understanding with gays and lesbians. Rather, Marco viewed this as a struggle of power against power. His primary orientation was not to understand but to ensure the success of the Christian right agenda by destroying the power of "gay militants . . . *at its roots*." Marco's reflections illustrate that many, though perhaps not all, Christian right activists during this period used the rhetoric of equal rights as a strategic tool for undermining the prevailing view of gays and lesbians as an oppressed minority.

"No Special Rights"—Persuasive, Not Manipulative

When combined with the inconsistencies in Christian right rhetoric, the self-reflections of these activists bolster the claim that the rhetoric of "No Special Rights" was strategic, and not a deliberative form of persuasion aimed at understanding. But it was also, in my analysis, not manipulative. Like manipulation, this rhetoric was oriented toward winning and depended on insincerity. Central to both the Christian Coalition's manipulative stealth campaigns and CFV's strategically persuasive rhetoric of "No Special Rights" was the use of insincere statements that activists did not fully believe. Christian Coalition activists pretended to be ordinary Republicans, while CFV activists pretended to be genuinely committed to protecting the rights of "legitimate" minorities.

Yet this distinction between the Christian Coalition's manipulative form of insincerity and CFV's persuasive form of insincerity arises from the political context within which these rhetorical approaches emerged. CFV's rhetoric of "No Special Rights" arose within an open context of strategic persuasion. Its activists relied on insincere claims about the importance of minority rights protections but did not use these claims to covertly interfere with other citizens' capacities to choose. Unlike the "stealth" strategy, CFV's rhetoric was not based on lying. Although the rhetoric of "No Special Rights" failed to cohere with other Christian right discourses, this inconsistency did not require the intentional propagation of information known to be false. While the rhetoric of "No Special Rights" may have opposed the other beliefs of CFV activists, we have no evidence that activists viewed their rhetorical claims as false. In fact, they may not have even been conscious of this inconsistency.

Nor did CFV's rhetoric of "No Special Rights" arise from a manipulative strategy of concealment. In contrast to the Christian Coalition, which encouraged candidates to hide their true political agendas, CFV was clear and direct about its political ambitions. It communicated to fellow citizens that its message of "No Special Rights" was intended to achieve one primary political goal—to pass Amendment 2. This was not a bait-and-switch. It was not an attempt to convey a false impression to fellow citizens and then enact a set of hidden policies once elected. Although the activists insincerely presented themselves as committed to protecting minority rights, we have no evidence that they sought to hide their positions on other issues that might undermine these claims. Thus we have no reason to believe that these claims were part of an intentional strategy to distort the choices of voters by hiding relevant information.

The stealth tactics of the Christian Coalition arose within a more covert context of manipulation. Rather than openly expressing their political intentions and group affiliation, Christian Coalition activists sought to hide these aspects of themselves from other citizens. In this sense, their insincerity was not merely strategic; it was manipulative. For it relied on strategies of concealment and lying to interfere covertly in other citizens' capacity to choose. Their strategy of concealment *was* a bait-and-switch: candidates presented themselves as moderates during the election and then, once elected, revealed themselves to be hard-line religious conservatives.

So while CFV's rhetoric of "No Special Rights" was strategic, it was not manipulative. Its use of this rhetorical trope during the 1992 election arose as an open appeal to fellow citizens. The message was not based on covert tactics intended to interfere with the capacity of fellow citizens to choose autonomously. It was based on a strategic effort to win over mainstream voters by appropriating the liberal vocabulary of civil rights.

Deliberative Persuasion: "It's All about the Kids"

If the early 1990s marks the Christian right's appropriation of civil rights, the present era marks a second shift toward the language of social science and humanism. Gone is the rights-based rhetoric against homosexuality. When speaking in public settings, Focus on the Family and other contemporary Christian right political organizations now express a more consequentialist set of arguments.[75] As Michael Brewer, public policy director for the GLBT Community Center of Colorado, observes,

> I've noticed how they've changed their focus over the last several years to now focus on "It's all about the kids. We don't care about the homosexuals. We don't like them necessarily. We don't think they are good for society. They are unhealthy. But it's really all about the kids."[76]

This new, more empirically based, message retains the two-tiered structure of the Christian right's earlier rhetoric, with one important difference: its public arguments now express a distinctively utilitarian concern for the destructive effects of the gay agenda on human interests, particularly those of children.

In a 2003 memo on same-sex marriage, for instance, Focus on the Family's Glenn Stanton encourages members to express their concerns by appealing to the following empirical claims:

- No child development theory says children need two parents of the same gender, but rather that children need their mothers and fathers.
- Same-sex "marriage" will subject generations of children to the status of lab rats in a vast, untested social experiment.
- Thousands of published social science, psychological and medical studies show that children living in fatherless families, on average, suffer dramatically in every important measure of well-being. These children suffer from much higher levels of physical and mental illness, educational failure, poverty, substance abuse, criminal behavior, loneliness, as well as physical and sexual abuse.[77]

These claims are based not on the non-consequentialist language of rights but on the consequentialist consideration that same-sex marriage has negative effects on families and children.

Stanton describes this as a shift to the language of humanism. In a 2006 essay titled "The Conservative Humanist," he explains:

"Doc" [Dobson] represents a generation that took fundamentalism beyond its cultural isolation and engaged many sectors of culture: politics, academia, industry, the arts, law, and entertainment. . . . What is the next generation called to do? I propose that we need to go upstream again, this time from the family to humanity itself. . . . What if there were a movement dedicated to the question, *What does it mean to be human?* Asking such a question would lead us to explore and demonstrate what it means to live, to feel, to hope, to love, to give, to receive, to be wounded, and to be healed. . . . These are not narrow, issue-based questions. They are not questions for the pro-family movement alone. They are human questions.[78]

Stanton's words redescribe the conventional idea of humanism. The *Oxford English Dictionary* defines "humanism" as "any system of thought or action which is concerned with merely human interests (as distinguished from divine), or with those of the human race in general (as distinguished from individual)."[79] Stanton's conception of humanism rejects the first part of the definition—the concern for "merely human interests" as distinguished from divine. His concerns for fellow humans are deeply rooted in faith. Nevertheless, he embraces the second part of the humanist ideal, which emphasizes the promotion of general human, rather than purely individual, interests.

This emphasis on humanism departs radically from the thinking of early Christian right leaders. For them, humanism was the great enemy of evangelical Christianity. Tim LeHaye, author of the *Left Behind* series, blamed "humanism" for having "moved our country from a Biblically based society to an amoral 'democratic' society during the past forty years."[80] Even James Dobson once worried about the corrosive effects of humanism. In his 1990 book, *Children at Risk*, he laments, "The humanistic system of values has now become the predominant way of thinking in most of the power centers of society. It has outstripped Judeo-Christian precepts."[81] Just as the Christian right sought to appropriate the once hostile language of civil rights, however, Stanton has sought to appropriate the language of humanism.

I argue that in contrast to the rhetoric of "No Special Rights" in the early 1990s, the Christian right's humanist arguments against same-sex marriage, while not fully deliberative, come closer to embracing the ideal of deliberative persuasion. My argument consists of three parts. First, I argue that unlike the rhetoric of the early 1990s, the current rhetoric of humanism displays a greater level of discursive consistency. Second, I argue that the self-reflections of activists who employ this rhetoric express an intent to achieve understanding, not simply to win. Finally, however, I present evidence that complicates the simple conclusion that these activists fully embrace the ideal of deliberative persuasion. I argue that while this rhetoric is sincere, it is less clear whether it embodies a full orientation toward understanding and the deliberative spirit of openness to revision.

Rhetorical Consistency

Consider first the relation between the Christian right's public rhetoric of humanism and the rhetoric it uses in other discursive settings. Two questions guide this analysis. The first is: do these humanist arguments against same-sex marriage cohere with the internal rhetoric of Christian right organizations? Within their own sphere, groups like Focus on the Family still emphasize religious reasons to oppose same-sex marriage. As Dobson wrote in a 2003 newsletter to members,

Throughout Scripture, God's intention for human sexual relationships is clearly limited to the heterosexual union between a man and a woman in marriage (see Genesis 1:27–28, and 2:18, 23–24). By stark contrast, sex outside of that relationship, whether it be of a heterosexual or homosexual nature, is clearly identified as a sin. With particular regard to homosexuality, Paul warns: " . . . God gave them over to shameful lusts. Even their women exchanged natural relationships for unnatural ones. In the same way the men also abandoned natural relations with women and were inflamed with lust for one another. Men committed indecent acts with other men, and received in themselves the due penalty for their perversion" (Romans 1:26b–27, NIV).[82]

Yet Dobson's internal rhetoric on same-sex marriage is not confined to Biblical principles. One paragraph later, he appeals to his members using the very arguments that Focus on the Family uses in public discourse. As he declares,

> If the God-ordained basis for the family does indeed fail on a large scale, children will pay a terrible price. Social science confirms that two parents of the same sex, however loving or nurturing they may be, cannot meet the unique needs of children in the same way that a mother and a father can.[83]

That Dobson's internal rhetoric appeals to these more public considerations may not prove that his rhetoric of humanism is deliberative. It does, however, give us reason to believe that his public arguments represent genuine concerns—that they are more than a simple strategic ploy.

The Christian right's current public arguments also cohere with internal theological claims. Unlike the "No Special Rights" approach of CFV, current activists like Stanton make explicit connections between the humanist vocabulary of social science and religion. As he told me,

> We don't just have a belief in fideism—of pure faith. It's faith tied to something. The value of Christianity is that at the center of it is the incarnation— the fact that the God of Christianity became the creation. There is a deeply intimate connection. The incarnation is the demonstration that there is a very tight connection between those things. That God is intimately in touch with the creative world. Whereas a lot of faiths focus on the value of Christianity transcending the world, the way I look at it is that Christianity brings these worlds together. We cannot be disinterested in what God created or designed, what he is redeeming, what he became, and what he is one day going to renew. So this is a Christianity that is very well connected with fleshly everyday earthly existence.[84]

In Stanton's theology, the Biblical principles of God are tightly connected to "fleshly everyday earthly existence." This perspective makes it possible for the conclusions of social science and other humanist concerns to be not simply an auxiliary set of arguments, used solely to convince non-believers, but an important part of a religious worldview. On Stanton's view, faith and real-world human interests are tightly intertwined.

The second question concerning the discursive consistency of the Christian right's rhetoric is: do these humanist arguments against same-sex marriage cohere with the Christian right's public rhetoric on other social issues? I argue that when confronting a vast array of other social issues, groups like Focus appeal to a similar set of concerns about the promotion of human interests. Consider, for example, Focus's arguments on core social issues, aimed primarily at fellow Christians, as they appear on its political website *CitizenLink*:

- **Opposing Pornography**: "To win the battle against the consumption and disposal of human beings so common to pornography, we must rediscover what it means to be human—and live with the purpose of treating others—and ourselves—as such."[85]
- **Opposing Gambling**: "For millions of Americans, gambling addiction leads to hopeless pain and misery; for some it leads to death. Gambling-related suicides are an increasingly common phenomena as legalized gambling continues to spread throughout America."[86]
- **Promoting Abstinence**: "Modern contraceptive inventions have given many an exaggerated sense of safety and prompted more people than ever before to move sexual expression outside the marriage boundary. When adhered to strictly, marital fidelity has always protected individuals and society."[87]

These arguments are united by the notion that pornography, gambling, and extramarital sex are wrong because they erode families and hurt individuals. They are wrong because they fail to promote human interests. In this sense, these arguments reflect a consistent concern for promoting the welfare of humanity that Focus expresses when opposing same-sex marriage.

Deliberative Self-Reflections

Now consider the self-reflections of Christian right activists when asked about the orientation of this humanist public message. When I asked Stanton, "How do you go about constructing what you call 'universal human arguments' that appeal to all citizens?" he explained,

> It's not tricky. It is just thinking, "All right, what do we all have in common?" If you go into a room and they are all Elvis fans, use a rationale like his favorite

book was such and such. In the culture war, why can't we have more of that? Let's find our common starting place rather than starting with our divisions.[88]

Within the conditions of pluralism, he insists, "You have to be very careful. You have to start at an incontrovertible common starting point to even get off the ground."[89] While such attempts to find common ground could be purely strategic, my sense as an interviewer is that with Stanton it represents a more genuine effort to engage citizens with different religious convictions.

At another point in our interview, Stanton was even more explicit about his efforts to use rhetoric promoting understanding. As he declared, "If we were all on the same page, then, yes, I would speak our common [religious] language, but there's a whole bunch of people in this room all coming from different perspectives. So if you're going to make progress, let's start with the thing that we all hold in common and start from there."[90] If these reflections indicate something more than a desire to trick an interviewer, and I think they do, they suggest that at least some Christian right activists offer "universal human arguments" not simply as an attempt to win politically but to increase understanding—to engage in a more constructive dialogue with others who do not share their religious convictions.

Other Focus activists like Daniel Weiss share Stanton's emphasis on using public arguments to achieve greater levels of mutual understanding:

> I think it's respectful to the culture [not to use religious claims] and I don't think that it's a betrayal of our beliefs either. It's a more effective way of communicating. . . . Would we like to talk that way in the public square? Well, that's not really our aim in the public square—to proselytize and convert. We do see our political philosophies and theologies combine in the sense that we believe that there's a certain order in society that needs to be upheld. You don't have to believe in Christ to see the benefits of an ordered society and the benefits of a society trying to strengthen marriages rather than weaken them. . . . Of course, theology animates and inspires that, but the goal isn't through policy to convert people over to the faith.[91]

Here too, Weiss insists that the Christian right's actions are not solely concerned with winning. He also argues that the use of "universal human arguments" is "respectful to the culture." Such statements indicate that these attempts to communicate in a language that all citizens can understand are motivated by at least some orientation toward understanding.

Weiss also expressed theological reasons for the use of such public arguments. As he explained,

In the Book of Acts, the apostle Paul is credited largely with the amazing spread of Christianity throughout the Roman Empire because he traveled everywhere and was such an eloquent and prolific writer. Paul goes to one town in Greece, spends some time there, and then goes to the market place where all of the folks talk and he starts talking to them about their own traditions. He's speaking to them in their own language—Greek was the common language—he's referencing their gods and he's making a reasoned case for believing in Jesus Christ as the true God based on their own faith, their own philosophers. So he's speaking the way they can understand. Now I think right now—for good or ill—not a lot of people understand the way Christians talk, so we speak their language.[92]

In his view, the contemporary Christian right's emphasis on humanism is not motivated solely by a desire to win or to transform America's democracy into theocracy but is also grounded in a theological account of how Christians ought to engage others in the public political forum.

There are two important caveats to this analysis of the Christian right's deliberative self-reflections. First, my non-randomized sampling method may have resulted in a bias toward interviewing activists who embrace a more deliberative mode of speaking. The activists who declined my requests for interviews may have been more dogmatic in their beliefs and more suspicious of outsiders. By contrast, those who agreed to meet with an outsider, such as me, may have had a more open and deliberative approach to politics. This possibility points to the suggestive nature of my conclusions and indicates that some Christian right activists may use such humanist arguments with a purely strategic intent. For analytic purposes, however, even one instance suffices to illustrate the nature and possibility of arguments directed at understanding.

Second, while these self-reflections imply a more deliberative mode of speaking, they do not rule out the possibility of purely strategic intent. Stanton's desire to "find our common starting place rather than our divisions" might have been a purely strategic attempt to win the debate. He might have discovered that finding common ground was the best way to ensure that his side prevails and embraced that approach only for that reason. While plausible, such an interpretation neglects the important differences between the self-reflections of Focus activists and those of CFV. Recall the declaration of CFV's strategist Tony Marco. He viewed CFV's mission as one of "destroying" the power of "gay militants . . . *at its roots*." Such purely strategic self-reflections stand in stark contrast to the statements of Stanton and Weiss. Their humanist rhetoric may be tinged with strategic intent, but their expressed desire to "respect" the culture and to find "common ground" come closer to realizing the deliberative qualities of sincerity and an orientation toward understanding.

My own, perhaps incomplete, judgment regarding these remarks is that they were sincere. The self-reflections of Christian right activists coupled with the consistency between the language of humanism and other Christian right discourses suggests that Focus's contemporary rhetoric of humanism, as used by the activists I interviewed, is more sincere than their earlier appeals to "No Special Rights." This analysis suggests that, in at least some instances, the Christian right's humanist rhetoric against same-sex marriage seeks understanding. In contrast to the purely strategic arguments of the early 1990s, this humanist rhetoric represents an effort to engage the opposition on familiar terms, find common ground, and open a constructive space for deliberation.

Openness to Revision
The humanist rhetoric of contemporary Christian right activists appears to embody the deliberative quality of sincerity. Yet to embody fully the qualities of deliberative persuasion, activists must also use this rhetoric with an openness to revise existing beliefs and preferences. Recall that in deliberative persuasion, the general orientation toward understanding of this form of speech arises from three primary aspects of speech: (1) the sincerity of speakers' arguments, (2) their focus on the merits,[93] and (3) their willingness to engage *deliberatively* in democratic conversation—to seek understanding with an openness to the possibility of revising their own beliefs and arguments. When viewed against this final aspect of the deliberative orientation toward understanding, the Christian right's humanist rhetoric yields mixed results.

First, consider the recent transformations in the Christian right's use of empirical research. In my interactions with their activists and opponents, both agree that the Christian right's appeals to empirical research have undergone a gradual process of revision and transformation over the last thirty years. During the 1980s and 1990s, groups like Focus and CFV appealed to empirical "research" that reinforced the stereotype of gays as deviants and sexual predators. To shock and disgust potential voters, for instance, CFV's 1992 election tabloid detailed lurid statistics concerning the sexual habits of gay men.[94] The source of many of the Christian right's "scientific" claims about gays and lesbians during this era was Paul Cameron—a Christian right psychologist prominently touted during the 1990s as an authority on homosexuality. Among other things, Cameron's studies, which relied on deeply flawed methodology, purported to show that homosexuals are ten to twenty times more likely than straight males to be child molesters, twenty times more likely to commit bestiality, and fifteen times more likely to commit murder.[95]

As the Christian right has evolved, this rhetorical emphasis on the "deviant" sexual habits of gays and lesbians has mostly disappeared. Pat Steadman, one of Colorado's leading lobbyists for gay and lesbian issues, told me, "You don't really see that negative rhetoric anymore, especially from Focus and some of the more polished people who are connected to them."[96] As we have seen, rather than using empirical research to expose the sexual patterns of gays and lesbians, groups like Focus now use empirical research to demonstrate the alleged risks that same-sex marriage and adoption pose to children.

The motivation behind this gradual revision in the Christian right's empirical appeals is unclear. Did this shift result from a deliberative effort to understand fellow citizens or a purely strategic effort on the part of activists to enhance their chances of political success? On the deliberative interpretation, this shift toward more accurate and respectful public arguments illustrates the willingness of activists to revise existing beliefs and arguments in the course of public debate. The fact that Christian right activists voluntarily revised the inaccuracies and divisiveness of their prior rhetoric shows that they have engaged in debate with a deliberative ethos of openness.

Yet political opponents of the Christian right point to an alternative, more strategic, interpretation. They argue that this shift was motivated not by the desire to better understand opponents but by sheer political necessity. As public attitudes toward homosexuality shifted over the last fifteen years, they argue, the Christian right was forced to abandon its prior empirical claims against gays and lesbians. As Michael Brewer, a leading Colorado advocate for gay and lesbian rights, told me,

> [This shift in rhetoric] has a lot to do with the growing acceptance and tolerance for gay people in society. More and more people know gay people and probably will not tolerate or be moved by that kind of rhetoric. It seems now, even compared to ten years ago, that it's the low road approach to attack people for who they are.[97]

In this interpretation, these transformations in the Christian right's appeals to empirical evidence derive from the general public's growing tolerance toward gays and lesbians, not from the growing deliberative spirit of the Christian right.

While it may be impossible to determine which interpretation most closely matches reality, these opposing views raise important questions.

They show that while the rhetoric of contemporary Christian right activists is more sincere than past appeals to "No Special Rights," it may not clearly emerge from the deliberative commitment to openness to revision.

A second complication arises from the Christian right's tenuous commitment to the attitudes of rigor, self-criticism, and openness to revision implicit in the scientific project.[98] An important tension lurks beneath the Christian right's appeals to scientific empirical evidence. The ethos of science includes a determination to follow the evidence where it leads and an openness to having one's views refuted. Yet many Christian right leaders, as conservative Christians, believe in the primacy of revealed religion and of truths known prior to and independently of scientific investigation.[99]

How do Christian right activists who believe in revealed truth reconcile this belief in Biblical literalism and inerrancy with the scientific method? I asked both Glenn Stanton of Focus and Paul Cameron of the Family Research Institute to describe their understanding of the relationship between faith and science. In both cases, they argued that they see these two worlds as tightly connected—that empirical research and religious convictions go hand-in-hand. Recall, for instance, Stanton's remark "We just don't have a belief in fideism—of pure faith. It's faith tied to something. This is a Christianity that is very well connected with fleshly everyday earthly existence."[100] Stanton's reflections need not suggest that Focus manipulates or "massages" data to bring it into conformity with God's will. These remarks on their face reflect a view of science and faith as interconnected.[101]

The risks of Stanton's holistic view of the relation between science and religion, however, are that dogmatic religious conviction may furnish a ground for discounting the reliability of evidence that does not fit Biblically revealed truths. This risk is particularly acute in the "research" of some of the Christian right's more radical activists. Paul Cameron, the researcher behind many of the Christian right's most lurid claims against the homosexual lifestyle, for instance, sees faith and scientific empirical research as so tightly intertwined that the findings of sound empirical research cannot conflict with religious precepts. "In the ultimate sense," he explained to me, "assuming that we have correctly gotten material from the real world, as a Christian I believe that it cannot be incompatible with God's intent and what the universe is about."[102] Cameron is quite explicit about the primacy of faith in his empirical research. As he told me, "Religious convictions are foundational in that they suggest where I should spend my energy. Obviously, you could ask questions about trees and use the same methodology. I'm interested in homosexuality because the Christian tradition and scripture have pointed to it as a terrible evil. And I want to see to what degree that's the case."[103]

Cameron's reflections reinforce the notion that in their appeals to empirical research, the commitment of at least some Christian right activists to the deliberative ideal of openness to revision may only be partial. His statement that empirical research "cannot be incompatible with God's intent," for example, displays a potential unwillingness to revise existing beliefs. It shows that on the radical fringe of the Christian right movement, researchers and activists may engage in scientific exploration and deliberation to promote their preexisting beliefs—that they may have no intention of revising their religious or political convictions based upon the results of deliberation.

Along with the unclear motives behind the recent transformations in Christian right rhetoric, these reflections complicate the simple conclusion that all contemporary Christian right activists engage in deliberative persuasion. While the humanist rhetoric of groups like Focus may often be sincere, it may not always satisfy deliberative persuasion's requirement that speakers engage in debate with an openness to revising existing beliefs and arguments and with the goal of achieving understanding. To be sure, some rank-and-file members and elites may act with this attitude of openness. Yet we have seen that the deliberative ethos of openness to revision is not ubiquitous. Some Christian right activists, especially those on the radical fringes of the movement, seem unwilling to question or revise beliefs grounded in revealed religion.

Table 3.1.   Three Moments in the Christian Right's Two-Tiered Rhetoric

	1. Self-Description of Intent	2. Discursive Inconsistency	3. Use of Hidden or Irrational Tactics?	Form of Speech
The Christian Coalition's "Stealth" Rhetoric	Intent to Win at All Costs (Using Hidden Force)	Yes	Yes	Manipulation
Colorado for Family Values's Rhetoric of "No Special Rights"	Intent to Win	Yes	No	Strategic Persuasion
Focus on the Family's Rhetoric of Humanism	Intent to Understand	No	No	Deliberative Persuasion*

The above table represents the qualities of speech that arise in each of these three cases of the Christian right's two-tiered rhetoric. While such real-world instances of rhetoric may not wholly embody the qualities of deliberative, strategic, and manipulative speech, these categories provide an important moral spectrum. They offer a theoretical framework for distinguishing morally ideal forms of speech from those that are morally decent or morally problematic. The asterisk after "Deliberative Persuasion" refers to the fact that Focus on the Family's rhetoric only partially realizes this ideal. While its activists appear to express a sincere orientation toward understanding, a tenuous relation to science calls into question whether these activists employ humanist arguments with a true openness to revising their claims.

These three cases illustrate that the Christian right's two-tiered rhetoric can, depending on context and intent, embody the qualities of all three modes of speech designed to change minds. The Christian Coalition used a two-tiered strategy to manipulate; Colorado for Family Values used it to persuade strategically; and Focus on the Family used it to persuade more deliberatively. These distinctions are not based simply on the self-reflections of Christian right activists, which could easily be manipulated, but rather on a mixture of investigations into the political context, discursive consistency, and self-reflections of Christian right activists. Understanding the moral dimensions of rhetoric requires going beyond the content of what is said at a particular moment to a deeper investigation of context and intent.

In everyday politics, our evaluations of these dimensions of speech will often be more indeterminate than the conclusions that arise in these three cases. Only extensive access to internal communications and reflections, as in the case of the Christian Coalition, allows us to identify manipulative acts with a high likelihood of accuracy. As we have seen, even with such information, the lines between deliberative, strategic, and manipulative speech are often blurred. Evaluations of the manipulative character of speech will always yield, to a greater or lesser degree, indeterminate results.

Yet the inevitability of indeterminacy does not require abandoning all efforts to detect and mitigate the threat that manipulative speech poses for democracy. In the chapters that follow, I argue that while manipulative speech is often difficult to identify, its dangers can be mitigated by thinking in a more Madisonian, institutionally grounded, way. This approach marks a shift away from evaluating specific forms of manipulative speech toward a broader evaluation of discursive context. It argues that in addition to improving our theoretical understanding of strategic and manipulative speech, we should also explore structural conditions that diminish the power of manipulative speech and discourage would-be manipulators.

Notes

1. Glenn T. Stanton, *Why Marriage Matters* (Colorado Springs, CO: Navpress Publishing Group, 1997); Glenn T. Stanton and Bill Maier, *Marriage on Trial: The Case against Same-Sex Marriage and Parenting* (Downers Grove, IL: Intervarsity Press, 2004).

2. Glenn T. Stanton, "Debate-Tested Sound Bites on Defending Marriage," 2003. Internal training memo on file with author.

3. Interview with Glenn Stanton, June 6, 2006.

4. Telephone interview with Alan Wisdom, June 28, 2005.

5. Interview with Daniel Weiss, July 6, 2006.

6. For Rawls's discussion of public reason, see John Rawls, *Political Liberalism* (New York: Columbia University Press, 1993); and John Rawls, "The Idea of Public Reason Revisited," in *The Law of Peoples with "The Idea of Public Reason Revisited"* (Cambridge: Harvard University Press, 1999).

7. For a more detailed analysis of the parallels between the Christian right's two-tiered rhetoric and Rawls's conception of public reasons, see Nathaniel J. Klemp and Stephen Macedo, "The Christian Right, Public Reason, and American Democracy," ed. Stephen Brint and Jean Schroedel, *Evangelicals and Democracy in America*, vol. 2 (New York: Russell Sage Foundation, 2009).

8. For discussions of this shift, see Jean Hardisty, *Mobilizing Resentment* (Boston: Beacon Press, 1999); Didi Herman, *The Antigay Agenda: Orthodox Vision and the Christian Right* (Chicago: University of Chicago Press, 1997); Allen D. Hertzke, *Representing God in Washington* (Knoxville: University of Tennessee Press, 1988); Nathaniel J. Klemp, "Beyond God-Talk: Understanding the Christian Right from the Ground Up," *Polity* 39 no. 4 (October 2007); Michael Moen, *The Transformation of the Christian Right* (Tuscaloosa: University of Alabama Press, 1992); Michael Moen, "From Revolution to Evolution: The Changing Nature of the Christian Right," in *The Rapture of Politics*, ed. Peter Kivisto, Steve Bruce, and William H. Swatos Jr. (New Brunswick, NJ: Transaction Publishers, 1995). For an empirical study of political groups that do the opposite, emphasizing private reasons in public and public reasons in private, see Nina Eliasoph, *Avoiding Politics* (New York: Cambridge University Press, 1998).

9. James Dobson, "Marriage on the Ropes," Focus on the Family newsletter, September 2003.

10. Interview with Glenn Stanton, June 6, 2006.

11. Hardisty, *Mobilizing Resentment*, 114; Chris Hedges, *American Fascists: The Christian Right and the War on America* (New York: Free Press, 2007), 16.

12. Rawls, "The Idea of Public Reason Revisited."

13. Rawls, "The Idea of Public Reason Revisited," 137.

14. For detailed criticism of the empirical application of Habermas's theory see Robert Wuthnow, James Davidson Hunter, Albert Bergesen, and Edith Kurzweil, *Cultural Analysis* (Boston: Routledge & Kegan Paul, 1984).

15. Jurgen Habermas, *The Theory of Communicative Action*, trans. Thomas McCarthy (Boston: Beacon Press, 1984), 286.

16. Habermas, *The Theory of Communicative Action*, 286.

17. Kenneth Burke, *A Grammar of Motives* (Berkeley: University of California Press, 1969), xv. For other reflections on the investigating motives, see C. Wright Mills, "Situated Actions and Vocabularies of Motive," *American Sociological Review* 9, no. 1 (1940); Steve Bruce and Roy Wallis, "Rescuing Motives," *British Journal of Sociology* 34, no. 1 (1983).

18. I interviewed the following Christian right activists:
   - Ed Brookover (chairman of political practice at Greener and Hook, Arlington, VA)

- Paul Cameron (director of the Family Research Institute, Colorado Springs, CO)
- Bruce Hausknecht (legal council for Focus on the Family, Colorado Springs, CO)
- Glenn Stanton (interviewed three times; head of marriage and sexuality at Focus on the Family, Colorado Springs, CO)
- Daniel Weiss (interviewed two times; director of pornography policy at Focus on the Family, Colorado Springs, CO)
- Alan Wisdom (vice president of the Institute on Religion and Democracy, Washington, DC)

19. I interviewed the following Colorado Springs lawmakers:
- Jerry Heimlicher (city council member, Colorado Springs, CO)
- Scott Hente (city council member, Colorado Springs, CO)
- Mary Lou Makepeace (former mayor, Colorado Springs, CO)

20. I interviewed the following liberal opponents of Focus on the Family:
- Ryan Acker (director of the Pikes Peak Gay and Lesbian Organization, Colorado Springs, CO)
- Greg Borum (former executive director of the Citizens Project, Colorado Springs, CO)
- Michael Brewer (public policy director of the GLBT Community Center of Colorado, Denver, CO)
- Jen Caltrider (executive producer at ProgressNow.org, Denver, CO)
- Jean Dubofsky (head legal council in *Romer v. Evans*, Boulder, CO)
- Nancy MacDonald (former director of P-FLAG, Norman, OK)
- Mary Lou Makepeace (executive director of the Gay and Lesbian Fund, Colorado Springs, CO)
- Nori Rost (founder and executive director of Just Spirit, Colorado Springs, CO)
- Jason Salzman (director of Cause Communications, Denver, CO)
- Richard Sleght (former president of the Pikes Peak InterFaith Council, Colorado Springs, CO)
- Pat Steadman (Menedez Steadman and Associates, Denver, CO)
- Dean Tollefson (community chaplain, Colorado Springs, CO)
- Barb Van Hoy (interim director of the Citizen's Project, Colorado Springs, CO)
- James White (former pastor of the First Congregational Church, Colorado Springs, CO)
- Mel White (former ghost writer for Pat Robertson and head of Soulforce.org, Lynchberg, VA)
- Heath Wickline (director of the SPIN Project, San Francisco, CA)

21. These secondary sources include Sara Diamond, *Not By Politics Alone* (New York: Guilford Press, 1998); Matthew Freeman, *The San Diego Model: A Community Battles the Religious Right* (Washington, DC: People for the American Way, 1993); Jean Hardisty, "Constructing Homophobia: Colorado's Right-Wing Attack on Homosexuals," in *Eyes Right!* ed. Chip Berlet (Boston: South End Press, 1995); Jean Hardisty, *Mobilizing Resentment* (Boston: Beacon Press, 1999); Didi Herman, *The Antigay Agenda: Orthodox Vision and the Christian Right* (Chicago: University of Chicago Press, 1997); Allen D. Hertzke, *Representing God in Washington* (Knoxville: University of Tennessee Press, 1988); Clyde Wilcox and Carin Larson, *Onward Christian Soldiers?* (Boulder, CO: Westview Press, 2006); Julia Lesage, "Christian

Coalition Leadership Training," in *Media Culture and the Christian Right*, ed. Linda Kintz and Julia Lesage (Minneapolis: University of Minnesota Press, 1998); Michael Moen, *The Transformation of the Christian Right* (Tuscaloosa: University of Alabama Press, 1992); and James Penning, "Pat Robertson and the GOP: 1988 and Beyond, " *Sociology of Religion* 55, no. 3 (1994).

22. Erving Goffman, *The Presentation of Self in Everyday Life* (New York: Doubleday, 1959), 106–11.

23. "Inconsistency," *Oxford English Dictionary*, 2008.

24. Ludwig Wittgenstein, *Philosophical Investigations* (New York: Prentice Hall, 1999), 71.

25. Dennis F. Thompson, "Hypocrisy and Democracy," in *Liberalism without Illusions*, ed. Bernard Yack (Chicago: University of Chicago Press, 1995), 179.

26. While my research and observations are likely to be tinged by my political and philosophical biases, I do not use randomized sampling methods to mitigate these biases. One reason is that interviews with political elites resist this kind of randomized procedure. Face-time with political leaders and activists (especially those in the Christian right) is difficult to get, which means that it is nearly impossible to come up with a random selection of political elites and be assured of meeting with those selected. For more on elite interviewing, see Robert L. Peabody, Susan Webb Hammond, Jean Torcom, Lynne P. Brown, Carolyn Thompson, and Robert Kolodny, "Interviewing Political Elites," *PS: Political Science and Politics* 23, no. 3 (1990). As many journalists note, securing an interview with James Dobson is just as difficult, if not more so, than securing an interview with the president of the United States. See, for example, Dan Gilgoff, *The Jesus Machine* (New York: St. Martin's Press, 2007). To diminish selection bias, however, I worked to research the rhetoric of the Christian right from a variety of oppositional and sympathetic political perspectives. This attempt to balance opposing perspectives coheres with many approaches in historiography, see Ian S. Lustic, "History, Historiography, and Political Science: Multiple Historical Records and the Problem of Selection Bias," *American Political Science Review* 90, no. 3 (1996). Despite these efforts to mitigate bias, the small size of the sample means that my empirical conclusions should be viewed as suggestive rather than definitive.

27. The section-heading quotation is taken from Ralph Reed, former head of the Christian Coalition, discussing his organization's "stealth" tactics. "The Religious Right Is Flying Low," *St. Petersburg Times*, August 9, 1995, 7E.

28. Penning, "Pat Robertson and the GOP," 337.

29. Penning, "Pat Robertson and the GOP," 338.

30. Moen, *The Transformation of the Christian Right*, 108.

31. Freeman, *The San Diego Model*, 9.

32. Freeman, *The San Diego Model*, 19.

33. "Christian Group Coaches School Board Candidates," *New York Times*, June 14, 1995, B8.

34. Diamond, *Not By Politics Alone*; Freeman, *The San Diego Model*; Hardisty, "Constructing Homophobia"; Wilcox and Larson, *Onward Christian Soldiers?*; Penning, "Pat Robertson and the GOP."

35. "How to Participate in a Political Party," internal memo obtained by People for the American Way and used at the Iowa Republican County Caucus, March 1986. On file with author.

36. Seth Mydans, "Evangelicals Gain with Covert Candidates," *New York Times*, October 27, 1992, 1A.

37. Freeman, *The San Diego Model*, 20.

38. Freeman, *The San Diego Model*, 19–23.

39. Freeman, *The San Diego Model*, 18–19.

40. Freeman, *The San Diego Model*, 45–46.

41. "How to Participate in a Political Party."

42. Freeman, *The San Diego Model*, 19.

43. Mydans, "Evangelicals Gain with Covert Candidates."

44. Joan Lowy, "Stealth Christian Coalition Is Making Inroads in Politics," *Houston Chronicle*, January 3, 1993, 4A.

45. Lowy, "Stealth Christian Coalition."

46. Mydans, "Evangelicals Gain with Covert Candidates."

47. Freeman, *The San Diego Model*, 16; Penning, "Pat Robertson and the GOP," 338.

48. Alan Dershowitz, "Beware of the Stealth Candidates," *Buffalo News*, August 9, 1995, 3B.

49. "How to Participate in a Political Party."

50. "How to Participate in a Political Party."

51. The *Oxford English Dictionary* definition of "intentional" stresses this phrase, see *Oxford English Dictionary*, 2007.

52. Freeman, *The San Diego Model*, 18.

53. Hardisty, *Mobilizing Resentment*, 110.

54. "How to Participate in a Political Party."

55. "How to Participate in a Political Party."

56. Mydans, "Evangelicals Gain with Covert Candidates."

57. "Mobilizing the Christian Right," *Campaigns and Elections*, October/November, 1993.

58. Aside from Moen's book, Allen Hertzke makes a similar claim about the Christian right's shift toward more public rhetoric, see Hertzke, *Representing God in Washington*. See also Moen, "From Revolution to Evolution."

59. Hertzke, *Representing God in Washington*, 195.

60. Moen, *The Transformation of the Christian Right*, 129.

61. Though the National Legal Federation, a prominent conservative legal group, advised CFV to avoid this phrasing in the text of the amendment, they confirmed that the "No Special Rights" slogan served as the perfect centerpiece for public messaging; see Hardisty, "Constructing Homophobia," 102.

62. Interview with Jean Dubofsky, June 23, 2006. For another important analysis of the "special rights" spin, see Diamond, *Not By Politics Alone*, 156–72.

63. See "STOP Special Class Status for Homosexuality: Vote YES! On Amendment 2," 1992. Campaign mailer used by CFV during the 1992 election. On file with author. See also Herman, *The Antigay Agenda*, 118.

64. Lesage, "Christian Coalition Leadership Training," 340.

65. Hardisty, "Constructing Homophobia," 103. Emphasis mine.

66. "STOP Special Class Status for Homosexuality: Vote YES! On Amendment 2," 1992. Emphasis mine.

67. "STOP Special Class Status for Homosexuality: Vote YES! On Amendment 2," 1992. Emphasis mine.

68. "STOP Special Class Status for Homosexuality: Vote YES! On Amendment 2," 1992.

69. Herman, *The Antigay Agenda*, 130.

70. Herman notes that Perkins expressed these sentiments in an interview with her. See Herman, *The Antigay Agenda*, 130.

71. Herman, *The Antigay Agenda*, 131.

72. Herman, *The Antigay Agenda*, 131.

73. Moen, *The Transformation of the Christian Right*, 132.

74. Herman, *The Antigay Agenda*, 114. Emphasis in original.

75. For a discussion of consequentialism see Philip Pettit, "Consequentialism," in *A Companion to Ethics*, ed. Peter Singer (Oxford: Blackwell Publishers, 1991).

76. Telephone interview with Michael Brewer, July 6, 2006.

77. Glenn T. Stanton, "Talking Points: Same-Sex Marriage," *Citizen Magazine*, 2005.

78. Glenn T. Stanton, "The Conservative Humanist," Christian Vision Project, 2006, www.christianvisionproject.com/2006/04/the_conservative_humanist_1.html.

79. "Humanism," *Oxford English Dictionary*, 2007.

80. Diamond, *Not By Politics Alone*, 70.

81. James Dobson, *Children at Risk* (Dallas: Word Publishing, 1990), 22.

82. Dobson, "Marriage on the Ropes."

83. Dobson, "Marriage on the Ropes."

84. Interview with Glenn Stanton, June 6, 2006.

85. "Pornography Home," Focus on the Family, March 26, 2007, www.citizenlink.org/FOSI/pornography/.

86. "Gambling and Suicide," Focus on the Family, March 26, 2007, www.citizenlink.org/FOSI/gambling/A000002167.cfm.

87. "Abstinence Policy," Focus on the Family, March 26, 2007, www.citizenlink.org/FOSI/abstinence/.

88. Interview with Glenn Stanton, June 6, 2006.

89. Interview with Glenn Stanton, June 6, 2006.

90. Interview with Glenn Stanton, June 6, 2006.

91. Interview with Daniel Weiss, July 6, 2006.

92. Interview with Daniel Weiss, July 6, 2006.

93. I focus primarily on the first and third quality of deliberative persuasion not because the second quality—a focus on the merits—is less important but to offer a more focused and in-depth analysis. The first and third qualities illustrate the tension that arises in the Christian right's rhetoric. They show that while this rhetoric tends to embody sincerity, it often departs from a full realization of the deliberative ideal of openness to revision.

94. Here are just a few of CFV's empirical claims:

- "Overall, surveys show that 90% of gay men engage in anal intercourse—the most high-risk sexual behavior in society today. (No wonder 83% of Colorado AIDS cases have occurred in gay males—it's a tragedy, but it's true.)"
- "80% of gay men surveyed have engaged in oral sex upon the anus of partners."
- "Well over a third of gays in 1977 admitted to 'fisting.'"

See "STOP Special Class Status for Homosexuality: Vote YES! On Amendment 2," 1992.

95. Chris Bull and John Gallagher, *Perfect Enemies* (New York: Madison Books, 1996), 27.

96. Interview with Pat Steadman, July 10, 2006.

97. Telephone interview with Michael Brewer, July 8, 2006.

98. I am grateful to Stephen Macedo for many insights in this discussion of the intersection between faith and science. For an in-depth discussion of these issues, see Klemp and Macedo, "The Christian Right, Public Reason, and American Democracy."

99. This tension between the use of empirical evidence and religion is further reinforced by survey data on the beliefs of conservative Christians. First, these surveys show that a small majority of conservative Christians believe in the literal and inerrant truth of the Bible. Greeley and Hout find that while the belief in Biblical literalism has declined somewhat throughout the last thirty years. 54 percent of conservative Protestants endorse the statement "The Bible is the actual word of God and is to be taken literally, word for word." Andrew Greeley and Michael Hout, *The Truth about Conservative Christians* (Chicago: University of Chicago Press, 2006), 15. Christian Smith reaches similar conclusions about the percentage of conservative Christians who embrace Biblical literalism. He finds 52 percent of "evangelicals" and 61 percent of "fundamentalists" believe that the Bible is "literally true." Christian Smith, *American Evangelicalism* (Chicago: University of Chicago Press, 1998), 2.

100. Interview with Glenn Stanton, June 6, 2006.

101. They also express a very different understanding of the relation between faith and science from the views that Christian Smith reports in his study of liberal Protestants. Smith quotes one of his interviewees as describing these two realms of understanding as entirely separate: "I have never had any intellectual conflicts between my faith and my science, because I am very successful at wearing a multitude of hats and playing a multitude of roles . . . My faith and science may never come together, which is fine." Smith, *American Evangelicalism*, 58.

102. Telephone interview with Paul Cameron, July 10, 2006.

103. Telephone interview with Paul Cameron, July 10, 2006.

PART III

THE MORAL QUALITIES
OF RHETORICAL CONTEXT

CHAPTER FOUR

~

Contextualizing Rhetoric

From Contestatory to
One-Sided Information Spaces

Unless opinions favourable to democracy and to aristocracy, to property
and to equality, to co-operation and to competition, to luxury and to
abstinence, to sociality and individuality, to liberty and discipline, and
all the other standing antagonisms of political life, are expressed with
equal freedom, and enforced and defended with equal talent and energy,
there is no chance of both elements obtaining their due; one scale is sure
to go up, and the other down.

—John Stuart Mill, "On Liberty"[1]

Mill's words offer an important reminder that questions concerning the
morality of spin extend beyond a simple analysis of ideal speech types. Understanding when deliberative, strategic, and manipulative forms of speech
enhance or diminish democracy requires investigating the conditions in
which opposing positions are or are not, as Mill puts it, "expressed with equal
freedom."

In previous chapters, I have often assumed a simplified discursive situation—an exchange between a single speaker and listener—to illuminate the
moral qualities of these three ideal speech types. As Mill reminds us, however, political life consists of an abundance of "antagonisms." Political debate
in practice arises in a vast array of complex and overlapping discursive environments, rich with a myriad of speakers, offering conflicting political ideals.

To address the contextual complexities of political life, this chapter asks
how the moral qualities of deliberative, strategic, and manipulative rhetoric

are influenced by the broader deliberative context. Following Mill and others, I argue that the moral quality of speech is shaped not simply by how it corresponds to the three ideal speech types but also by the quality of the discursive environment within which it emerges. My claim is that *contestatory spaces*—where diverse views are exchanged under conditions of fair competition—enhance democracy. Such contexts bolster the moral quality of persuasive speech and strategic speech, and may even allow for the emergence of morally legitimate forms of manipulative speech. The flip side of this claim is that *one-sided information spaces*—where a single political, religious, or ethical perspective is insulated from oppositional views—undermine democracy. When such contexts arise in the public arena of deliberation, they have corrosive effects on even the most ideal forms of deliberative persuasion and deepen the dangers of manipulative rhetoric.

This chapter has two sections. In the first, I outline two arguments for contestatory deliberative spaces: the *epistemic claim* and the *non-domination claim*. In the second section, I argue that these two arguments for contestation point toward three principles for evaluating deliberative context: (1) the Principle of Fair Competition, (2) the Principle of Rhetorical Diversity, and (3) the Principle of Independent Public Scrutiny. Finally, I consider the interactions between this contextual ideal and the three ideal speech types presented in chapter 2. These principles, I argue, show that deliberative context plays a profound role in determining the moral value of all three ideal forms of speech.

Two Arguments for Contestation

In what follows, I outline two arguments for contestatory spaces. The first argument—*the epistemic claim*—views the clash of opposing interests as a means for uncovering errors and improving the general public's understanding of political matters. Throughout the history of political thought, theorists have appealed to some variation of the epistemic claim to justify debate between citizens and lawmakers holding a diversity of views. Recall that in *The Politics*, Aristotle likens the combination of minds to a potluck dinner: "The many, of whom none is individually an excellent man, nevertheless can when joined together be better—not as individuals but all together—than those [who are best], just as dinners contributed [by many] can be better than those equipped from a single expenditure."[2]

Most modern deliberative democrats share these epistemic commitments. "Through the give and take of argument," explain Gutmann and Thompson, "participants can learn from each other, come to recognize their individual and collective misapprehensions, and develop new views and policies that can more successfully withstand critical scrutiny."[3]

At the individual level, deliberative democrats claim that deliberation exposes citizens to the interests of others; it clarifies the interests and values at stake for various parties; and it helps transform and shift poorly informed preferences and correct epistemic errors. At the social level, they argue that deliberation corrects errors and enriches the public marketplace of ideas. When contestation and debate flourish, they claim, socially held beliefs are reexamined, flawed beliefs are uncovered, and new and better arguments rise to the surface.[4]

In "On Liberty," Mill offers perhaps the most robust defense of this epistemic claim. His contention is that anti-contestatory conditions, limiting the free flow of ideas, have negative effects on the public's political understanding. For Mill, any effort to censor opinions is "robbing the human race." As he puts it, "If the opinion is right, they are deprived of the opportunity of exchanging error for truth: if wrong, they lose, what is almost as great a benefit, the clearer perception and livelier impression of truth, produced by its collision with error."[5]

Mill's words illuminate the two pillars of his epistemic argument for contestation. The first is that anti-contestatory conditions suppress the free expression of true opinions. As a result, the errors and falsehoods pervading the public consciousness are likely to go unchecked and uncorrected. True opinions will be less likely to emerge. Mill attributes this problem to the partiality and one-sidedness of human beings. Each individual, he argues, has a "world" of knowledge and experience shaped by contingency and historical accident. The "world" of each individual is "the part of it with which he comes in contact; his party, his sect, his church, his class of society."[6] Problems arise because humans tend to reify their partial "worlds" into something universal and absolute. Their particular beliefs become beliefs that all humans should hold. Their "world" takes on a presumption of infallibility. As Mill explains, "He devolves upon his own world the responsibility of being in the right against dissentient worlds of other people; and it never troubles him that mere accident has decided which of these numerous worlds is the object of his reliance."[7]

Mill thinks that the best antidote to the partiality and one-sidedness of each person's world is free and open public discussion. When a diversity of opinions and views enters the public arena, this partiality and one-sidedness can be challenged, contested, and corrected. "The only way in which a human being can make some approach to knowing the whole of a subject," Mill declares, "is by hearing what can be said about it by persons of every variety of opinion, and studying all modes in which it can be looked at by every character of mind."[8] In other words, only discussion and contestation in a context of diverse opinions can dissolve the partiality of the human mind and open the possibility of correcting errors and arriving at truth.

Mill's epistemic argument for contestation also involves a second claim. Mill tells us that even if the public holds true beliefs, anti-contestatory conditions limiting the expression of false beliefs erode the vitality of these truths. The truths will become lifeless abstractions. They will lose meaning and cease to be held as real knowledge. However true any given belief may be, Mill insists, "If it is not fully, frequently, and fearlessly discussed, it will be held as a dead dogma, not a living truth."[9] So contestation not only weeds out errors and misapprehensions; it also forces us to continually reevaluate our truest beliefs and, in so doing, cultivates a living and vital form of knowledge.

Finally, Mill highlights a third consideration. In addition to situations where received opinions are either true or false, we often encounter instances where opinions involve fragments of the truth. In such instances, orthodox and heretical doctrines cannot neatly be sorted into truth and falsity. Instead, each contains a fragment of the whole truth. Mill claims that in the actual practice of politics, this "case is hitherto the most frequent, as, in the human mind, one-sidedness has always been the rule, and many-sidedness the exception."[10] The crucial point is that, as in the other cases, robust public contestation is the best method for combining these "incomplete truths" and moving closer to beliefs that approximate the whole truth.[11]

While Mill's claims for contestation are largely theoretical, a growing literature on group behavior confirms his basic insight: one-sidedness and partiality erode the epistemic benefits of deliberation.[12] In homogenous groups, where members share similar knowledge and biases, contestation and debate appear not to enhance but to actively diminish the likelihood of uncovering epistemic errors. Consider what occurred when sixty citizens in Colorado were put in ten deliberative groups.[13] In this experiment, participants were divided into "red state groups," consisting of conservatives from Colorado Springs, and "blue state groups," consisting of liberals from Boulder. Members of these groups were asked to state their opinions on questions about same-sex marriage, affirmative action, and global warming before and after fifteen minutes of discussion within their groups.

What were the effects of deliberation? As Cass Sunstein explains, "In almost every group, members ended up with more extreme positions after they spoke with one another. Discussion made civil unions more popular among liberals; discussion made civil unions less popular among conservatives."[14]

This study along with others shows that in many circumstances, deliberation within like-minded groups has polarizing effects.[15] Along with pushing groups toward extreme positions, such deliberations tend to ossify, rather than correct, epistemic errors and biases. When groups lean toward the wrong answer, the polarizing effects of deliberation can push groups further toward bad informational outcomes.[16]

The potential for deliberative distortion is not unique to homogeneous groups. Even in heterogeneous groups, a number of factors limit the diversity and multisidedness of contestation. One problem arises from "hidden profiles."[17] Hidden profiles occur when accurate information exists in the group but cannot be obtained because of several empirical barriers. One problem is that, as Tocqueville might remind us, majorities can have tyrannical effects on the minority in the group, silencing ideas and information that fall outside the majority opinion.[18] This silencing effect occurs because those in the minority have incentives to stay quiet: opposing the majority places their reputation in jeopardy; supporting it does not. Mill understood this problem. A social state that encourages this kind of "intellectual pacification," he argues, "cannot send forth the open, fearless characters, and logical, consistent intellects who once adorned the thinking world."[19]

Another problem Mill does not address is that information may be concealed because low-status members with relevant information often defer to high-status members.[20] When confronted with the assertions of confident high-status members, minorities, women, and others with lower social status often accept, rather than actively challenge, these assertions.

Taken together, these findings support Mill's claim that one-sided information spaces limiting the diversity and openness of discussion diminish epistemic outcomes. Contemporary empirical research suggests that anti-contestatory conditions—such as group polarization and conditions that produce hidden profiles—undermine the epistemic benefits of deliberation. In short, whether contestation enhances or erodes collective understanding is deeply contextual; it depends on the openness and diversity of opinion in the deliberative context.[21]

Contestation as Non-Domination

The second argument—*the non-domination claim*—offers a more fundamental defense of robust public contestation between diverse interests. This claim asserts that the primary value of public contestation lies in its capacity to diminish the likelihood of any individual or group wielding absolute or arbitrary forms of power over others. This claim is based on Madison's insight in

Federalist 51 that to avoid tyranny, the branches of government ought to be separated so that "ambition must be made to counter ambition."[22] Like the formal separation of powers, diverse contestatory spaces place checks on the rhetorical power of individuals and groups. They also create disincentives that discourage the use of manipulative rhetoric.

While I rely on Madison to draw out this claim, Mill often hints at the role of contestation in preventing potential abuses of power. As he declares in "On Liberty":

> In politics . . . it is almost a commonplace, that a party of order or stability, and a party of progress or reform, are both necessary elements of a healthy state of political life. . . . Each of these modes of thinking derives its utility from the deficiencies of the other; but it is in a great measure the opposition of the other that keeps each within the limits of reason and sanity.[23]

As we shall see, Mill's words echo Madison's insight that the fair competition of rival interests places implicit checks on the emergence of corruption and tyranny.

To illuminate the theoretical foundations of this argument, consider Madison's reflections on the separation of powers. Although Madison's primary interest in Federalist 51 is not political rhetoric but the structure of the federal system of government, his insights yield important implications for our analysis of ideal contextual conditions. In the tradition of Locke and Montesquieu, Madison tells us that to avoid tyranny, the powers of government must be separated. He begins his argument with a claim about human nature. When the power of the state is vested in a single body, he argues, there can be no assurance of good government because ambition—or love of power—is an inescapable feature of the human condition. The very fact that we need government, he thinks, is proof that humans tend to be selfish and power hungry—that we are not "angels." "If men were angels," Madison insists, "no government would be necessary."[24] Since those involved in politics are easily swept up by ambition, placing political authority in the hands of a single branch opens the door to tyranny; it leaves the potentially repressive will of this single branch unchecked and ripe for exploitation.

To protect the people from tyranny, Madison recommends that each branch be given a "will of its own" as well as the "constitutional means and personal motives to resist the encroachment of others."[25] This arrangement aims to structure political institutions so the self-serving motives of each branch act as a check on the others. "The constant aim," he declares, "is to divide and arrange the several offices in such a manner as that each may be a check on the other—that the private interest of every individual may be a sentinel over the public rights."[26] In effect, Madison solves the problem of tyranny by dividing potential tyrants into three opposing camps and structuring institutions so each camp has significant incentives to thwart attempts by each of the others to overreach its powers. The resulting framework of political institutions ensures "that the private interest of every individual may be a sentinel over public rights."[27]

Implicit in Madison's argument for the separation of powers is a republican claim against conditions of tyranny. In the vocabulary of contemporary republican theorists, Madison's account is an institutional strategy for securing non-domination.

On Philip Pettit's view, domination consists of three conditions. In conditions of domination, an agent exercises power where

1. the agent has the capacity to interfere
2. on an arbitrary basis
3. in certain choices that the other is in a position to make.[28]

Before applying this formulation to political rhetoric, it is worth unpacking each of Pettit's three conditions. The first condition stipulates that one agent has the capacity to interfere with or to distort other agents' choices or range of options. In Pettit's words, "All interfering behaviors, coercive or manipulative, are intended by the interferer to worsen the agent's choice situation by changing the range of options available, or by altering the expected payoffs assigned to those options, or by assuming control over which outcomes will result from which options and what actual payoffs, therefore, will materialize."[29]

Yet not all agents with the capacity to interfere in the choices of others are engaged in domination. Pettit's second condition stipulates that in domination, this capacity to interfere has an arbitrary quality. It must, as Pettit puts it, arise in situations where the agents were "in a position to choose" whether or not to interfere "at their pleasure."[30] The slave master dominates his slaves not simply because he has the capacity to interfere in their choices but because his interfering actions cannot be contested or challenged. Such agents exert arbitrary power over others. The opposite of arbitrariness is responsiveness, which promotes non-domination.[31] When the capacity of groups or individuals to interfere with the choices of others is subject to significant challenge and contestation, the arbitrariness of their power dissolves. Such agents must contend with the objections and challenges of rival interests and thus can no longer interfere with the choices of others "at their pleasure."

Finally, this conception of domination asserts that domination may only interfere with "certain" choices. Pettit's point is that the dominating agent need not have the potential to interfere with all of the other agent's choices. Instead, dominating relationships may only affect a small sphere of others' choices.

These three conditions outline a conception of freedom that departs from the traditional liberal ideal of non-interference. Liberal conceptions of non-interference simply stipulate that freedom exists in the absence of the interference of other agents. Pettit's conception of non-domination, by contrast, outlines an ideal of freedom that accounts for more implicit forms of control. As Pettit puts it, "What constitutes domination is the fact that in some respect the power-bearer has the capacity to interfere arbitrarily, even if they are never going to do so."[32] The crucial difference is that Pettit's view accounts for *potential* interference, where agents can interfere in others' choices at moments of their own choosing. When a politician can manipulate citizens in a situation where they do not have the information or resources to contest or resist his will, for instance, domination is present, even if he never actually engages in manipulation.

Pettit's conception of domination clarifies and reinforces Madison's argument for decentralized checks and balances. Though Madison never mentions it explicitly, the idea of domination arises implicitly in his objections to what he calls "pure democracy." In Federalist 10, Madison worries that by centralizing the power of the state in a single set of hands, such pure democracies will undermine the "rights of other citizens." Within such democracies, he tells us, "a common passion or interest will, in almost every case, be felt by a majority of the whole . . . and there is nothing to check the inducements to sacrifice the weaker party or an obnoxious individual."[33] In Pettit's terms, the problem with "pure democracy" is that it creates a power relationship in which a single group—the majority—can interfere in the choices of other citizens without facing significant challenge or contestation. To prevent such conditions, Madison calls for a "republic" where the sheer size of the citizenry, its representative structure, and separation of powers among branches of government ensures that no individual or faction wields absolute power over other citizens.

Rhetorical Conditions of Non-Domination

In Robert Dahl's critical account, he worries that Madison's argument "exaggerates the importance, in preventing tyranny, of specified checks to governmental officials by other specified government officials; it underestimates the importance of the inherent social checks and balances existing in every pluralistic society."[34] Madison, he argues, fails to extend his insight to the implicit checks that arise from "such things as loss of status, respect, prestige, and friendship."[35]

While it was not his primary focus, I argue that Madison does seek to extend his reflections on the separation of powers beyond the formal structures of government. In fact, he extends this insight to the focus of our inquiry: the informal system of political debate and communication. In Federalist 51, he explicitly declares that the checking function of ambition is not just a peculiarity of government. It applies throughout the political and social world: "This policy of supplying, by opposite and rival interests, the defect of better motives," he remarks, "might be traced through the whole system of human affairs, private as well as public."[36]

When applied to the exchange of political rhetoric in the deliberative system, Madison's conclusion that "ambition must be made to counter ambition" calls for robust conditions of contestation and debate.[37] In the closing lines of Federalist 10, Madison hints at the implications of his institutionally oriented approach for debate and deliberation. "Besides other impediments," Madison declares, "it may be remarked that where there is a consciousness of unjust or dishonorable purposes, communication is always checked by distrust in proportion to the number whose concurrence is necessary."[38] To prevent rhetorical domination, Madison suggests that in a republic with a wide array of factions and individuals competing for public approval, "communication is always checked by distrust." This distrust, cultivated through contestation and political competition, leads rival interests to scrutinize and check the rhetorical strategies of the other.

The extension of Madison's view beyond the formal structures of government to the more informal sphere of debate and deliberation can also be justified by the similarities between the governmental system, the focus of Madison's inquiry, and the deliberative system. First, each of these systems consists in part of opposing interests vying against one another for influence.[39] Just as the executive may challenge legislative power, one party may challenge opponents by exposing the flaws in their arguments. Second, both the governmental and deliberative systems allow those working within them to exercise influence and power over "the people." While members of the executive, legislative, and judicial branches engage in explicit rule, rhetoricians and orators influence "the people" more implicitly. As Garsten points out, "In trying to bring an audience from the conventional wisdom to thoughts or intentions they might not otherwise have adopted, rhetoric intends to wield influence over them."[40] Like more direct forms of political power, persuasive and manipulative rhetoric enable the speaker to incite profound changes in the listener's actions, beliefs, or values.

Applied to deliberative context, Madison's view suggests that we ought to aspire toward conditions of robust contestation—conditions where rhetoric can be publicly countered and scrutinized by oppositional groups. Like his proposal for separating the branches of government, this call for contestation applies to the non-ideal circumstances of everyday politics. Instead of calling on interest groups and candidates to bracket their self-interest and ambition, it seeks to channel these motives of political actors toward outcomes that protect, rather than undermine, the common interest. In this sense, my claim for contestation maintains Madison's skepticism about human nature. Politicians, candidates, and interest group leaders—all will inevitably be tempted to use strategic speech and manipulation. Madison's ideal of contestation indicates that such motives can be redirected to ensure that expressions of rhetorical power are subject to challenge in deliberation. In Pettit's language, this account views contestation as a tool for dissolving the arbitrariness of rhetorical power and cultivating non-domination in the deliberative system (see figure 4.1).

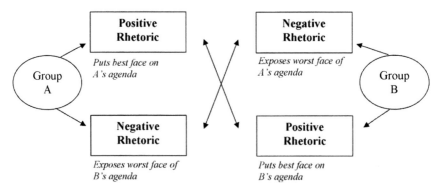

Figure 4.1.   This figure illustrates ideal discursive conditions that emerge from a Madisonian understanding of rhetoric. Driven by the motivation to succeed politically, each group offers a positive rhetoric in defense of their view and a negative rhetoric that puts their opposition's view in its worst light. As a result, the public is shown the "best face" and "worst face" of each group's agenda. This structure exposes and discourages manipulative speech. If Group A suspects Group B of manipulation, its negative rhetoric will expose these manipulative tactics. In this way, competition between rival interests promotes the exchange of persuasive, rather than manipulative, rhetoric.

The Dangers of One-Sided Information Spaces

The accounts of Madison and Pettit point to the virtues of contestation in securing non-domination. This argument for contestation is reinforced by an examination of the dangers that emerge in the absence of public scrutiny and debate.[41] The antithesis of contestation arises from *one-sided information spaces* in the public arena of deliberation. In such spaces, the perspective of a single group or individual is unchecked and unchallenged by rival interests. Not all one-sided information spaces diminish democracy. When they arise in the public arena of deliberation, however, they create structural conditions that enable a single perspective to prevail and fail to check rhetorical domination. In short, such spaces enable those controlling them to interfere with the choices of others, if they so choose, without challenge or contest.

Such one-sided information spaces may arise throughout the deliberative system but are most likely to emerge in public deliberations at local levels. On the broad scale of federal politics, oppositional interests fiercely contest the rhetoric of rival politicians, candidates, and interest groups. At local levels, however, oppositional interests and other sources of public scrutiny may disappear. Madison was acutely aware of this proclivity toward unchecked rhetorical power at local levels. The theme also arose in my interviews with contemporary political activists and public relations professionals. As Republican public relations strategist Ed Brookover told me, "The smaller the audience, the more likely it [manipulation] is to occur. The most vicious campaigns are the ones in a small city council trying to decide what to do about some zoning rights. That gets more vicious than anything that takes place on the floor of Congress. It's that lack of public scrutiny that allows them to get away with these things."[42] Like Madison, Brookover worries that as the size of the audience declines, the possibilities for unjust rhetorical tactics increase.

In what follows, I outline two problems that arise in one-sided information spaces. The first—*the problem of one-sided persuasion*—arises when an individual or group can persuade in the public arena without encountering the arguments or reasons of the other side. The second—*the problem of rhetorical corruption*—arises when individuals or groups can engage in the unchecked dissemination of manipulative rhetoric (lies, concealments, and distractions).

The Problem of One-Sided Persuasion

Over the last twenty years, a growing literature in psychology and political science has illuminated the powerful effects of the framing of an issue or idea on public opinion. Framing effects take two forms. The first is what James Druckman calls "equivalency frames." These frames arise when subjects change their mind when presented with identical information packaged in a slightly different way. As Druckman explains, "People reject a policy program when told that it will result in 5 percent unemployment but they prefer it when told that it will result in 95 percent employment."[43] These two statements are, of course, logically equivalent. But by framing information in a positive or negative light, they elicit markedly different responses.

Framing effects also arise from what Druckman calls "issue frames."[44] As he explains, "Issue framing effects refer to situations where, by emphasizing a subset of potentially relevant considerations, a speaker leads individuals to focus on these considerations when constructing their options."[45] Frank Luntz's now infamous reframing of the "estate tax" as the "death tax" had precisely this effect.[46] These two frames refer to the same taxation policy. Yet by highlighting the word "death" rather than "estate," Luntz's frame successfully portrayed this policy in its worst possible light.[47]

The literature on framing offers an ideal testing ground for understanding the dangers of one-sided information spaces. To evaluate such framing effects, the majority of these experiments create an artificial information space where only one side of the issue is presented. As Sniderman and Theriault explain, framing studies have "restricted attention to situations in which citizens are artificially sequestered, restricted to hearing only one way of thinking."[48] Such studies do not address situations of robust debate and contestation where citizens encounter both frames and counter-frames, but concentrate on problems that arise in one-sided information spaces. In such situations, Sniderman and Theriault explain, "Citizens in large numbers can be readily blown from one side of an issue to the very opposite depending on how the issue is specifically framed."[49] The worry is that the rhetorical frame rather than the substance of the issue plays a primary role in shaping public opinion. Such frames could undermine the capacity of citizens to make informed choices about important political matters.

Yet these effects diminish or disappear when competition and contestation are built into the experimental setting. To be sure, competition between rival framing strategies is not the only antidote to framing effects. As Druckman shows, framing effects may also diminish as a result of citizen predispositions, political information, and the credibility of the frame's source.[50] Yet competition—where frames are countered by rival frames—has the biggest impact on mitigating framing effects. In Sniderman and Theriault's experiments with frame competition, they found that when citizens are exposed to a complete rather than an edited version of political debate, they do not succumb to ambivalence or fall into confusion. On the contrary, even though as part of the process of debate they are exposed to an argument at odds with their general orientation, they tend to "go to home," to pick out the side of the issue that fits their deeper-lying political principles.[51]

These experimental results reinforce the argument for robust contestation and debate. They show that one-sided information spaces often create anti-democratic conditions where a single group or individual can shift public opinion by the clever packaging of arguments and reasons. Such one-sided spaces enable elites who control the information space to, as Schumpeter would put it, "manufacture" public opinion through the skillful use of rhetoric. Contestatory spaces counter the framing problem. They help ensure that citizens arrive at political decisions based on substantive political principles, rather than the skillful use of issue or equivalency frames.

The Problem of Rhetorical Corruption
One-sided information spaces not only strengthen framing effects, they also counter structural disincentives to lying and other forms of rhetorical manipulation. Just as Madison argued that unchecked power facilitates tyranny, I argue that one-sided information spaces facilitate manipulative speech. In the absence of robust contestation and public scrutiny, the lies, concealments, and distractions of political actors often go unnoticed and unchecked. In such environments, the primary antidote to manipulative speech—the threat of exposure by independent media outlets or oppositional parties—ceases to exist. As a result, political actors no longer face strong disincentives to manipulation. In what follows, I outline two empirical cases—one at the local level and another at the federal level—that illuminate both the danger of one-sided information spaces and the essential role that robust contestation plays in discouraging manipulative speech.

The first case involves the "stealth" tactics of the Christian Coalition, discussed at length in chapter 3. Recall that the Christian Coalition encouraged its activists and local-level candidates to "hide your strength," to not "flaunt your Christianity," and to "give the impression that you are there to work for the Party, not to push an ideology."[52] Such candidates relied on a manipulative strategy of concealment to hide their true religious agenda from the voting public. These tactics illuminate a paradigm case of manipulation. They also help to illuminate several important contextual points.

First, this case illustrates the efficacy of manipulative speech in one-sided information spaces. During the 1990 election in San Diego County, the

Christian Coalition silently employed its "stealth" strategy. Recall that its activists and candidates exploited two aspects of the local-level political context to ensure the success of its strategy of concealment. First, voters have little interest in midterm elections, so few people turn out. Second, those who do turn out are not likely to have scrutinized the issues in elections for school board, Republican Party committee posts, and other lower-level offices.[53] With the general public relatively unaware of its efforts, the Christian Coalition successfully used its "stealth" strategy in a midterm election to elect two-thirds of its candidates for local school board posts (roughly sixty out of ninety candidates). Its candidates also won enough party seats to control the San Diego County Republican Central Committee, which controlled candidate recruitment and Republican Party fundraising.

Second, however, this case also illuminates the disincentives to manipulation that arise from robust contestation. After the 1990 election, the Christian Coalition's victories transformed the context of public political debate. Coalition activists and candidates sought to extend their gains by continuing to "hide" their affiliations with Christian right organizations and their religious agenda. Yet the Christian right's victories in 1990 raised the level of public awareness and scrutiny. It heightened contestatory conditions. As Matthew Freeman of People for the American Way put it, "The plain difference between 1990 and 1992 was awareness. That in turn led to a massive mobilization of San Diego moderates. Having awakened the day after the 1990 election to a drastically reshaped government, San Diegans resolved to fight back."[54]

To challenge the Christian right and raise the public awareness of its tactics, moderate activists formed three organizations before the 1992 election: the Community for Responsible Education, the Mainstream Voters Project, and the Community Coalition Network. These organizations exposed the manipulative tactics of "stealth" candidates. The Community for Responsible Education monitored school board meetings and reported instances where "stealth" candidates expressed their overtly religious agenda. They also led a public relations campaign to expose the ties between local-level candidates and nationally known Christian right organizations like the Christian Coalition and Operation Rescue.[55] As Freeman puts it, these groups highlighted "candidates' affiliations with national Religious Right groups, their general integrity, and their general support for public education as symbolized by whether they sent their own children to public or private schools."[56]

The opposition groups also exposed the narrowcasting tactics of "stealth" candidates discussed in chapter 3. They informed local church leaders about

these "stealth" tactics and made public many of the targeted marketing flyers coalition candidates placed on the car windshields of "Christian" voters
during church services.

As a result of exposure and increased public awareness, the Christian Coalition's "stealth" tactics during the 1992 election cycle lost much of their
efficacy. While not all "stealth" candidates were defeated, the Christian right
saw a 50 percent decline in the number of candidates elected to local school
boards.[57] As the efficacy of its strategy declined in the mid-1990s, Christian
right organizations such as the Christian Coalition abandoned the strategy.

The lesson of the Christian Coalition's "stealth" strategy is twofold. On
one side, this case shows that absent competition and contestation—in
one-sided information spaces—political actors face few disincentives to
manipulative tactics. In fact, the case of the Christian Coalition shows that
manipulative tactics led to stunningly successful electoral results, at least in
the short term. On the other side, this case illustrates the power of robustly
contestatory discursive environments. Once the "stealth" tactics were exposed and challenged by oppositional groups, much of their power dissolved.
Christian Coalition candidates lost their credibility with mainstream voters
and could no longer "pretend" to be ordinary Republicans with no ulterior
agenda. With the rise in public scrutiny and contestation, the manipulative
tactics of such candidates worked against, rather than for, them.

The conclusion that robust contestation discourages manipulative speech
is further supported by a national-level example of manipulation: the now infamous Willie Horton ad. As I mentioned in chapter 2, the Bush campaign's
use of this ad to appeal implicitly to race was an instance of manipulative
distraction, an attempt to elicit the latent racial prejudices of voters without
their full awareness or understanding. So rather than explicitly mention
that Dukakis gave a "weekend pass" to a *black* man who assaulted and raped
a *white* woman, the ad highlighted Horton's race simply by displaying the
menacing image of his mug shot.

As Tali Mendelberg points out, in the initial phases of the campaign
when its racial strategy remained implicit, the Bush campaign successfully
appealed to voters' resentment against minority groups. Yet on October 21,
just weeks before the election, Jesse Jackson began speaking against the racial
undertones of the Horton ad. At this point, the media coverage of the ad
shifted from implicit to explicit discussions of race. The fact that Horton was
a black man became a central part of the public conversation, and the Bush
campaign's racial strategy was exposed. This exposure did not cost Bush the
election. It did, however, erode his support among Democrats, Republicans,
and Independents who resent blacks.[58] As Mendelberg explains, "The more

consciously white voters hear 'race,' the less effective the message becomes at conveying derogatory racial meaning."[59]

Like the case of the Christian Coalition, the Horton ad illuminates the disincentives to manipulation that arise from robust contestation. When rival parties expose the motives behind attempts to manipulate public opinion, the speakers often lose credibility and public esteem. In Mendelberg's words, "What makes implicit appeals distinctively effective is also their Achilles [heel]. To counter an implicit appeal, one can render it explicit."[60]

The Christian Coalition's "stealth" rhetoric and the Horton ad demonstrate that robust contestation is the primary antidote to manipulation and rhetorical corruption. Through the public scrutiny of independent media or rival partisan groups, the motives of political actors can be exposed. As a result, those trying to manipulate fellow citizens pay a high price. Once they are exposed, the effectiveness of their manipulative actions is often overshadowed by the loss of credibility accompanying exposure. Such implicit disincentives are a check on rhetorical domination. By subjecting the speaker to significant challenge and contestation, they dissolve the capacity of political actors to wield manipulative power. The checks that arise through contestation create conditions where those who manipulate lose credibility.

The Christian Coalition's 1990 campaign, however, reminds us that in one-sided information spaces free of robust contestation, the implicit appeals, lies, and distractions of political actors are likely to go unnoticed, at least for a time. This creates problematic structural conditions, allowing political actors to engage in relatively unchecked manipulation and rhetorical domination.

The Democratic Virtues of One-Sided Information Spaces

The dangers posed by one-sided spaces should not lead us to promote robust contestation in all spheres of life and reject all one-sided informational environments. While one-sided spaces fail to discourage manipulation when they arise in the public political forum, they play an important role in promoting non-domination when they arise in the internal culture of associations and groups.

One-sided group spaces help promote non-domination in two primary ways. First, they provide individuals of shared ethnicity, religion, or political persuasion with a space for resisting conditions of domination. As Tocqueville declares, "It is clear that, as each citizen individually becomes weaker and consequently less capable of preserving his liberty single-handed, either he must learn the art of joining with his fellow men to defend it, or tyranny must increase with equality."[61] Tocqueville suggests that by joining together and creating an association of like-minded individuals, citizens can ensure the preservation of liberty and resist tyranny.

Tocqueville's claim is a general one about association, but theorists of difference point to the one-sided information spaces within groups as playing an essential role in promoting non-domination. Nancy Fraser calls such groups "subaltern counterpublics," defined as "parallel discursive arenas where members of subordinated social groups invent and circulate counterdiscourses to formulate oppositional interpretations of their identities, interests, and needs."[62] Fraser claims that such insulated spaces provide excluded groups with a private space for constructing distinctive tactics, interests, and discourses.

Mansbridge calls such spaces "deliberative enclaves of resistance."[63] In her description of the "enclave theory of change" she remarks,

> In a larger culture permeated by a hegemonic ideology, counter-hegemonic ideas are most likely to appear when subordinates in a system of domination can engage in interactions of high intensity, in settings with barriers that keep the outside out and inside in, with incentives for experimentation and change, and with a lowered fear of punishment. Such "safe spaces" usually produce both creativity and commitment.[64]

These theorists focus primarily on enclaves of left-leaning gender groups and ethnic minorities, but such enclaves may also emerge on the right. As discussed in chapter 5, many conservative Christians feel they have been dominated by a similarly hegemonic ideology—that Christian values and the traditional family structure are under attack from liberal elites in the media, academia, and the courts.[65]

In these enclaves of resistance on the right and the left, the one-sided exchange of like-minded opinions plays an important role. As Mansbridge and Fraser point out, such practices cultivate shared purpose, passion, and encouragement that enhances the cohesion and power of political groups and ensures that their ideas, values, and concerns are represented in public debate. Such enclave structures are representational catalysts. They enable citizens with shared interests to express more effectively their reasons, arguments, and rhetoric in the democratic process.

The one-sided information spaces within groups also play a second role in securing non-domination: they catalyze active political participation. Active participation in the political process plays a vital role in countering domination. It ensures that groups have the capacity to challenge and con-test existing policies and institutions—to guard against arbitrary exercises of political power. Tocqueville, for instance, views active participation as one of the most essential safeguards to conditions of despotism and political domination. To counter the "regulated, mild, peaceful servitude" that arises from conditions of equality in modern democracy, Tocqueville turns to par-ticipation. As he puts it,

> Ordinary citizens, by associating, can constitute very opulent, very influential, and very powerful entities. . . . A political, industrial, commercial, or even scientific or literary association is an enlightened and powerful citizen that cannot be made to bow down at will or subjected to oppression in the shadows, and by defending its rights against the exigencies of power it saves common liberties.[66]

Tocqueville suggests that participation in a variety of associations, not just political ones, is a safeguard against despotism.[67]

One-sided information spaces, which insulate group members from en-gaging directly with oppositional views, cultivate active participation. The literature on the political implications of social networks shows that citizens with more crosscutting ties—exposed to oppositional views and inhabiting diverse information spaces—are less likely to vote in presidential and con-gressional elections.[68] Members of more insular groups, with homogenous social networks, by contrast, are more likely to show up on Election Day.

One important reason for this difference is, as Diana Mutz observes, that "political activists are likely to inhabit an informational environment full of like-minded others who spur them on to additional political activity."[69] Group interaction in one-sided information spaces sustains high levels of political participation by activists on the right, in organizations like Focus, and activists on the left, in organizations like MoveOn, the Sierra Club, and PETA.

Two features of group behavior explain the participatory benefits of one-sided deliberations in homogeneous groups. The first is informational. As Cass Sunstein observes in his work on "group polarization," discussion in homogeneous groups involves "limited argument pools."[70] As a result, group members have minimal engagement with alternative views and have a strong sense of confidence in their existing beliefs and preferences.

The second is reputational. When interacting in groups, individuals have incentives to maintain their reputation with group members. In crosscutting groups, individuals are less likely to express extreme views that might offend others. In such settings, Mutz suggests, "One feels uncomfortable taking sides in the face of multiple constituencies"—a feature that helps explain why crosscutting ties diminish the likelihood of political participation.[71]

In homogeneous groups, reputational pressures have the opposite effect. Rather than creating incentives to abstain from active participation or the expression of extreme views, such environments reward these qualities and sanction those who fail to toe the party line. As Mansbridge observes in *Why We Lost the ERA*, "Among proponents [of the ERA], the pressure to conform was probably strongest in the radical women's movement, where 'betraying the women's movement' by not taking the correct ideological line could be 'as terrifying as betrayal of your family, your closest friends.'"[72] Such reflections illuminate the kinds of reputational incentives that encourage like-minded group members to engage passionately in political activities that promote the group's agenda.[73]

Reconciling One-Sided and Contestatory Spaces

The virtues of one-sided information spaces show that robust contestation is not an unqualified democratic good. In many contexts, contestation plays an essential role in preventing one-sided persuasion and in discouraging manipulation. Yet extending conditions of robust contestation between diverse interests into the internal deliberations of minority groups and associations can also diminish democracy. Such contestation may limit the capacity of such groups to form counter-narratives of resistance and discourage active participation.

These contextual complications raise an important question: When should we encourage robust contestation and when should we encourage one-sided information spaces? The answer is contextual. In the public arena of deliberation, we should encourage robust contestation. In the internal deliberations of groups and associations, we ought to encourage a mixture of in-group deliberation in one-sided information spaces and out-group deliberation in more public contestatory spaces. To clarify this idea, consider a visual representation of three possible models for balancing one-sided and contestatory spaces (see figure 4.2).

The first model—the *insulated enclave model*—consists of insulated enclaves that rarely enter the public deliberative arena. This model preserves the virtues of one-sided information spaces. It enables groups to form strong narratives of resistance and to mobilize political engagement. Yet such conditions of collective isolation cultivate a number of problems. On the one side, such conditions cultivate intolerance and social fragmentation. In the

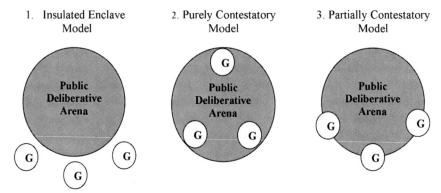

Figure 4.2. **The above figure displays three possible models of the relationship between contestation in the public arena (represented by the large gray circle) and the one-sided spaces of groups (represented by the small white circles). The first model displays a relation where groups are fully insulated from direct engagement in the public arena. The second displays the opposite: a model where groups are fully engaged but lack a private space for deliberation. The third represents a balance between the two, where groups both engage other citizens and have a private space for in-group deliberation.**

language of Robert Putnam, such enclave conditions facilitate social networks based solely on "bonding."[74] By discouraging active engagement with a diversity of ideas and perspectives, they create cultural enclaves that are "inward looking and tend to reinforce exclusive identities and homogeneous groups." As a result, such groups cultivate "in-group loyalty" and "out-group antagonism," which result in polarization and intolerance toward other groups.[75] On the other side, the lack of direct engagement between groups, lawmakers, and ordinary citizens erodes the quality of contestation in the public arena. It diminishes the number of voices in the public dialogue and thus weakens disincentives to manipulative speech.

The second model—the *purely contestatory model*—suffers from the opposite problem. On this model, the contestatory arena of public debate extends into the internal deliberations of groups and associations. To be sure, this model has several virtues. First, the all-pervasiveness of robust contestation discourages manipulative forms of speech throughout the deliberative system. Second, it promotes an extreme form of what Putnam calls "bridging." In contrast to bonding, bridging arises in the practices of "cross-cutting groups" with diverse ambitions and membership. Such groups are more likely to encourage openness to diverse members and ideas to achieve solidarity, tolerance, and mutual understanding by reaching across social cleavages. Yet this model takes bridging to an extreme. It extends public contestation so deeply into the internal culture of groups and associations that it diminishes the virtues that arise from in-group deliberations. It runs the risk of silencing minority groups struggling to formulate a compelling public message, while also diminishing the power of such groups to mobilize members into political action.

The problems that arise from these admittedly extreme models point toward a more balanced approach. The third model—the *partially contestatory model*—seeks to preserve the benefits that arise both from robust contestation in the public arena and from one-sided information spaces in the group sphere. It calls for a public forum of deliberation where diverse groups have the space to engage both in private in-group deliberations and in broader debates in the public arena. This model preserves the virtues of one-sided discussion in groups and associations. It enables like-minded citizens to construct narratives of resistance and provides an insulated space for inspiring political action. Yet it also preserves the virtues of contestatory public spaces. By encouraging all groups to engage one another, this model creates robust discursive incentives that prevent the problems of one-sided persuasion and rhetorical corruption.

The virtues of this partially contestatory model point toward an important distinction between one-sided public and one-sided private information spaces. As we have seen, one-sided private information spaces, which arise in partially insulated group interactions, can benefit democracy. Yet these benefits do not arise when one-sided information spaces emerge in the broader public arena of deliberation. Such one-sided public spaces emerge when a single group or individual controls the public discourse at the national or local level. Unlike one-sided private spaces, the emergence of such one-sided conditions throughout the public forum creates a dangerously anti-contestatory set of conditions. As we have seen throughout the chapter, it erodes the epistemic benefits of public debate, while also diminishing the implicit checks against manipulation and other forms of rhetorical corruption that arise from robust contestation.

Three Principles of Public Contestation

To guard against such one-sided public information spaces, I propose three principles for structuring the public arena of debate and contestation. These principles echo the call running throughout the epistemic and non-domination arguments for contestatory public spaces. They seek to ensure conditions where the rhetoric of individuals or groups encounters oppositional rhetoric. This need not entail putting an end to partisanship or impassioned political action. Instead, it is a call for structural incentives that channel the rhetoric of partisan political actors toward outcomes that enhance, rather than diminish, the common interest. In what follows, I discuss each contextual principle and consider their effect on the moral quality of the three ideal speech types outlined in chapter 2.

The Principle of Fair Competition

This principle stipulates that citizens and groups ought to receive a fair hearing when expressing their perspectives or challenging the perspective of others in the public political forum. In defining fairness, I follow Knight and Johnson's suggestion that full fairness and equality requires "equal opportunity of access to political influence."[76] In this view, fairness in the deliberative realm entails that each individual or group have an *equal capacity* to advance their claims. In Knight and Johnson's words, "Equality entails that the possibility that a participant might influence the preferences of other deliberators be roughly the same for all participants."[77] Cultivating fair competition according to this conception of equal capacities need not necessarily require securing equal outcomes or equal resources. Given the complex and uncertain nature of democratic politics, Knight and Johnson argue that equal outcomes cannot be guaranteed.[78] Moreover, the simple equality of resources may not result in an equal capacity to influence. While resources play an important role, a group's capacity to influence also arises from its community connections, prestige, and intellectual capital.

To achieve fair competition, therefore, groups ought to have *roughly* equal capacities to exert influence in the public political forum. I emphasize the word "roughly" here because achieving full fairness in the realm of deliberation may be beyond realization in practical politics. Nevertheless, this aspiration toward roughly equal capacities means that we ought to correct conditions in which vast asymmetries of power exist, which enable certain groups to exert disproportionate influence. When a single individual or group controls the discourse and creates barriers to other citizens expressing objections or challenges, fair competition is impossible. Such settings enable a single group to exert unchecked rhetorical power. They undermine the capacity of all citizens and groups to challenge and contest the political ambitions of more powerful groups. In short, such one-sided spaces undermine the idea that each group ought to have an equal capacity to exert influence.

The one-sided discursive space created by the Christian Coalition's "stealth" campaign, for instance, undermined fair competition. By concealing their religious agenda from fellow citizens, such "stealth" candidates dramatically reduced the capacity of fellow citizens to challenge and contest their explicitly religious platform. Their manipulative strategy made it almost impossible for others to engage them in the fair competition of ideas. Fair competition calls on citizens and the democratic state to rectify such deliberative situations where groups or individuals exert influence using uncontested manipulative or coercive measures.[79]

The Principle of Rhetorical Diversity

Fair competition alone is an insufficient guarantee that contestatory spaces will reflect a diversity of interests. The principle of rhetorical diversity stipulates that in addition to fair competition, we should also ensure the pluralism of groups in the market of public ideas reflects the actual diversity of opinions and interests in the democratic state. This call for rhetorical pluralism echoes Mill's sentiment in the quotation at the beginning of the chapter. For Mill, it is essential that "opinions favourable to democracy and to aristocracy . . . to liberty and discipline, and all the other standing antagonisms of political life, are expressed with equal freedom."[80] In a democracy as vast as America, for instance, it is not enough to have two parties competing against one another for public influence. Such competition may prevent the emergence of rhetorical domination, but it leaves a myriad of perspectives unexpressed and unexamined in the public dialogue.

To achieve rhetorical diversity, underrepresented groups ought to receive the resources and tools necessary for advancing their perspective. As Jane Mansbridge puts it, "Effective deliberation requires that those with information the public should know have the minimum resources necessary to make their evidence and views heard."[81] This may involve allocating public funding for groups or interests whose perspective is underrepresented in public political debate. To ensure fair competition between underrepresented groups and powerful corporate lobbying organizations, for instance, the state might allocate resources for mobilizing less powerful groups or mandate that such groups receive free airtime on media outlets.[82]

Cultivating rhetorical diversity requires more than resources; it also requires more powerful actors to listen to thought and argumentation that may depart from the norms of rational-critical debate, which often privilege dominant groups and exclude difference. As Iris Marion Young argues, "Most theorists of deliberative democracy assume a culturally biased conception of discussion that tends to silence or devalue some people or groups."[83] To include groups on the periphery of the democratic conversation, Young argues that public deliberation should include not only reasoned arguments but also alternative forms of speech such as "greeting," "rhetoric," and "story telling."[84] The key insight of such theorists of difference is that full inclusion of a diversity of groups may require more powerful political actors to accept forms of speech and rhetoric different from their own.

Cultivating rhetorical diversity helps mitigate rhetorical domination and enhances the epistemic quality of public political debate. In one-sided information spaces, the lack of rhetorical diversity creates conditions where framing effects can sway public opinion. Lack of rhetorical diversity also limits the capacity of citizens to challenge and contest manipulative speech. When diverse and opposing groups participate in the public conversation, the power of framing effects will decline and the barriers to manipulative speech will increase. Diverse contestatory spaces also have important epistemic benefits. Problems of "group polarization" and "hidden profiles" both arise from a lack of rhetorical diversity. Under conditions of group polarization, the expressions of like-minded group members radicalize collective opinion and lead to epistemic error. Similarly, hidden profiles arise when members with diverse perspectives withhold crucial information from deliberations for fear of challenging majority opinion. In both cases, epistemic distortions arise from lack of rhetorical diversity.

The Principle of Independent Public Scrutiny

The first two principles emphasize checking by the competition of diverse interests in the public form. The principle of independent public scrutiny, by contrast, calls for the creation of a secondary form of public scrutiny on the sidelines of this competitive system. It calls for relatively independent and non-partisan organizations that can scrutinize the rhetorical appeals of candidates, interest groups, and lawmakers. Such entities might be media outlets, academic centers, nonprofit groups, or even depoliticized government commissions.[85]

A robust network of such independent organizations benefits the deliberative conditions of democracy. First, such organizations reinforce the structural incentives that discourage would-be manipulators from rhetorical corruption. Such organizations increase the threat of exposure, raising the probability that the credibility of manipulators will suffer when their rhetorical tactics are exposed. Second, such organizations strengthen the epistemic conditions of deliberation. By highlighting falsehoods and inaccuracies, such organizations help uncover errors and enhance the veracity of public discussion.

Within contemporary American politics, an array of non-partisan independent entities serve this checking function. The Annenberg Public Policy Center's FactCheck.org, PolitiFact.org, and OpenSecrets.org all scrutinize the claims of candidates and elected officials. Media organizations have also created blogs and columns evaluating the validity of arguments and reasons offered by political actors. The *Washington Post* gives "Pinocchio Awards" to the most audacious political "fibs."

While existing entities play an important role in checking the rhetorical appeals of political actors, the scope of their efforts is often confined to national politics. So lies, concealment, and other forms of manipulation at local levels may go unchecked by independent organizations. As we have seen, it is at the local level that rhetorical corruption is most likely to arise. To ensure independent scrutiny throughout the deliberative system, this principle calls for support for the creation of a more robust network of independent checking organizations at the state and local level.

Application to Ideal Speech Types

Now consider the application of this contextual ideal of contestation to the three ideal speech types discussed in chapter 2. While I touched on the contextual qualities of manipulative speech in that chapter, these three contextual principles enable a deeper analysis that extends to all three ideal speech types. The primary lesson of this chapter's contextual analysis is that robust contestation between diverse interests in public spaces enhances democracy and discourages manipulation. Such conditions improve the epistemic outcomes of deliberation and create structural disincentives against manipulation and rhetorical corruption. By contrast, one-sided information spaces that arise throughout the public arena of deliberation diminish deliberative democratic conditions. They often enable domination and poor epistemic outcomes.

What effect does the quality of deliberative context have on the moral value of deliberative persuasion, strategic persuasion, and manipulation? Figure 4.3 represents interactions between the three ideal speech types (represented by the three dotted lines) and the quality of contextual conditions in the public arena of deliberation. My claim here is that the moral value of these three ideal speech types arises, at least in part, from the quality of the deliberative context. As deliberative contexts become more contestatory, the moral value of all three forms of speech increases. Conversely, as deliberative contexts become increasingly one-sided, the moral value of all three forms of speech decreases.

This means that one-sided public information spaces may diminish the moral quality of even the most ideal forms of deliberative persuasion. To illuminate this possibility, recall Sunstein's experiment on "group polarization" in which liberals from Boulder and conservatives from Colorado Springs were asked to deliberate about same-sex marriage.[86] Imagine that within

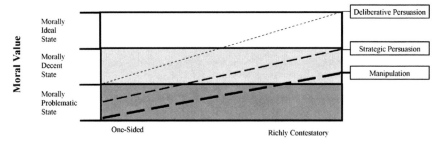

Figure 4.3.

these groups, members appealed to ideal forms of deliberative persuasion that offered sincere arguments and sought to understand the perspectives of others. In the case of the liberals from Boulder, this would mean that each group member offered genuine arguments for same-sex marriage and was open to revising his or her view.

In my view, the exchange of rhetoric within these two groups would still be morally problematic. The problem does not arise from the form of speech, for all participants in this example adhere to the deliberative ideal of persuasion. Instead, the problem arises from the context. It is the one-sided information space within which these conversations occur that diminishes the moral value of such homogeneous group deliberations. As Sunstein has shown, the social pressures and limited argument pools within such one-sided settings cultivate polarization, intolerance, and social fragmentation.[87] The problems that emerge in such spaces help illuminate the influence of deliberative context on the moral quality of rhetoric. They show that such one-sided spaces distort the moral quality of even the most ideal forms of deliberative persuasion.

The impact of context on these ideal speech types also works the other way. Under ideal contextual conditions in which diverse views are expressed on roughly equal terms, seemingly immoral forms of manipulation may become morally decent, although perhaps not admirable. The negotiations of a congressional subcommittee, for instance, may offer an idealized contestatory context that diminishes the immoral effects of manipulative speech. Imagine that two powerful representatives engage in manipulative rhetorical tactics to outwit the other in the course of a publicly televised negotiation. In this context, manipulative forms of rhetoric are unlikely to severely diminish the choices of others or exert invisible influence. Given that all actors can challenge one another and given the intense public scrutiny of these deliberations, the power of manipulative rhetoric is greatly diminished.

This chapter has sought to illuminate a basic insight—namely, that context matters. Contestatory spaces in the public arena of deliberation enhance democracy, while one-sided information spaces diminish democracy. Part of the argument for this conclusion is epistemic: contestatory spaces tend to mitigate the problems of group polarization and hidden profiles. The other part of the argument is Madisonian: contestatory spaces, with their implicit rhetorical checks and balances, tend to mitigate the problems of framing and rhetorical domination.

Notes

1. John Stuart Mill, "On Liberty," in *John Stuart Mill on Liberty and Other Essays* (New York: Oxford University Press, 1998), 54.

2. Aristotle, *The Politics*, trans. Carnes Lord (Chicago: University of Chicago Press, 1984), 101, 1281b1.

3. Amy Gutmann and Dennis Thompson, *Why Deliberative Democracy?* (Princeton: Princeton University Press, 2004), 12; Jane Mansbridge, "Using Power/Fighting Power: The Polity," in *Democracy and Difference*, ed. Seyla Benhabib (Princeton: Princeton University Press, 1996), 47.

4. Allen Buchanan, "Political Liberalism and Social Epistemology," *Philosophy and Public Affairs* 32, no. 2 (2004); Amy Gutmann and Dennis Thompson, *Democracy and Disagreement* (Cambridge: Belknap Press, 1996); Gutmann and Thompson *Why Deliberative Democracy?*

5. Mill, "On Liberty," 21.

6. Mill, "On Liberty," 22.

7. Mill, "On Liberty," 23.

8. Mill, "On Liberty," 25.

9. Mill, "On Liberty," 40.

10. Mill, "On Liberty," 52.

11. Mill, "On Liberty," 52.

12. For a review of this literature, see Tali Mendelberg, "The Deliberative Citizen: Theory and Evidence," in *Political Decision Making, Deliberation and Participation* (New York: Elsevier Science, 2002).

13. Cass Sunstein, *Infotopia* (New York: Oxford University Press, 2006).

14. Sunstein, *Infotopia*, 45–46.

15. Rupert Brown, *Group Processes* (Oxford: Blackwell, 2001); Cass Sunstein, "Deliberative Trouble? Why Groups Go to Extremes," *Yale Law Journal* 110, no. 1 (2000); Cass Sunstein, *Republic.com* (Princeton: Princeton University Press, 2001).

16. Sunstein, *Infotopia*, 96.

17. Daniel Gigone and Reid Hastie, "The Common Knowledge Effect," *Journal of Personality and Social Psychology* 65 (1993); Garold Stasser and William Titus, "Hidden Profiles: A Brief History," *Psychological Inquiry* 14 (2003); Garold Stasser and William Titus, "Pooling of Unshared Information in Group Discussion," *Journal of Personality and Social Psychology* 48 (1985); Sunstein, "Deliberative Trouble?"; Sunstein, *Infotopia*.

18. Alexis de Tocqueville, *Democracy and America*, trans. Arthur Goldhammer (New York: Library of America, 2004); Sunstein, "Deliberative Trouble?"; Sunstein, *Infotopia*.

19. Mill, "On Liberty," 38.

20. Sunstein, *Infotopia*, 86–88; Jane Mansbridge, *Beyond Adversary Democracy* (Chicago: University of Chicago Press, 1983); Lynn M. Sanders, "Against Deliberation," *Political Theory* 25, no. 3 (1997).

21. Mendelberg, "The Deliberative Citizen."

22. James Madison, *The Federalist Papers* (New York: Penguin Books, 1987), 319.

23. Mill, "On Liberty," 53.

24. Madison, *The Federalist Papers*, 319.

25. Madison, *The Federalist Papers*, 319.

26. Madison, *The Federalist Papers*, 320.

27. Madison, *The Federalist Papers*, 320.

28. Philip Pettit, *Republicanism* (New York: Oxford University Press, 1997), 52.

29. Pettit, *Republicanism*, 53.

30. Pettit, *Republicanism*, 55.

31. Alex Zakaras, "Expensive Speech, Illegitimate Power: Corporations and the First Amendment," working paper (2008).

32. Pettit, *Republicanism*, 63.

33. Madison, *The Federalist Papers*, 126.

34. Robert A. Dahl, *A Preface to Democratic Theory* (Chicago: University of Chicago Press, 1956), 22.

35. Dahl, *A Preface to Democratic Theory*, 20.

36. Madison, *The Federalist Papers*, 320. Madison's willingness to extend his theory of ambition beyond the affairs of government connects his separation of power analysis in "Federalist 51" with his discussion of factions in "Federalist 10." One of Madison's primary remedies for the potentially tyrannical whims of factions is to extend the sphere of the republic—to increase the size and diversity of the citizenry. As David Epstein notes, the mechanism Madison relies on to discourage tyranny in government mirrors the mechanism that he relies on to prevent majority factions in civil society: "In each case the problem is that a society of men cannot act as a whole in ruling itself; it is divided into majority and minority, and into rulers and ruled . . . The remedy for the problems posed by those ineradicable divisions is a further division of the more dangerous part—multiplying interested or passionate groups in society, and multiplying ambitious men in government." What connects factions and ambitious politicians is that both groups have a two-sided potential: depending

on the institutional context, their ambitious projects can either destroy or reinforce the republic. For Madison, justice demands good government and it also demands a good civil society: "Justice is the end of government," he insists, "it is the end of civil society" (Madison, *The Federalist Papers*, 322). For an excellent reading of "Federalist 10" and "Federalist 51," see David F. Epstein, *The Political Theory of The Federalist* (Chicago: University of Chicago Press, 1984), 146.

37. Garsten makes a similar claim for a Madisonian discursive space to prevent and moderate "demagoguery and faction." See Bryan Garsten, *Saving Persuasion* (Cambridge: Harvard University Press, 2006), 200–204.

38. Madison, *The Federalist Papers*, 127–28.

39. While politics often entails competition between opposing interests, it also includes moments that are non-conflictual—moments where all parties seek to arrive at the common good. For more on the distinction between such adversarial and deliberative modes of politics, see Mansbridge, *Beyond Adversary Democracy*; Jane Mansbridge, "Conflict and Self-Interest in Deliberation," in *Deliberative Democracy and Its Discontents*, ed. Samantha Besson and Jose Luis Marti (New York: Ashgate Publishing Group, 2006).

40. Garsten, *Saving Persuasion*, 6.

41. For an account of the one-sided information space in the women's movement during the campaign for the Equal Rights Amendment, see Jane Mansbridge, *Why We Lost the ERA* (Chicago: University of Chicago Press, 1986).

42. Interview with Ed Brookover, May 17, 2006.

43. James N. Druckman, "Political Preference Formation: Competition, Deliberation, and the (Ir)Relevance of Framing Effects," *American Political Science Review* 98, no. 4 (2004): 671.

44. Druckman, "Political Preference Formation."

45. Druckman, "Political Preference Formation," 672.

46. For his account of his "death tax" framing strategy, see Frank Luntz, *Words That Work* (New York: Hyperion, 2007).

47. While many argue that this reframe of the "estate tax" led to an increase in opposition, Larry Bartels shows that Americans' opposition to the "estate tax" has remained relatively consistent; see Larry Bartels, *Unequal Democracy: The Political Economy of the New Gilded Age* (Princeton: Princeton University Press, 2008).

48. Paul M. Sniderman and Sean M. Theriault, "The Structure of Political Argument and the Logic of Issue Framing," in *Studies in Public Opinion*, ed. Willem E. Saris and Paul M. Sniderman (Princeton: Princeton University Press, 2004), 141. See also Druckman, "Political Preference Formation."

49. Sniderman, "The Structure of Political Argument," 133–34.

50. Druckman, "Political Preference Formation."

51. Sniderman, "The Structure of Political Argument," 148.

52. "How to Participate in a Political Party." Internal Christian Coalition memo obtained by People for the American Way and used at the Iowa Republican County Caucus, March 1986. On file with author.

53. Matthew Freeman, *The San Diego Model: A Community Battles the Religious Right* (Washington, DC: People for the American Way, 1993), 10.

54. Freeman, *The San Diego Model*, 58.

55. Freeman, *The San Diego Model*, 30.

56. Freeman, *The San Diego Model*, 44.

57. Freeman, *The San Diego Model*, 58.

58. Mendelberg points out that the preference for Bush among Republicans who resented blacks fell from 89 percent during the period where the racial frame was implicit to 78 percent during the period where the racial frame was made explicit. Similarly, the preference for Bush among Independents who resented blacks fell from 72 percent to 61 percent and the preference for Bush among Democrats who resented blacks fell from 56 percent to 44 percent. See Tali Mendelberg, *The Race Card* (Princeton: Princeton University Press, 2001), 175–78.

59. Mendelberg, *The Race Card*, 269.

60. Mendelberg, *The Race Card*, 10.

61. Tocqueville, *Democracy and America*, 595.

62. Nancy Fraser, "Rethinking the Public Sphere: A Contribution to the Critique of Actually Existing Democracy," in *Habermas and the Public Sphere*, ed. Craig Calhoun (Cambridge: MIT Press, 1992), 123.

63. Mansbridge, "Using Power/Fighting Power," 47.

64. Jane Mansbridge, "Cracking Through Hegemonic Ideology: The Logic of Formal Justice," *Social Justice Research* 18, no. 3 (2005).

65. For a critical analysis of this "victim narrative" of the Christian right, see Nathaniel Klemp and Stephen Macedo, "The Christian Right, Public Reason, and American Democracy," in *Evangelicals and Democracy in America*, ed. Steve Brint and Jean Schroedel (New York: Russell Sage Foundation, 2009).

66. Tocqueville, *Democracy and America*, 824.

67. Echoes of this argument run throughout modern democratic theory as well as the empirical work of scholars like Robert Putnam on social capital. See Robert Putnam, *Bowling Alone: The Collapse and Revival of American Community* (New York: Simon and Schuster, 2000).

68. Diana Mutz, *Hearing the Other Side* (New York: Cambridge University Press, 2006), 111.

69. Mutz, *Hearing the Other Side*, 113.

70. Sunstein, "Deliberative Trouble?," 75; Sunstein, *Infotopia*.

71. Mutz, *Hearing the Other Side*, 107.

72. Mansbridge, *Why We Lost the ERA*, 181.

73. Mutz, *Hearing the Other Side*, 32; Sunstein, "Deliberative Trouble?"

74. Robert D. Putnam, *Making Democracy Work: Civic Traditions in Modern Italy* (Princeton: Princeton University Press, 1994), 86–98.

75. Putnam, *Bowling Alone*, 22–23.

76. Note that Knight and Johnson focus on "equality" rather than "fairness." I base my conception of "fair competition" on their capacity-based conception of

equality in the deliberative realm. Jack Knight and James Johnson, "What Sort of Equality Does Deliberative Democracy Require?" in *Deliberative Democracy*, ed. James Bohman and William Rehg (Cambridge: MIT Press, 1997), 280.

77. Knight and Johnson, "What Sort of Equality?", 293.

78. Knight and Johnson, "What Sort of Equality?", 296.

79. I am grateful to Jane Mansbridge for her essay on the need to address such forms of power from the deliberative arena. See Jane Mansbridge, "A Deliberative Theory of Interest Representation," in *The Politics of Interests*, ed. Mark Petracca (Boulder, CO: Westview Press, 1992), 48.

80. Mill, "On Liberty," 54.

81. Mansbridge, "A Deliberative Theory of Interest Representation," 48.

82. Cass Sunstein calls for similar measures to ensure that media outlets and Internet news sites present all sides of the issue. See Sunstein, *Republic.com*.

83. Iris Marion Young, "Communication and the Other: Beyond Deliberative Democracy," in *Democracy and Difference*, ed. Seyla Benhabib (Princeton: Princeton University Press, 1996), 120. See also Fraser, "Rethinking the Public Sphere."

84. Young, "Communication and the Other," 130.

85. Pettit, for instance, calls for "depoliticized" public commissions to deal with issues easily hijacked by the fear-based appeals of politicians such as redistricting, prostitution, and drug policy. See Philip Pettit, "Depoliticizing Democracy," *Ratio Juris* 17, no. 1 (2004).

86. Sunstein, *Infotopia*.

87. Sunstein, "Deliberative Trouble?"; Sunstein, *Republic.com*; Sunstein, *Infotopia*.

~

CHAPTER FIVE

Countercultural Christian Enclaves

Focus on the Family's Anti-Contestatory Practices

Over the last thirty years, media savvy conservative Christians have created what radio-host Michael Medved calls "a conservative religious counter-culture"—a culture that he deems "far more powerful and more significant than anything in the stupid counter-culture of the 1960s."[1] At the institutional level, Medved has an important point. Lacking the 1960s generation's flashy public displays of civil disobedience, rebellion, and free love, the conservative Christian political movement evolved in a more subtle fashion. Yet it now consists of a vast network of media, political, and religious institutions, guaranteeing influence in the present and a long-lasting cultural presence.

This chapter uses the theoretical principles of the previous chapter to evaluate the contextual quality of the discursive space created by this network of sub-cultural institutions. In the first section, I provide a brief background on Focus on the Family, the Christian right organization used as the basis for this case study. In the second section, I argue that the emerging conservative Christian "counterculture" promoted by Focus and other groups has created an *enclave infrastructure*—an insulated cultural space that minimizes direct engagement with oppositional views. This enclave infrastructure represents a paradigm case of a one-sided information space.

In the third section, I evaluate the effects of this enclave infrastructure on the contextual quality of the larger deliberative system. I argue that the enclave infrastructure of Focus as well as many of its rivals on the left poses two primary threats to contestatory democratic conditions. First, such spaces cultivate anti-contestatory attitudes of polarization and intolerance, which diminish the likelihood of cross-cutting conversations with fellow citizens. Second, these enclave spaces cultivate anti-contestatory practices like info-blasting, which tend to diminish the openness and competitiveness of public political debate at local levels.

In the final section of the chapter, I present a democratic paradox. While such enclave infrastructures demean the ideal of robust public contestation, they also cultivate an essential democratic virtue: active political engagement. These one-sided information spaces enable organizations like Focus to overcome political apathy and mobilize their membership into political action. I argue that the participatory virtues of such enclave spaces, while important, must be reconciled with their anti-contestatory democratic vices and that we ought to aspire toward a balance between the values of participation and deliberation.

The Case: Focus on the Family

While chapter 3 examined the rhetoric of three Christian right organizations, this chapter uses a single organization—James Dobson's Focus on the Family—to evaluate the contextual qualities of the Christian right.[2] It should also be noted that while Dobson founded Focus and served as its radio host and chairman of the board during my fieldwork, he stepped down in 2009 to found a new organization called Family Talk with Dr. Dobson.

Dobson, who founded Focus on the Family in 1976, has become one of the most powerful figures in conservative Christian politics. In recent years, as the Christian Coalition's annual budget has plummeted, Focus has consistently generated around $146 million in annual revenue.[3] While most conservative Christian political organizations consist of a small cadre of lobbyists in Washington, DC, Focus has perfected a grass-roots model. It employs nearly 1,400 people (along with 400 volunteers) at its Colorado Springs headquarters and receives so much mail from constituents that it has its own zip code.

What makes Dobson unique, however, is that despite his enormous influence in national politics, he insists that Focus is not a political organization. He emphasizes that Focus devotes only 6 percent of its $146 million annual budget to political activities.[4] Dobson describes Focus as, unlike other political groups, a Christian "ministry" forced out of necessity into the sordid wars of partisan politics. When I first toured the organization in June of 2004, my guide insisted, "Focus on the Family is not a political organization, and it is not our intention to become one. Dr. Dobson did not choose to go into the political arena, but rather the political arena has imposed itself on the family and we feel that the family is in mortal danger."[5]

So Focus is a far more complex organization than most traditional political interest groups. It has three objectives. First, it has constructed a nationwide counseling center using Dobson's principles to counsel people on parenting troubles, divorce, or homosexuality. On any given day, Focus estimates that over 10,000 letters, 7,000 phone calls, and 10,000 e-mails deluge its Colorado Springs offices.[6] One out of every ten contacts is routed to a team of sixty specialists, who send pre-packaged materials with Dobson's advice on related matters. A smaller percentage of these "pain mail" requests are handed to a group of sixteen state-licensed councilors who conduct a short phone-therapy session with the caller and refer them to a Focus-approved counselor in their area.[7]

The sheer mass of these inquiries has enabled Focus to assemble a database of over five million names. In concrete political terms, this counseling operation enables the organization to transform personal trauma into a powerful instrument for political action. Helping families through crises creates a personal bond between the ministry and its members—bolstering their attachment to Focus's values and also increasing their likelihood of engaging in political activities. As Focus on the Family's senior analyst for pornography policy, Daniel Weiss, told me,

> The only reason that Dr. Dobson has this kind of influence is that he's earned those people's trust by all the non-policy work. All the work he's done to help marriages stay together. All the work he's done to help parents know how to parent their kids. That's the hallmark of this ministry. It's not the political juggernaut that is presented in the press. We are all about meeting needs. And I think that's the only reason that anyone responds to the policy stuff. It's because they trust that you've helped us in our time of trouble and we know that you are legitimate—that you are not some political shill.[8]

The political upshot is that Dobson can mobilize thousands of phone calls, e-mails, and letters to legislators in a matter of hours and energize millions of voters to go to the polls in election years.[9]

Focus on the Family's second aim, discussed in greater detail in the next section, is the construction of a conservative Christian media infrastructure. Focus currently dominates the market for family values publishing. It distributes twelve magazines and countless DVDs, publishes books on everything from divorce to same-sex marriage, and dominates the Christian radio market.[10]

Focus on the Family's third aim is political influence. In spite of its tax status as a nonprofit Christian ministry, on issues like same-sex marriage, stem cell research, and abortion, Focus voices the Christian pro-family perspective in the mainstream political discourse. Glenn Stanton, director of social research and cultural affairs and senior analyst for marriage and sexuality at Focus, explains that the way to influence politics "is to assemble people together to try to speak to them, which Focus on the Family has done very well with our radio broadcast that goes out to millions of people a day and our magazines."[11] Focus uses this network to foment outrage and a positive political vision that equips members with the political tools to fight back: "You've got to speak to someone, you've got to tell them something, and they've got to be able to do something with the information that you give them," Stanton says. "And that's the game of politics in a large sense. What we are trying to do is help educate citizens—to make their voice heard on the pertinent issues that relate to the family and to give them the means and the avenues to come forth and do that." Stanton's three-part political mantra is "Amass, Educate, and Mobilize."[12]

Focus on the Family's Enclave Infrastructure

Focus's radio programs, film productions, and publications have helped create an *enclave infrastructure* in the conservative Christian community. They have created a network of media resources that provide an insulated cultural space. *Breakaway*, Focus's magazine for teens, was founded to encourage Christian teens to rebel against the mainstream by establishing a relationship with Jesus. As its mission statement declares, "Since 1990, *Breakaway* magazine has been encouraging teen guys to break away from the pressures of the world around them and to get real in a relationship with Jesus. As our theme verse says, 'Do not conform any longer to the pattern of this world, but be transformed by the renewing of your mind. Then you will be able to test and approve what God's will is—his good, pleasing and perfect will' (Romans 12:2)."[13] The name of the magazine itself—*Breakaway*—suggests an ethos of distance and detachment from the secular world.

Throughout the Christian right, Christian radio plays a pivotal role in sustaining this enclave infrastructure. In 1972, America had 399 Christian radio stations.[14] Over the last thirty-five years, that number has increased by a factor of five to nearly 2,000 Christian radio stations throughout America.[15] While Christian radio personalities abound, James Dobson has become the primary voice of conservative religious broadcasting. By its own estimates, which are prone to hyperbole, Focus on the Family's broadcast goes on two thousand stations throughout America and reaches 200 million people worldwide through international broadcasts in ninety-eight countries. In addition to Dobson's daily radio show, Focus produces *Family News in Focus*, a shorter, family-values-oriented news show airing daily on seven hundred radio stations, reaching nearly one million listeners.

Focus on the Family also publishes hundreds of books, DVDs, and videos, and distributes twelve magazines with a nationwide paid circulation of 3.5 million people.[16] Its magazines reach all sectors of the conservative Christian market. *Clubhouse* and *Clubhouse Jr.* cater to small children, *Brio* and *Breakaway* meet the needs of Christian teens, and *LifeWise* addresses the over-fifty crowd. Focus also publishes magazines directed at pastors and doctors, providing professional advice from the conservative family values perspective. As Kurt Bruner, vice president of Focus's publishing and film production, explains, these magazines inform members in a way that reinforces conservative Christian values. "This organization is largely built on counterculture," says Bruner. "The trend and the message of the culture has always been permissive parenting, and Dr. Dobson said, 'No: Dare to discipline.' Then feminist ideology was on the rise, and he was affirming motherhood. It's the backlash supporting those ideas that has caused the growth and impact of this organization, because there's a large segment of the population that says, 'I don't want my family going in the direction of the culture at large.'"[17]

This enclave infrastructure creates a one-sided information space. While Focus's membership may not be completely insulated from oppositional views, this infrastructure creates an information environment where conservative Christian political and religious agendas go relatively unchallenged and unchecked by rival interests. Like other one-sided information spaces that emerge within groups and associations, this enclave infrastructure offers group members a refuge from what leaders such as Dobson deem the permissive ethos of the American mainstream. It also offers members an opportunity to construct and reinforce counter-narratives that emphasize the importance of traditional family values.

The Anti-Contestatory Effects of Focus's Enclave Infrastructure

I discuss the democratic virtues of Focus's enclave infrastructure at the close of the chapter. For now, consider two democratic dangers posed by its one-sided internal group culture. The first is the *problem of polarization*. By insulating group members from oppositional perspectives, such enclave spaces foster conditions that radicalize the views of adherents and heighten intolerance.

The popular press is captivated by this idea of polarization. Pundits and political reporters often present America as deeply polarized, divided between liberal voters in blue states and conservative voters in red states. Yet Morris Fiorina has found that polarization is less widespread than we might think. He argues that the divisiveness discussed on talk shows and in op-eds does not exist to such a degree among ordinary citizens. That divisiveness is largely confined to the "political class"—"the collection of officeholders, party and issue activists, interest group leaders, and political infotainers who constitute the public face of politics in contemporary America."[18] The case of Focus on the Family shows that conditions of polarization also arise at the grass roots—that everyday activists and members of such insular groups, who are by no means political elites, may also display intolerance and polarization.

As mentioned in chapter 4, a growing literature on group interaction indicates the "bonding" discussion of homogeneous groups cultivates polarization. In such homogenous groups, discussion does not produce moderation but instead pushes group members toward extreme positions—toward what Sunstein calls "group polarization."[19]

This effect also surfaces in the specific case of Focus on the Family's enclave practices. In my interview with Focus's Glenn Stanton, he worried that polarization between his community and those on the left prevents healthy contestation and debate. In his words,

> I think the problem is that we don't talk. And the fact that we don't talk is the atmosphere in which the stereotypes and the misunderstanding exist. For camps that we don't understand, we assume that everyone is the same. For our camp [Focus members], it is that all homosexuals are looking to have as much sex as they possibly can with as many people that they can. Well, you get in there and you realize that that's true for some, but it's not true for all. You come here [to Focus on the Family] and you think, "All these people believe X." No, they don't. They all believe in God. They pretty much all have warm feelings about Jesus, but they have different views of it.[20]

Stanton's words reinforce the conclusion that misunderstandings and stereotypes arise on the left and on the right, at least in part, because of the isolation that enclave conditions promote. Citizens detached from direct engagement with others stop talking to one another and become increasingly intolerant.

Opponents of Focus on the Family also point to attitudes of polarization and intolerance. Jen Caltrider of ProgressNow attributes the polarized attitudes of Focus activists to the authoritarian structure of Dobson's message:

Anybody that says, "I'm right, nobody else is; listen to what I have to say" is damaging because it's taking away people's ability to think for themselves, and it creates these kinds of cult-like leaders that people can't question. Anytime you encourage people to cease thinking for themselves and follow blindly, it's a bad thing. And I think that Focus on the Family does that with the oldest trick in the book, which is "The bible says, God says."[21]

Mary Lou Makepeace, former mayor of Colorado Springs, also attributes intolerance to the authoritarian and over-simplified messages that Focus uses to inspire members:

Dobson represents a kind of authority of the church, and I think that many people don't want to think about complex issues. They don't want to think about the complexities of faith and so it's much easier if you have this trust in someone. If they say black is black—it's black. Because life is complicated and I think there are a lot of people who would like that kind of father figure authority figure to tell them what is right and what is wrong.[22]

While the authoritarian structure of his message may cultivate these attitudes, a deeper problem is that Christian right leaders like Dobson promote stereotypes that reinforce polarization and intolerance. In many of Focus's radio productions and publications, opponents of the organization are portrayed as cynical, manipulative, and misguided. Gay and lesbian rights groups bear the brunt of Focus's polarizing messages. Consider Dobson's portrayal of same-sex marriage activists in a 2003 newsletter to members:

The history of the gay and lesbian movement is that its adherents quickly move to the goal line as soon as one has been breached, revealing even more shocking and outrageous objectives. In the present instance, homosexual activists, heady with power and exhilaration, feel the political climate is right to tell us what they have wanted all along. This is the real deal: most gays and lesbians do not want to marry each other. That would entangle them in all sorts of legal constraints. Who needs a lifetime commitment to one person? The intention here is to destroy marriage altogether.[23]

The image of "gay activists" emerging from Dobson's rhetoric demeans the gay community. It suggests that gays and lesbians are inherently promiscuous and uninterested in marriage. Instead, Dobson claims that such activists are engaged in an intentional conspiracy to destroy marriage.

More research is needed on toleration among Christian right activists, but the few surveys conducted confirm that such activists display heightened levels of intolerance. A 1990–1991 survey of members of Beverly LaHaye's Concerned Women for America and Focus on the Family found that only 2 percent of Concerned Women for America members and 6 percent of Focus on the Family members agreed with the statement "A diversity of moral views is healthy."[24]

Another large study of attitudes of Christian right activists found that they are less tolerant than other segments of the public. Wilcox and Larson note that when asked about members of liberal groups such as the National Organization for Women, American Civil Liberties Union, and People for the American Way, "only 61 percent of Christian right activists would allow them to speak in their communities, 57 percent would allow them to demonstrate, and a disconcerting 14 percent would allow them to teach in public schools."[25] While liberal groups often attack the Christian right with equal animosity, this study found that left-leaning activists are more likely to grant their opponents basic political rights. Of course, such studies do not show causality. They do not prove that the Christian right's emerging media infrastructure has heightened polarization and intolerance. They do, however, illustrate the pervasiveness of such attitudes in groups like Focus with a powerful enclave infrastructure.

My argument is not that Focus is unique in presenting its members with political messages that encourage polarization and intolerance. MoveOn.org, PETA, the AFL-CIO, and other left-leaning groups construct their internal rhetoric around similar over-simplifications and stereotypes. As James While, former minister of one of Colorado Spring's more liberal denominations, told me, "Someone said to me that right-wing and left-wing operatives are gathering people together and just enforcing their points of view and entrenching folks more and more. And I thought well, God, I'm doing the same damn thing here. I'm just reinforcing all these liberals and their anti-Bush views. So I think polarization is going on pretty big."[26] Critic of the Christian right and gay and lesbian lobbyist Pat Steadman shares this view. He declares, "I think we've come a long day since the Lincoln-Douglas debates, but this is politics in twenty-first century America. This is how we play this game: misinformation, attacks, propaganda, robo-calls, and direct mail."[27] So while Dobson's language promotes polarization and intolerance, the practice is not unique to the Christian right or Focus on the Family.

The emergence of polarization in organizations like Focus on the Family undermines the contextual ideal of robust contestation and the deliberative ideal of persuasion. On the contextual side, these attitudes have feedback effects. When polarization and intolerance arise out of enclave conditions, they reinforce members' aversion to cross-cutting discussions and strengthen the collective insulation of the enclave. As Stanton puts it, "The problem is that we don't talk." This lack of cross-cutting discussion creates misunderstandings and stereotypes about members of opposition groups, fomenting greater insularity and collective isolation. The result of this feedback loop is a diminished public contestatory space that fails to adhere to the principle of rhetorical diversity. Rather than encompassing an array of competing interests, the public conversation is fragmented into self-contained pockets of like-minded individuals.

The problem of polarization also undermines the deliberative virtues of "civic friendship" and openness to revision. Such virtues play a vital role in the deliberative ideal of persuasion. Intolerance and polarization in groups like Focus on the Family stand in stark contrast to such citizen virtues. The out-group antagonism that arises in enclave structures contradicts the notion that citizens ought to engage with one another in what Rawls calls the spirit of "civic friendship."[28] Such attitudes also foster the antithesis of what Gutmann and Thompson regard as one of deliberation's primary purposes: "to promote mutually respectful processes of decision making."[29] Rather than helping "participants recognize the moral merit in their opponents' claims when those claims have merit,"[30] the enclave infrastructure of groups like Focus and some of its contemporaries on the left promotes the idea that opponents' claims are baseless and motivated by sinister intentions. This antagonism diminishes the likelihood that members of such organizations will engage others with an openness to admitting their own errors or revising their existing preferences.

This tension between the attitudes of Focus members and deliberative ideals raises further questions about the deliberative nature of Focus's use of public reasons. In chapter 3, I outlined several reasons that call into question the deliberative nature of Focus's approach. I argued that its shift from the vocabulary of civil rights and its unified view of religion and science call into question the activists' sincerity and their willingness to revise existing beliefs. The pervasiveness of attitudes of intolerance and polarization within groups like Focus reinforces these worries. It suggests that many activists lack a genuine desire to achieve mutual understanding with opponents—that the use of public reasons by at least some Focus activists is spurred by a strategic intent to win rather than a deliberative intent to understand.

The Problem of Info-Blasting

The attitudes of polarization and intolerance that arise in enclave spaces also cultivate anti-contestatory practices. The *problem of info-blasting* highlights a practice that emerges from Focus's enclave structure and polarized membership. This tactic involves mobilizing group members to intimidate those who disagree with Focus's agenda by deluging their offices with e-mails, faxes, and phone calls. At local levels, this tactic results in a diminished contestatory environment. It creates incentives for lawmakers, candidates, and interest groups to avoid challenging the political agenda of such powerful organizations.

Using this tactic, groups with large grassroots followings like Focus direct thousands of e-mails, letters, and phone calls at the opposition in minutes. As Colorado Springs city councilman Jerry Heimlicher explained, "They [Focus] go to what I would call a phone bank or an e-mail bank and then we are bombarded with hundreds of phone calls and hundreds of e-mails, especially on the issue of benefits for gays and lesbians. And that is no small bit of influence because the e-mails come from all around the world, not just Colorado Springs."[31]

There is nothing new or unique about info-blasting. Encouraging group members to contact legislators and political opponents has long been a trusted tool of political organizing. Such tactics are also not unique to conservatives. Liberal activists use similar tactics to influence lawmakers, media outlets, and oppositional groups. Info-blasting can also serve a useful purpose. It can incite debate, inform citizens, and make lawmakers aware of constituents' grievances.

Yet in some contexts, info-blasting erodes free and open debate. In the context of asymmetrical power relations, this tactic can silence debate. When powerful groups like Focus on the Family use this tactic at local levels, it often creates an intangible atmosphere of intimidation. The knowledge that speaking out against the family values agenda might result in an info-blasting campaign with worldwide reach can discourage relatively powerless local groups and lawmakers from speaking out on these issues.

To illuminate the dangers of info-blasting, consider an instance when Focus on the Family employed this tactic. On March 8, 2006, when the Jack Abramoff scandal reached its apotheosis, a group called DefCon (the Campaign to Defend the Constitution) ran a full-page ad in the New York Times implicating three prominent Christian right leaders. Lou Sheldon, Ralph Reed, and James Dobson, they claimed, were complicit in Abramoff's ploy to support anti-gambling campaigns to force his Indian casino clients to pay for additional lobbying services.

DefCon claimed that Dobson knowingly participated in the creation of radio ads for Abramoff bankrolled by the Indian gaming industry. As they put it,

"Gambling—all types of gambling—is driven by greed and subsists on greed."
—James Dobson, 2006

This is the same James Dobson whose voice you could have heard on radio commercials paid for by Jack Abramoff's Indian casino clients. These casinos gave millions to Jack Abramoff to limit competition.[32]

News of the DefCon attack spread quickly. Soon, a host of other groups jumped on the anti-Dobson bandwagon. ProgressNow, a leading progressive Colorado media organization, spread the story throughout the liberal blogosphere. "When they were having hearings in Congress," Jen Caltrider, an executive producer at ProgressNow, told me, "we called for them to call Dobson in to make him talk about the gambling ads. He did the gambling ads for one of the Indian tribes. Dobson provided anti-gambling ads that were basically paid for with gambling money."[33]

Two days later, Dobson responded to the attacks of DefCon and ProgressNow by devoting an entire radio broadcast to the subject. Dobson was insistent: "We have a serious gambling problem. I have been fighting the gambling industry for at least 15 or 20 years because I know what it does to families. The notion that somehow I am linked to gambling is just breathtaking. . . . I've never heard of Jack Abramoff and I've never taken a cent from him."[34]

Following the DefCon attack, Focus on the Family sent an "Action Alert" to its members, asking them to call, write, and e-mail DefCon and Progress-Now. In moments, a deluge of phone calls, faxes, and e-mails began. "When we called for Congress to bring Dobson in," Caltrider told me, "they sent out a letter to the Focus members and said they were being attacked by Progress-Now questioning Dobson's character. We got inundated with e-mails and phone calls and comments on our blogs attacking us—thousands of them."[35]

Offering a look behind the scenes of Focus's political practices, ProgressNow gave me a sample of the over one thousand e-mails they received. These e-mails express a wide range of concerns. Some members voice outrage, others laud Dobson and his organization, and still others threaten ProgressNow to rethink its attacks. But all staunchly support Dobson and Focus on the Family.

In most e-mails, Dobson is praised as a great man—often as a man of God—who spent years helping American families. One female e-mailer writes, "I have never known such a wonderful man (except for my husband) as Dr. Dobson. . . . Thank you, Dr. Dobson, for your hard work. I stand with you in all you do!"[36] Other members emphasize Dobson's integrity. "We, my wife and I, know that Dr. Dobson is a man of integrity and he is above reproach," remarked one man.[37]

Then there are those with a more hard-hitting approach: "YOU ARE SICK," exclaimed one member, "DR. DOBSON IS A GOOD MAN."[38]

Another calls into question the ethics of ProgressNow: "The only unethical behavior is coming from your organization!!! It's too bad you spend so much time trying to destroy decent people!!!"[39]

Finally, some e-mails go beyond critique, promising payback. One e-mailer warned, "Be aware when it comes to being held accountable, because there is a God who is just and He was there when the Constitution was being made and He WILL judge rightly."[40] Another comes close to an outright threat: "When a man's ways please the Lord, He causes adverse circumstances and even the sins of others to work together for good for His believing child. Dr. Dobson is precious to God. Be careful in your campaign to destroy him; you may get more than you bargained for."[41]

A small percentage of these e-mails went further, directly threatening the organization and its employees. As Caltrider told me, "We actually got a couple e-mails that were so threatening that my boss sent them to the FBI. But we never had physical attacks."[42]

When Focus on the Family uses this tactic to mobilize its worldwide network against local-level political actors, info-blasting creates an intangible atmosphere of intimidation that inhibits public debate. This tactic creates implicit disincentives that discourage lawmakers, oppositional groups, nonpartisan organizations, and corporations from challenging the family values agenda.

Ryan Acker, a leader in the Colorado Springs gay and lesbian community, described Dobson's influence in the community of Colorado Springs as "implicit—it's almost like a looming sense."[43] Mary Lou Makepeace, the former mayor of Colorado Springs, agreed: "In Colorado Springs there's kind of an intimidation factor on the part of elected officials, where it seems to me— and I'm not the only person who feels this way—that elected officials are a little bit afraid of the [Christian] right. And they don't want that backlash that occurs if you do something."[44]

This influence arises from two effects of info-blasting. First, by disrupting day-to-day operations, these campaigns impose significant resource costs. The flood of e-mails must be sorted; the thousands of phone calls must be answered. This is most disruptive at local levels, where individuals and organizations are understaffed and unprepared for deluges of information.

Yet the costs of info-blasting are not just material. As the campaign against ProgressNow illustrates, a small percentage of threatening calls and e-mails also impose more intangible psychological costs. Most of these threats are indirect, but some are more explicit. As Mel White, director of Soulforce.org, told me, "When I was on a seven-day fast for understanding in front of his [Dobson's] headquarters in Colorado Springs, he took out a full-page ad condemning me, calling me a liar. He used his broadcast to stir up hatred against me. We finally had to move into a hotel because of the death threats—literally—on local radio. One person calling in saying, 'Somebody ought to go up there and take him out,' referring to me."[45]

It is important to emphasize that Focus's leadership does not encourage threats. They end e-mail alerts with a plea for members to articulate their concerns respectfully. As one Focus Action Alert recommends, "Please take a moment to respectfully let DeGette; Abraham Foxman, national director of the ADL; and Michael Huttner, executive director of ProgressNow.org, know what you think of their politically motivated attempts to smear Dr. Dobson."[46] Yet with a large network of members and a polarizing political message, it is not surprising that a few members threaten rather than inform.

As a result, most local-level political opponents are not afraid of Focus on the Family itself but fear its more fanatical members. As Makepeace, who now heads the Gay and Lesbian Fund for Colorado, put it, "If I were going to be afraid of something, I wouldn't be afraid of Focus. I would be afraid of some unstable person who might hear the Focus talk and see this organization [the Gay and Lesbian Fund] as something that should be attacked."[47]

The resource and psychological costs of info-blasting erode free and open political debate. In the context of asymmetrical power relationships, this practice undermines fair competition. Faced with the possibility of becoming the target of an info-blasting campaign, rival groups and citizens may refrain from expressing their beliefs or challenging the conservative Christian agenda. In this sense, info-blasting is implicit coercion to silence the opposition. Focus never explicitly threatens other political actors, but its info-blasting campaigns remind those considering speaking out against its agenda that challenging the Christian right agenda may subject them to heavy costs.

Not all info-blasting campaigns undermine the principle of fair competition. The effects of this practice depend on the context. In national politics, such tactics are less likely to create an atmosphere of intimidation that silences debate. On the broad stage of national politics, equally powerful groups like People for the American Way and the Human Rights Campaign counter groups like Focus. However, at the local level, info-blasting can silence debate. When Focus mobilizes its network to deluge Colorado Springs political associations and lawmakers with phone calls and e-mails, it can create an anti-contestatory atmosphere of intimidation.

The Democratic Virtues of Focus's Enclave Infrastructure

Juxtaposed against the ideal of robust contestation, these enclave structures appear to diminish democracy. They cultivate polarization and political practices that inhibit free and open political debate. Yet a closer look at these practices reveals that the virtues of one-sided group spaces, discussed in chapter 4, also arise in the specific case of Focus.

First, the enclave infrastructure of Focus and other groups often has positive representational effects. Focus provides like-minded Christians with an insulated space for constructing narratives of resistance and ensuring that their message is heard in the public political forum. For activists and members of Focus, the desire to inject their views into the public forum is a pivotal political ambition. Motivated by the perception that Christians are excluded from full participation in American politics and culture by "liberal elites," groups like Focus seek to fight back by injecting family values into the cultural mainstream.

In "defending" its ideal of family values, Focus has successfully disseminated its message to the broader culture. Restrictions on abortion, prohibitions on same-sex marriage, and limits to stem cell research are now inescapable topics in the American political conversation. As opponents of Focus, such as Michael Brewer, the public policy director at the GLBT Community Center of Colorado, observed, "They [Focus] do fuel the flame of debate. Some evidence for that is their pushing of the same-sex marriage ban in Colorado. They are pushing that. I tell people, there is no gay couple in Colorado asking the legislature, or the courts, or the people to grant full-fledged marriage. It's their side saying, 'We're going to debate that and we're going to win.'"[48]

Focus's enclave infrastructure plays an important role in ensuring the representation of its views in the broader culture, but in some instances its efforts may go too far. Focus's vast financial resources, media infrastructure, and grass-roots following distinguish it from other organizations that struggle to express the grievances of underrepresented minorities. As a result of its power and polarized membership, Focus's practices often go beyond mere representation. They risk establishing a new "hegemonic ideology." Focus's practice of info-blasting at local levels, for instance, sometimes not only ensures that these interests are represented but that their interests are the *only* interests represented in public debates. So while many of Focus's efforts to receive a fair hearing in the public political forum are praiseworthy, these efforts occasionally diminish the capacity of other underrepresented groups (such as women and gays and lesbians) to express their perspective.

In addition to its representational effect, Focus's enclave infrastructure has a second democracy-enhancing effect: it helps catalyze active political participation. When viewed through what we might call the participatory ideal of democracy, its enclave infrastructure appears to enhance democracy by mobilizing citizens for political participation.[49] As Sara Diamond puts it, "Media outlets [of the Christian right] feed adherents a steady diet of information, entertainment, and spiritual uplift—just the right mix to keep people tuned in, loyal, and ready to act on what they hear."[50]

Unfortunately, there are no comprehensive studies of homogeneity and participation among Focus on the Family activists. Yet many of the group's practices support the notion that members are engaged in bonding activities and participate actively in politics. Focus's mission to provide members with an insulated "countercultural" Christian media infrastructure cultivates homogeneous information spaces and social practices of bonding rather than "bridging."

Moreover, the active engagement of Focus's membership in politics is well documented. As a result of such passionate engagement in voter drives, phone campaigns, and fundraising efforts, its members influence everything from media coverage to state and federal lawmakers and the Republican Party's agenda.[51] As Jen Caltrider, executive producer at ProgressNow, a left-leaning Colorado group that counters Focus, told me, "They have enormous influence because they have so many followers and James Dobson has such a huge personality and such far reach with his radio show and his ministries and his books and his websites. It's one thing to have 5 million people in a database. It's another to know that you have 5 million people 10 percent of which you know will be active when you make a call. They don't just have names in a database; they have people that will be active when they call for it."[52]

Even liberal opponents of Dobson, such as Pat Steadman, a leading Colorado lobbyist for gay and lesbian issues, admit that these enclave structures have positive participatory effects on democracy: "Having people care is important," Steadman told me. "Apathy is one of our biggest problems in policy decisions today. And so the fact that they [Focus] do make people engaged is a good thing, even if they are all misguided and on the wrong side of the issue in my opinion."[53]

Reconciling Participation and Contestation

The Christian right's practices highlight the tension described in chapter 4 between one-sided and robustly contestatory information spaces. On the one hand, the one-sided information space within Focus enables conservative Christians to empower their perspective and to mobilize fellow Christians into political action. On the other, Focus's enclave infrastructure cultivates polarization, intolerance, and anti-contestatory practices that diminish the contestatory nature of the public deliberative arena.

The case of Focus on the Family illustrates that in certain circumstances, there is a democratic trade-off between practices that cultivate active participation and those that cultivate robust and fair public contestation. How are we to reconcile the tension between participation and deliberation? As discussed in chapter 4, such trade-offs should not be resolved by embracing insulated enclaves that promote active participation or by embracing radically contestatory conditions that extend into the private sphere of in-group deliberations. Instead, we ought to encourage *partially contestatory* conditions where group members both interact with fellow citizens in the public deliberative arena and interact with like-minded members in the group's one-sided information space.

Focus on the Family seems to have failed to strike this balance. While its enclave infrastructure effectively inspires political action, its countercultural ethos is so strong that it appears to discourage direct engagement with other views. As a result, Focus's enclave infrastructure appears to play a primary role in cultivating anti-deliberative attitudes of intolerance and polarization. It may even motivate the small percentage of the e-mails, phone calls, and faxes that cause Focus's practice of info-blasting to intimidate opponents from voicing concerns about the family values agenda.

There is no easy solution to counteracting such imbalances, and this chapter cannot specify policy solutions in detail. Yet the best response to the participatory imbalances that arise from Focus's enclave infrastructure is less insulation and greater cross-cutting engagement. As Sunstein puts it, we should address such situations by ensuring

> that any such enclaves are not walled off from competing views, and that at certain points, there is an exchange of views between enclave members and those who disagree with them. It is total or near-total self-insulation, rather than group deliberation as such, that carries with it the most serious dangers, often in the highly unfortunate (and sometimes deadly) combination of extremism and marginality.[54]

This is not to say that we should discourage all enclaves and try to stop like-minded citizens from forming close associations with each other. It simply means that we should be wary of the dangers of such overly insular cultural spaces and think of institutional and structural conditions that might encourage citizens in such groups to directly engage a broad cross-section of citizens.

Using the case of Focus on the Family, this chapter has sought to bring the previous chapter's contextual principles to bear on the practices of one of America's most powerful political interest groups. Focus's vast media infrastructure is a powerful one-sided information space within the conservative Christian community. Viewed against the contextual ideals of fair competition and rhetorical diversity, the attitudes and practices that emerge from this enclave structure appear to diminish democracy. Yet such structures are not entirely destructive because they also incite engaged political participation. I argue that, while important, Focus's participatory practices often become so extreme that they erode the possibility of realizing deliberative democratic ideals. To correct this imbalance between participation and deliberation, groups like Focus on the Family and their counterparts on the left should be encouraged to engage a more diverse cross-section of citizens.

Notes

1. Adam Piore, "A Higher Frequency," *Mother Jones Magazine*, November/December, 2005.

2. The research methodology for this chapter is similar to that of chapter 4 in that I use the same approach and draw on the same data sources. For those interested in my field research methodology, my interview methods, and a complete listing of interviewees, see chapter 4.

3. Dan Gilgoff and Bret Schulte, "The Dobson Way," *US News and World Report*, January 17, 2005, 62.

4. Gilgoff and Schulte, "The Dobson Way," 62.

5. These quotes were taken from my tour of Focus on the Family headquarters, June 24, 2004.

6. Figures given during my tour of the Focus on the Family headquarters, June 24, 2004.

7. Gilgoff and Schulte, "The Dobson Way," 62.

8. Interview with Daniel Weiss at the Focus on the Family headquarters, July 6, 2006.

9. Gil Alexander-Moegerle, *James Dobson's War on America* (New York: Prometheus Books, 1997), 15.

10. Dale Buss, "The Counter Counterculture," *Primedia*, January 2002.

11. Interview with Glenn Stanton, June 24, 2004.

12. Interview with Glenn Stanton, June 24, 2004.

13. "About Breakaway," Focus on the Family, www.breakawaymag.com/aboutus/index.cfm, 2006.

14. Sara Diamond, *Not By Politics Alone* (New York: Guilford Press, 1998), 21.

15. Mariah Blake, "Stations of the Cross," *Columbia Journalism Review*, issue 3 (May/June, 2005).

16. Buss, "The Counter Counterculture."

17. Buss, "The Counter Counterculture."

18. Morris P. Fiorina, *Culture War? The Myth of a Polarized America* (New York: Pearson Longman, 2006), 1.

19. Cass Sunstein, *Republic.com* (Princeton: Princeton University Press, 2001), 65.

20. Interview with Glenn Stanton, June 6, 2006.

21. Interview with Jen Caltrider, June 11, 2006.

22. Interview with Mary Lou Makepeace, June 20, 2006.

23. James Dobson, "Marriage on the Ropes," *Dr. Dobson's Newsletter*, September, 2003.

24. Jean Hardisty, *Mobilizing Resentment* (Boston: Beacon Press, 1999), 20.

25. Clyde Wilcox and Carin Larson, *Onward Christian Soldiers?* (Boulder, CO: Westview Press, 2006), 183.

26. Interview with James White, July 7, 2006.

27. Interview with Pat Steadman, July 10, 2006.

28. John Rawls, "The Idea of Public Reason Revisited," in *The Law of Peoples with "The Idea of Public Reason Revisited"* (Cambridge: Harvard University Press, 1999), 137.

29. Amy Gutmann and Dennis Thompson, *Why Deliberative Democracy?* (Princeton: Princeton University Press, 2004), 11.

30. Gutmann and Thompson, *Why Deliberative Democracy?*

31. Interview with city councilman Jerry Heimlicher, June 28, 2006.

32. Paid advertisement, *New York Times*, March 8, 2006.

33. Interview with Jen Caltrider, June 11, 2006.

34. James Dobson, Focus on the Family broadcast, March 10, 2006, http://progressnow.org/digest/audio/defdob.mp3.

35. Interview with Jen Caltrider, June 11, 2006.

36. March 2006 e-mails from Focus on the Family members to ProgressNow. On file with author.

37. March 2006 e-mails from Focus on the Family.

38. March 2006 e-mails from Focus on the Family.

39. March 2006 e-mails from Focus on the Family.

40. March 2006 e-mails from Focus on the Family.

41. March 2006 e-mails from Focus on the Family.

42. Interview with Jen Caltrider, June 11, 2006.

43. Interview with Ryan Acker, June 20, 2006.

44. Interview with Mary Lou Makepeace, June 20, 2006.

45. Interview with Mel White, July 11, 2006.

46. "Defend Dr. Dobson's Stem Cell Comments," CitizenLink Action Alert, August 5, 2005.

47. Interview with Mary Lou Makepeace, June 20, 2006.

48. Interview with Michael Brewer, July 8, 2006.

49. I am grateful to Diana Mutz for the notion that such enclave practices often enhance democracy when viewed from the vantage point of participatory democracy; see Diana Mutz, *Hearing the Other Side* (New York: Cambridge University Press, 2006).

50. Diamond, *Not By Politics Alone*, 2.

51. Dan Gilgoff, *The Jesus Machine* (New York: St. Martin's Press, 2007).

52. Interview with Jen Caltrider, June 11, 2006.

53. Interview with Pat Steadman, July 10, 2006.

54. Cass Sunstein, "Deliberative Trouble? Why Groups Go to Extremes," *Yale Law Journal* 110, no. 1 (2000): 114.

~

Conclusion

When does political rhetoric enhance and when does it diminish democracy? This question has guided our inquiry into the moral dimensions of rhetoric. As we have seen, existing democratic theories fail to provide a compelling response. Deliberative theories of democracy offer important accounts of the constructive side of rhetoric—of its ideal possibilities. Yet they tend to overlook the important moral distinctions between the kinds of non-ideal rhetoric that so often arise in contemporary democratic politics.

These problems are not merely theoretical. They are also practical. By neglecting the moral qualities of rhetoric—as it exists in concrete political circumstances—such theories lack an account of the realities of deliberative practice. They offer an important set of ideals toward which to aspire but lack the conceptual tools for evaluating the moral qualities of real-world political speech.

This book proposes a constructive framework for distinguishing these moral dimensions of political rhetoric. The analysis works on two levels. The first level concerns the moral qualities of rhetorical speech itself. To disentangle morally acceptable from morally problematic forms of rhetoric, I have outlined a distinction between persuasion and manipulation. On my account, persuasion takes two primary forms. In *deliberative persuasion*, speakers seek to induce agreement with an orientation toward mutual understanding. In *strategic persuasion*, speakers seek to induce agreement with an orientation toward winning—toward inducing the listener to take up *their* view or agree with *their* proposed course of action. Manipulation, by contrast, arises when speakers intentionally exert irrational or hidden forms of force on listeners to interfere with their capacity to choose.

These moral distinctions between ideal speech types help illuminate the nature and form of various kinds of rhetorical speech. Yet in order to discourage and prevent the emergence of morally problematic forms of rhetoric, we must go beyond simply understanding when rhetoric turns manipulative. The practical task of discouraging manipulative speech requires a second, contextual level of analysis. To prevent manipulative rhetoric, I have argued that we must aspire toward public deliberative contexts that promote manipulation's most powerful antidote—the threat of exposure.

In *contestatory spaces*, the fair competition of diverse interests cultivates public scrutiny and exposure. In such spaces, self-interested partisans have incentives to uncover and to challenge the concealments, lies, and irrational appeals of oppositional groups. The threat of exposure, and the loss of credibility that goes along with it, is a powerful check against would-be manipulators. Within *one-sided public information spaces*, however, such incentive structures no longer exist. These spaces consist of minimal competition and public scrutiny. As a result, speakers within such spaces face few disincentives to manipulation.

To illuminate the moral qualities of rhetorical speech and context, I have sought to ground this analysis in a case study of the American Christian right. This case study has served two primary purposes. First, it has brought to life the conceptual qualities of my constructive theory of rhetoric. The evolution of the Christian right's rhetoric from its manipulative "stealth" tactics to its partially deliberative humanist rhetoric illuminates the various moral qualities of rhetorical speech. Further, the "counterculture" promoted by the enclave infrastructure of groups like Focus on the Family illuminates the dangers that insulated, one-sided information spaces pose to democracy.

This case study also serves as an assessment of one of the most powerful social movements in contemporary American politics. Over the last thirty years, groups like the Moral Majority, the Christian Coalition, and Focus on the Family have played a powerful role in mobilizing Christians into political action and influencing the broader culture. Unlike most critical accounts of the Christian right, this case study offers a more ambivalent assessment. On the one side, these organizations ought to be commended for their shift away from manipulative forms of "stealth" rhetoric toward more deliberative forms of speech. On the other, the enclave infrastructure and anti-contestatory tactics of such organizations pose a number of risks to the free and open conditions of public deliberation.

Political Implications

The primary task of this book has been one of disentangling the various moral qualities of rhetorical speech and the contexts within which it is exchanged. It is, however, worth briefly exploring the implications this account holds for the structure and practice of democracy. Applied to American politics, this analysis offers reasons for hope as well as concern. On the hopeful side, the case of the Christian right shows a gradual shift toward more deliberative rhetorical appeals. Rather than using the manipulative "stealth" appeals that typified the Christian right of the early 1990s, contemporary activists use more strategic and even deliberative forms of rhetoric.

The contestatory rhetorical context of American democracy helped bring this shift about. When the Christian Coalition used "stealth" rhetoric in the early 1990s, the contestatory nature of electoral politics ensured their political victories were short-lived. As we have seen, the use of manipulative appeals in the 1990 elections garnered huge electoral gains: sixty of the ninety San Diego–based Coalition candidates ended up winning their races for school board, city council, and local-level party leadership positions.[1] Yet this tide of electoral success led to increased public awareness and scrutiny: the success of these rhetorical concealments in the short term brought about their demise over the long run.

The victories of "stealth" Coalition candidates in 1990 inspired the rise of several opposition groups. They created a more richly contestatory context in which the manipulative basis of the "stealth" strategy started to come to light. Oppositional groups and candidates exposed the deep disconnect between the moderate rhetoric of Coalition candidates on the campaign trail and their overtly religious political agenda. As a result, the 1992 election led to a reversal of the Christian Coalition's gains. Just two years later, the number of candidates elected to local school boards declined by 50 percent.[2] The shockwaves from these and other defeats spread beyond San Diego and the Christian Coalition. The long-term failure of the "stealth" strategy inspired the broader Christian right to shift from manipulation toward more strategic and deliberative forms of rhetoric.

The Christian right's gradual rhetorical shift toward more deliberative forms of rhetoric offers hope for America's contestatory spaces. It gives us reason to think that rhetorical conditions may not be as bad as many think. It shows that the structures of contestation and debate offer powerful incentives against lies, concealments, and other forms of manipulation. Within the public sphere of political debate, the most powerful antidote to manipulation—the risk of exposure—remains alive and well.

Yet this hopeful assessment of the rhetorical conditions of American democracy is only part of the story. Chapter 5 shows that the one-sided information spaces within political parties and activist movements pose many risks to the health of deliberative democracy. Beneath the deliberative public exterior of groups like Focus on the Family, we often find a more radical internal rhetoric used to mobilize group members. Rather than promoting the deliberative virtues of mutual respect and toleration, this rhetoric promotes out-group antagonism and attitudes of intolerance.

The dangers of one-sided information spaces extend beyond the Christian right. With the rise of the Internet and cable news networks, the power of such spaces to disseminate manipulative forms of rhetoric has intensified. Consider the lingering debate over whether President Obama was born in the United States and thus eligible for the presidency. At the beginning of Obama's run for president, rumors surfaced among conservative bloggers and some supporters of his primary opponent Hillary Clinton questioning whether he was born in America. On June 12, 2008, the Obama campaign attempted to put an end to these rumors by releasing a copy of his certificate of live birth on the campaign website.[3] Rather than ending the controversy, this document fueled it. In fact, it inspired the rise of a political movement of self-described "birthers" dedicated to discrediting Obama's qualifications as a presidential candidate. The "birthers" claimed to have proof that Obama released a fraudulent birth certificate. They used the Internet and other tools to promote an atmosphere of suspicion and to shift the perception of Obama among mainstream voters.

This rhetoric started within the one-sided spaces of the blogosphere. Soon, however, it emerged in the rhetoric and policy arguments of more mainstream political actors. In March of 2009, Representative Bill Posey (R-FL) introduced an amendment to the Federal Campaign Act of 1976 inspired by the "birthers." This amendment sought to require all presidential candidates to submit "a copy of the candidate's birth certificate . . . to establish that the candidate meets the qualifications for the eligibility of the office of president under the Constitution."[4]

The issue reached its apex during the initial phase of the Republican presidential primary in the spring of 2011. Billionaire and reality-TV star Donald Trump based his brief run for president on the issue. He insisted, "I have a birth certificate. People have birth certificates. He [Obama] doesn't have a birth certificate. He may have one but there is something on that birth certificate—maybe religion, maybe it says he's a Muslim, I don't know. Maybe he doesn't want that. Or, he may not have one."[5]

On April 27, 2011, in an attempt to put this controversy to rest, Obama released the original long-form version of his birth certificate and held a press conference on the issue. "We do not have time for this kind of silliness," said Obama. "We've got better stuff to do. I've got better stuff to do. We've got big problems to solve."[6]

For our purposes, the rhetorical manipulation surrounding Obama's birthplace highlights a deep problem with the current contestatory structure of American democracy. It shows that in spite of robust contestation at the national level, the rhetorical distortions that start within deeply polarized, one-sided spaces can creep into the rhetoric and beliefs of mainstream Americans. At the height of this controversy, just before Obama released the long-form version of his birth certificate, CNN reported that only 72 percent of Americans and 52 percent of Republicans believed that Obama was "definitely" born in the United States. After Obama's release of the long-form birth certificate, a substantial number of Americans still harbored doubts about Obama's birthplace. The number of Americans believing Obama was born in the United States rose just eight points to 80 percent and the number of Republicans rose seventeen points to 69 percent.[7] This shows that even with robust contestation in the media and the release of concrete evidence that Obama was indeed born in Hawaii, the power of the rhetoric of the "birthers" continued to sway many Americans.

The case of the Christian right and the "birthers" leaves us with a mixed picture of the health of political rhetoric in America. While the contestatory structures of American democracy have their strengths, they also leave ample room for improvement. The theory outlined in this book offers several directions for future efforts to improve the moral quality of rhetoric in American democracy. At base, it shows that the best way to counter such manipulative rhetoric is to create incentives against manipulation and the one-sided information spaces that magnify its autonomy-diminishing effects.

Yet discouraging politicians, interest group leaders, and pundits from relying on manipulative rhetoric is no simple matter. While this theoretical account of manipulation helps to illuminate the dangers posed by such speech, like most political theories it will probably have minimal influence on the behavior of real-world political actors. Simply illuminating the dangers of manipulative speech will not change the powerful institutional incentives that shape the rhetorical tactics of modern political actors. As Bok explains,

> The social incentives to deceit are at present very powerful; the controls, often weak. Many individuals feel caught up in practices they cannot change. It would be wishful thinking, therefore, to expect individuals to bring about major changes in the collective practices of deceit themselves. Public and private institutions, with their enormous power to affect personal choice, must help alter the existing pressures and incentives.[8]

Bok's point harkens back to our discussion of Madison in chapter 4. Transforming the actions of concrete political actors often requires restructuring political institutions in ways that reshape the basic incentive structures motivating and constraining human action.[9]

A comprehensive discussion of these policy implications is beyond the scope of this analysis. Here, however, I outline a few possible reforms that might help mitigate the problems that diminish the efficacy of America's contestatory structures. Guiding each of these proposals is the idea that the behavior of political actors can be transformed by increasing the structural incentives against manipulative speech.

Media Diversification

Over the last thirty years, the ownership of major American media outlets has become increasingly consolidated. Whereas fifty major America media corporations existed in 1983, the "Big Six" media corporations (General Electric, Disney, TimeWarner, Viacom, News Corporation, and CBS) now own most media outlets.[10] This trend has not only affected national-level news outlets, it has also led to the consolidation of media outlets at the local level. In Los Angeles, for instance, the number of local newspapers fell from forty-nine in 1982 to eighteen in 2007. In New York, the number of newspapers fell from twenty-eight to thirteen over the same time period.[11]

This trend toward media consolidation has been facilitated by a number of policy measures, such as the 1996 Telecommunications Act. This act abolished most restrictions on media ownership and helped create new incentives that encouraged consolidation and discouraged diversity and competition within the media industry.

From the perspective of this analysis, the incentive structures created by such policies toward media consolidation are deeply problematic. As many media critics point out, this shift toward consolidation has led to a decline in the diversity of media outlets. With fewer media outlets, the decisions and actions of lawmakers at local levels face less scrutiny and contestation. This shift has also increased the pressures on news organizations to generate profits and improve ratings.[12] It has resulted in newspapers, radio stations, and television networks devoting their resources to "soft news" and scaling back on investigative journalism and foreign bureau staff. By discouraging competition, diversity, and robust public scrutiny, such transformations have diminished the kinds of contestatory spaces that place a check on manipulative speech. The decline in competition has created a media that, especially at local levels, fails to enforce the primary antidote to manipulative speech: the threat of exposure.

To mitigate this shift, we ought to consider new policies to encourage greater diversity and competition. Rather than encouraging media monopolies and consolidation, such policies ought to promote the formation of new independent media outlets and other measures that encourage vibrant competition and diversity within the public sphere.

Educational Reform

To ensure that citizens have the capacity to challenge manipulative forms of speech, educational institutions ought to raise awareness among citizens of manipulative speech and its potential dangers. First, secondary schools, universities, and professional schools ought to ensure that students understand the various forms of manipulation. While most citizens understand the manipulative potential of lies, they should also be instructed to spot less obvious forms of manipulation, such as efforts by speakers to hide information or to distract the listener.

Second, and perhaps most important, educational institutions should explore the potential dangers that such speech poses to both individual autonomy and democratic self-rule. On the individual level, manipulative speech erodes the capacity of citizens to choose for themselves. On the political level, manipulative speech interferes with the capacity of "the people" as a whole to engage in informed collective decision-making. Students should learn that at both levels, manipulative speech strips the capacity to choose from citizens and places it in the hands of the skillful manipulator.

The aim in cultivating this kind of awareness is twofold. First, citizens who understand the nature of manipulative speech will be better able to expose and contest instances in which candidates, interest groups, or lawmakers appeal to manipulative tactics. Second, citizens with this awareness will be more sensitive to the dangers that manipulative forms of speech pose both to their own autonomy and to democracy itself. They will understand that manipulative actions are not to be taken lightly—that they constitute a deep threat to individual and collective freedom.

To cultivate this kind of awareness, educational institutions ought to also examine the kinds of incentive structures created by their own policies and practices. As Bok explains, such institutions ought to ask, "How scrupulously honest are they in setting an example? How do they cope with cheating, with plagiarism, and with fraudulent research? What pressures encourage such behavior? To what extent, and in what disciplines, are deceptive techniques actually *taught* to students?"[13] By asking such questions, educational institutions can take an important first step in reshaping their own practices to ensure that they encourage honest and sincere speech and discourage manipulation.

Diversifying Enclave Spaces

Chapter 5 explored the democratic virtues and vices of the enclave space created by the Christian right organization Focus on the Family. As we have seen, Focus uses its vast media infrastructure to create a one-sided information space—a space that insulates group members from direct engagement with opposing views. Such enclaves not only cultivate polarization and intolerance, they also create an information space where manipulative forms of rhetoric go uncontested and unchallenged. To mitigate these problematic aspects of enclaves, we ought to encourage greater levels of direct engagement between group insiders and outsiders.

Consider two possible measures aimed at diminishing the levels of insulation from oppositional views within such groups:

- *Desegregating America's Residential Areas*: Residential patterns throughout America reinforce enclave communities such as the Christian right. Increasingly, American neighborhoods divide along the lines of race, education, and income.[14] With the rise of suburban housing developments, interstates, and the commuter culture, America's cities consist of more and more self-contained pockets of homogeneity. In 1992, for instance, 37.7 percent of Americans lived in politically homogeneous counties (counties that voted for a presidential candidate in a landslide). In 2004, that number rose to 48.3 percent.[15] Such trends show that those with similar ethnicities, incomes, political views, and religious affiliations are more likely to live among one another and thus to interact primarily with one another. The formation of such segregated residential patterns may not have been intentional. As Diana Mutz suggests, "The initial goal may not have been politically like-minded neighbors, but that is achieved to the extent that lifestyle considerations correlate with political perspectives."[16] To mitigate this effect and to encourage greater levels of interaction between oppositional perspectives, urban planning policy ought to promote more heterogeneous neighborhoods and city spaces. When possible, it should encourage the formation of residential spaces where members of different political, economic, religious, and ethnic groups live among one another.

- *Citizen-Based Deliberative Forums:* Another way to encourage interactions between diverse groups is to create opportunities for such groups to engage in respectful deliberation. A growing number of organizations now seek to create such public forums. America Speaks, the Civic Practices Network, the Deliberative Democracy Consortium, and the Kettering Foundation all seek to encourage such deliberative spaces. Although such formalized deliberative spaces may not result in long-lasting interactions between diverse groups, they offer an important first step to opening up the pathways of conversation and understanding.

Emerging New Contestatory Spaces

Over the last ten years, a number of new contestatory spaces have emerged on the Internet. Blogs, wikis, chatrooms, and other emerging new technologies now enable citizens throughout the country to interact and to engage in political discussion. In the political realm, blogs have had the most profound impact. As we saw in the rise of "birther" rhetoric, political bloggers have unearthed a number of instances of political misinformation and outright racial prejudice.[17]

During the 2004 election, for instance, bloggers were responsible for the so-called "Rather-Gate" scandal. CBS anchor Dan Rather presented a report calling into question President George W. Bush's service in the Air National Guard from 1972 to 1973. As evidence, the report displayed several allegedly authentic documents authored by Bush's commander, which called into question Bush's service in the military. One day after the story aired, a blogger named Buckhead pointed out that the documents were written in Palatino or Times New Roman font, neither of which existed in 1972.[18]

Bloggers also exposed Senate Majority Leader Trent Lott's racially tinged defense of Senator Strom Thurmond's pro-segregationist platform for president in 1948. At a private birthday party for Thurmond in 2002, Lott declared, "When Strom Thurmond ran for president, we voted for him. We're proud of it. And if the rest of the country had followed our lead, we wouldn't have all these problems over all these years either."[19] These comments were largely ignored by the mainstream media until they were picked up by a blog called talkingpointsmemo.com and heavily discussed throughout the blogosphere. Several weeks later, under intense pressure from President Bush's White House and fellow Republican lawmakers, Lott resigned from his position as Senate Majority Leader.

Such instances point to the promises and perils of the Internet as a tool for exposing manipulative forms of rhetoric. Consider the promises of these new contestatory spaces. First, blogs, YouTube, and other online spaces offer an important challenge to the primarily top-down power structure of traditional media outlets. Unlike the nightly news or the op-ed page of the *New York Times*, which restrict the creation of content to a handful of elites, such spaces enable all citizens to contribute. Citizens with relevant ideas or information can post their comments on established blogs, create their own blogs, or post their videos on YouTube. This bottom-up power structure more fully realizes the contestatory ideal of chapter 4. It enables all citizens—not simply media elites—to contest and challenge potentially manipulative forms of speech and to have their voices heard.

Second, these emerging Internet spaces expand the scope of public scrutiny beyond the newsrooms of traditional media outlets to the entire citizenry. This expanded sphere of scrutiny intensifies the primary disincentive to manipulation—the threat of exposure. As we have seen in chapter 4, traditional media outlets provide an effective form of public scrutiny at the national level. Yet they often fail effectively to scrutinize the rhetoric of speakers at local levels. Using the Internet, however, ordinary citizens can expand the sphere of public scrutiny and provide a more robust checking function on the rhetoric of elites. They can monitor the back-stage discussions and local-level appeals of representatives and, using these emerging Internet spaces, expose instances of manipulation.

While such technologies promise important benefits, they also pose several potential dangers to free and open public discussion. First, the more radically democratic bottom-up power structure of the Internet lacks the kinds of accountability structures that constrain the speech of traditional media figures. Newspaper reporters, news anchors, and pundits all face strong incentives to avoid falsehoods and slander. If their reporting were exposed as manipulative, they would lose their credibility and perhaps even their careers. Internet bloggers face fewer incentives to engage in honest reporting. As Sunstein points out,

> Participants in the blogospere [sic] usually lack an economic incentive. They are not involved in any kind of trade, and most of the time they have little to gain or to lose. If they spread falsehoods, or simply offer their opinion, they do not sacrifice a thing. Perhaps their reputation will suffer, but perhaps not; perhaps the most dramatic falsehoods will draw attention and hence readers.[20]

Sunstein's point is that these online spaces may not only lack disincentives to manipulation, they may actually encourage and reward such practices. So while the Internet may discourage manipulation at the elite level, it may introduce new forms of manipulation in the blogs and comment posts of ordinary citizens.

Second, the expanded scope of public scrutiny created by the Internet may erode the spontaneous and improvisational side of political rhetoric. By intensifying the level of scrutiny that candidates and lawmakers face, these new spaces create powerful incentives to avoid off-hand rhetorical miscalculations. Wary of following the fate of Trent Lott or Senator George Allen after his now infamous "macaca moment," candidates and lawmakers now approach even the most casual conversations with a carefully crafted set of rhetorical appeals. They avoid potentially controversial topics and engage in a heavily scripted form of political talk. As a result, elite discussion may often veer away from important topics such as drug policy, criminal justice reform, and race. The heavily crafted nature of elite rhetoric may also diminish the vitality and excitement of public political discussions.

Underlying each of these reforms is the idea that reshaping the qualities of deliberative context stands as the best way to encourage more-ideal forms of rhetoric. It is not enough to point out the moral distinctions between deliberative and manipulative speech. While important, such conceptual distinctions are unlikely to alter the actions of real-world political actors.

Given the imperfect nature of democratic politics, we cannot expect lawmakers, pundits, and interest group leaders to act solely on the basis of moral principle. This is why deliberative context matters. By reshaping the context of debate to include fair competition and a diversity of ideas, manipulative rhetoric loses its efficacy and power. In such contestatory spaces, the atmosphere of debate and challenge transforms the nature of manipulation. Manipulative rhetoric no longer operates as a clever but immoral means of winning at all costs. Robust contestation transforms it into a tool that, once exposed, can destroy the reputation and career of those who manipulate.

Notes

1. Matthew Freeman, *The San Diego Model: A Community Battles the Religious Right* (Washington, DC: People for the American Way, 1993), 10.

2. Freeman, *The San Diego Model*, 58.

3. David Weigel, "Birtherism Is Dead. Long Live Birtherism," *Slate*, April 27, 2011, www.slate.com/id/2292306/.

4. Weigel, "Birtherism Is Dead."

5. Glenn Kessler, "A Look at Trump's 'Birther' Statements," *Washington Post*, April 28, 2011, www.washingtonpost.com/blogs/fact-checker/post/a-look-at-trumps-birther-statements/2011/04/27/AFeOYb1E_blog.html.

6. Barack Obama, "Remarks by the President," April 27, 2011, www.whitehouse.gov/the-press-office/2011/04/27/remarks-president.

7. "Birth Certificate Erases Most—But Not All—Obama Doubts," *CNN*, May 6, 2011, http://politicalticker.blogs.cnn.com/2011/05/06/birth-certificate-eases-most-but-not-all-obama-doubts/.

8. Sissela Bok, *Lying* (New York: Vintage Books, 1999), 244.

9. James Madison, *The Federalist Papers* (New York: Penguin Books, 1987). For an excellent discussion of deliberation and the importance of examining such institutional incentives, see Stephen L. Elkin, "Thinking Constitutionally: The Problem of Deliberative Democracy," *Social Philosophy and Policy* 21 (2004).

10. Dell Champlin and Janet Knoedler, "Operating in the Public Interest or in Pursuit of Private Profits? News in the Age of Media Consolidation," *Journal of Economic Issues* 36, no. 2 (2002).

11. For more of the figures detailing the decline of newspapers and the consolidation of media ownership, see *Forbes Magazine*, www.forbes.com/2008/05/08/media-consolidation-map-ent-competition08-cz_ph_0508map.html.

12. For more detailed discussions of these transformations, see Robert Crandall, "Competition and Chaos: U.S. Telecommunications since 1996" (Brookings Institute, 2005); James Fallows, *Breaking the News* (New York: Pantheon Books, 1996); Robert McChesney, *Rich Media, Poor Democracy* (Urbana: University of Illinois Press, 1999); Justin Lewis, *Constructing Public Opinion* (New York: Columbia University Press, 2001); Bartholomew H. Sparrow, *Uncertain Guardians* (Baltimore: Johns Hopkins University Press, 1999).

13. Bok, *Lying*, 247.

14. See, for example, Douglas S. Massey and Nancy A. Denton, *American Apartheid* (Cambridge: Harvard University Press, 1993); Stephen Macedo, "School Reform and Equal Opportunity in America's Geography of Inequality," *Perspectives on Politics*, no. 1 (2003).

15. Bill Bishop, *The Big Sort* (Boston: Houghton Mifflin, 2008).

16. Diana Mutz, *Hearing the Other Side* (New York: Cambridge University Press, 2006), 47.

17. For an excellent discussion of the virtues and vices of blogs, see Cass Sunstein, *Infotopia* (New York: Oxford University Press, 2006), 180–96.

18. Sunstein, *Infotopia*, 182.

19. Sunstein, *Infotopia*, 183.

20. Sunstein, *Infotopia*, 187.

Works Cited

Ackerman, Bruce, and James S. Fishkin. "Deliberation Day." *Journal of Political Philosophy* 10, no. 2 (2002).

Alexander-Moegerle, Gil. *James Dobson's War on America.* New York: Prometheus Books, 1997.

Anderson, Scott. "Coercion." *Stanford Encyclopedia of Philosophy*, 2006.

Applbaum, Arthur Isak. *Ethics for Adversaries.* Princeton: Princeton University Press, 1999.

Aristotle. *The Politics.* Translated by Carnes Lord. Chicago: University of Chicago Press, 1984.

———. "Rhetoric." In *The Complete Works of Aristotle*, edited by Jonathan Barnes. Princeton: Princeton University Press, 1984.

Audi, Robert. *Religious Commitment and Secular Reason.* Cambridge: Cambridge University Press, 2001.

Bachrach, Peter, and Morton S. Baratz. *Power and Poverty.* New York: Oxford University Press, 1970.

Barber, Benjamin R. *Strong Democracy.* Berkeley: University of California Press, 2003.

Bartels, Larry. *Unequal Democracy: The Political Economy of the New Gilded Age.* Princeton: Princeton University Press, 2008.

Bessette, Joseph M. *The Mild Voice of Reason.* Chicago: University of Chicago Press, 1994.

Bishop, Bill. *The Big Sort.* Boston: Houghton Mifflin, 2008.

Blake, Mariah. "Stations of the Cross." *Columbia Journalism Review*, issue 3 (May/June, 2005).

Bok, Sissela. *Lying.* New York: Vintage Books, 1999.

Brown, Rupert. *Group Processes*. Oxford: Blackwell, 2001.

Bruce, Steve, and Roy Wallis. "Rescuing Motives." *British Journal of Sociology* 34, no. 1 (1983).

Buchanan, Allen. "Political Liberalism and Social Epistemology." *Philosophy and Public Affairs* 32, no. 2 (2004).

Bull, Chris, and John Gallagher. *Perfect Enemies*. New York: Madison Books, 1996.

Burke, Kenneth. *A Grammar of Motives*. Berkeley: University of California Press, 1969.

———. *A Rhetoric of Motives*. Berkeley: University of California Press, 1969.

Chambers, Simone. "Discourse and Democratic Practices." In *The Cambridge Companion to Habermas*, edited by Stephen K. White. New York: Cambridge University Press, 1995.

———. *Reasonable Democracy*. Ithaca, NY: Cornell University Press, 1996.

———. "Rhetoric, Public Opinion, and the Ideal of a Deliberative Democracy." *2006 Princeton Conference on Deliberative Democracy*.

Champlin, Dell, and Janet Knoedler. "Operating in the Public Interest or in Pursuit of Private Profits? News in the Age of Media Consolidation." *Journal of Economic Issues* 36, no. 2 (2002).

Christiano, Tom. "Authority." *Stanford Encyclopedia of Philosophy*, 2004.

Cicero. *De Oratore*. Cambridge: Harvard University Press, 1942.

Cohen, Joshua. "Deliberation and Democratic Legitimacy." In *Democracy*, edited by David Estlund. New York: Blackwell Publishers, 2002.

Connolly, William. *The Terms of Political Discourse*. Princeton: Princeton University Press, 1993.

Crandall, Robert. "Competition and Chaos: U.S. Telecommunications since 1996." *Brookings Institute*, 2005.

Dahl, Robert A. *Modern Political Analysis*. Englewood Cliffs: Prentice-Hall, 1984.

———. *A Preface to Democratic Theory*. Chicago: University of Chicago Press, 1956.

Dewey, John. *The Public and Its Problems*. Chicago: Gateway Books, 1946.

Diamond, Sara. *Not By Politics Alone*. New York: Guilford Press, 1998.

Dobson, James. *Children at Risk*. Dallas: Word Publishing, 1990.

Druckman, James N. "Political Preference Formation: Competition, Deliberation, and the (Ir)Relevance of Framing Effects." *American Political Science Review* 98, no. 4 (2004).

Dryzek, John. *Deliberative Democracy and Beyond*. New York: Oxford University Press, 2002.

Eisgruber, Christopher. *Constitutional Self-Government*. Cambridge: Harvard University Press, 2001.

Eliasoph, Nina. *Avoiding Politics*. New York: Cambridge University Press, 1998.

Elkin, Stephen L. "Thinking Constitutionally: The Problem of Deliberative Democracy." *Social Philosophy and Policy* 21 (2004).

Elster, Jon. "The Market and the Forum: Three Varieties of Political Theory." In *Deliberative Democracy*, edited by James Bohman and William Rehg. Cambridge: MIT Press, 1997.

Epstein, David F. *The Political Theory of the Federalist*. Chicago: University of Chicago Press, 1984.

Estlund, David. "Beyond Fairness and Deliberation." In *Deliberative Democracy*, edited by James Bohman and William Rehg. Cambridge: MIT Press, 1997.

Fallows, James. *Breaking the News*. New York: Pantheon Books, 1996.

Fiorina, Morris P. *Culture War? The Myth of a Polarized America*. New York: Pearson Longman, 2006.

Fraser, Nancy. "Rethinking the Public Sphere: A Contribution to the Critique of Actually Existing Democracy." In *Habermas and the Public Sphere*, edited by Craig Calhoun. Cambridge: MIT Press, 1992.

Freeman, Matthew. *The San Diego Model: A Community Battles the Religious Right*. Washington, DC: People for the American Way, 1993.

Freeman, Samuel. "Deliberative Democracy: A Sympathetic Comment." *Philosophy and Public Affairs* 29, no. 4 (2000).

Garsten, Bryan. *Saving Persuasion*. Cambridge: Harvard University Press, 2006.

Gigone, Daniel, and Reid Hastie. "The Common Knowledge Effect." *Journal of Personality and Social Psychology* 65 (1993).

Gilgoff, Dan. *The Jesus Machine*. New York: St. Martin's Press, 2007.

Goffman, Erving. *The Presentation of Self in Everyday Life*. New York: Doubleday, 1959.

Goodin, Robert. *Manipulatory Politics*. New Haven: Yale University Press, 1980.

Greeley, Andrew, and Michael Hout. *The Truth about Conservative Christians*. Chicago: University of Chicago Press, 2006.

Greenawalt, Kent. *Private Consciences and Public Reasons*. New York: Oxford University Press, 1995.

Gutmann, Amy, and Dennis Thompson. *Democracy and Disagreement*. Cambridge: Belknap Press, 1996.

———. *Ethics and Politics: Cases and Comments*. New York: Wadsworth Publishing, 2005.

———. *Why Deliberative Democracy?* Princeton: Princeton University Press, 2004.

Habermas, Jurgen. *Between Facts and Norms*. Translated by William Rehg. Cambridge: MIT Press, 1998.

———. "Hannah Arendt: On the Concept of Power." Translated by F. G. Lawrence. In *Philosophical-Political Profiles*, edited by Jurgen Habermas. Cambridge: MIT Press, 1985.

———. *Justification and Application*. Translated by Ciaran Cronin. Cambridge: Polity Press, 1993.

———. *Moral Consciousness and Communicative Action*. Translated by Christian Lenhardt and Shierry Weber Nicholsen. Cambridge: Polity Press, 1990.

———. "Religion in the Public Sphere." *European Journal of Philosophy* 14, no. 1 (2006).

———. *The Structural Transformation of the Public Sphere*. Cambridge: MIT Press, 1991.

———. *The Theory of Communicative Action*. Translated by Thomas McCarthy. Boston: Beacon Press, 1984.

Hall, Cheryl. "Recognizing the Passion in Deliberation: Toward a More Democratic Theory of Deliberative Democracy." *Hypatia* 22, no. 4 (2007).

Hardisty, Jean. "Constructing Homophobia: Colorado's Right-Wing Attack on Homosexuals." In *Eyes Right!* edited by Chip Berlet. Boston: South End Press, 1995.

———. *Mobilizing Resentment*. Boston: Beacon Press, 1999.

Hedges, Chris. *American Fascists: The Christian Right and the War on America*. New York: Free Press, 2007.

Herman, Didi. *The Antigay Agenda: Orthodox Vision and the Christian Right*. Chicago: University of Chicago Press, 1997.

Hertzke, Allen D. *Representing God in Washington*. Knoxville: University of Tennessee Press, 1988.

Hobbes, *De Cive*. Oxford: Clarendon Press, 1983.

———. *The Elements of Law*. London: Elibron Classics, 2000.

Kant, Immanuel. *Grounding for the Metaphysics of Morals*. Indianapolis: Hackett Publishing, 1993.

———. "What Is Enlightenment?" In *Kant: Political Writings*, edited by H. S. Reiss. New York: Cambridge University Press, 1991.

Kastely, James L. "In Defense of Plato's *Gorgias*." *PMLA* 106, no. 1 (1991).

Kennedy, George A. *A New History of Classical Rhetoric*. Princeton: Princeton University Press, 1994.

Klemp, Nathaniel J. "Beyond God-Talk: Understanding the Christian Right from the Ground Up." *Polity* 39, no. 4 (October 2007).

Klemp, Nathaniel, and Stephen Macedo. "The Christian Right, Public Reason, and American Democracy." In *Evangelicals and Democracy in America*, edited by Steve Brint and Jean Schroedel. New York: Russell Sage Foundation, 2009.

Knight, Jack, and James Johnson. "What Sort of Equality Does Deliberative Democracy Require?" In *Deliberative Democracy*, edited by James Bohman and William Rehg. Cambridge: MIT Press, 1997.

Korsgaard, Christine M. "The Right to Lie: Kant on Dealing with Evil." *Philosophy and Public Affairs* 15, no. 4 (1986).

Krause, Sharon. *Civil Passions*. Princeton: Princeton University Press, 2008.

Larmore, Charles. *Patterns of Moral Complexity*. Cambridge: Cambridge University Press, 1987.

Lesage, Julia. "Christian Coalition Leadership Training." In *Media Culture and the Christian Right*, edited by Linda Kintz and Julia Lesage. Minneapolis: University of Minnesota Press, 1998.

Lewis, Justin. *Constructing Public Opinion*. New York: Columbia University Press, 2001.

Lukes, Steven. *Power: A Radical View*. New York: Palgrave Macmillian, 2004.

Luntz, Frank. *Words That Work*. New York: Hyperion, 2007.

Lustic, Ian S. "History, Historiography, and Political Science: Multiple Historical Records and the Problem of Selection Bias." *American Political Science Review* 90, no. 3 (1996).

Macedo, Stephen. "School Reform and Equal Opportunity in America's Geography of Inequality." *Perspectives on Politics* 1 (2003): 743–55.

Madison, James. *The Federalist Papers*. New York: Penguin Books, 1987.

Manin, Bernard. "Democratic Deliberation: Why We Should Promote Debate Rather than Discussion." Working paper (2005).

———. "Conflict and Self-Interest in Deliberation." In *Deliberative Democracy and Its Discontents*, edited by Samantha Besson and Jose Luis Marti. New York: Ashgate, 2006.

———. "Cracking Through Hegemonic Ideology: The Logic of Formal Justice." *Social Justice Research* 18, no. 3 (2005).

———. "Deliberative Neo-Pluralism." Unpublished manuscript (2007).

———. "A Deliberative Theory of Interest Representation." In *The Politics of Interests*, edited by Mark Petracca. Boulder, CO: Westview Press, 1992.

———. "Everyday Talk in the Deliberative System." In *Deliberative Politics*, edited by Stephen Macedo. New York: Oxford University Press, 1999.

———. "On Legitimacy and Political Deliberation." *Political Theory* 15, no. 3 (1987).

Mansbridge, Jane. *Beyond Adversary Democracy*. Chicago: University of Chicago Press, 1983.

———. "Practice-Thought-Practice." In *Deepening Democracy*, edited by Archon Fung and Erik Olin Wright. New York: Verso, 2003.

———. "Using Power/Fighting Power: The Polity." In *Democracy and Difference*, edited by Seyla Benhabib. Princeton: Princeton University Press, 1996.

———. *Why We Lost the ERA*. Chicago: University of Chicago Press, 1986.

Massey, Douglas S., and Nancy A. Denton. *American Apartheid*. Cambridge: Harvard University Press, 1993.

McChesney, Robert. *Rich Media, Poor Democracy*. Urbana: University of Illinois Press, 1999.

Mendelberg, Tali. "The Deliberative Citizen: Theory and Evidence." In *Political Decision Making, Deliberation and Participation*. New York: Elsevier Science, 2002.

———. *The Race Card*. Princeton: Princeton University Press, 2001.

Mill, John Stuart. "On Liberty." In *John Stuart Mill on Liberty and Other Essays*. New York: Oxford University Press, 1998.

———. "On Representative Government." In *John Stuart Mill on Liberty and Other Essays*. New York: Oxford University Press, 1998.

Mills, C. Wright. "Situated Actions and Vocabularies of Motive." *American Sociological Review* 9, no. 1 (1940).

Moen, Michael. "From Revolution to Evolution: The Changing Nature of the Christian Right." In *The Rapture of Politics*, edited by Peter Kivisto, Steve Bruce, and William H. Swatos Jr. New Brunswick, NJ: Transaction Publishers, 1995.

———. *The Transformation of the Christian Right*. Tuscaloosa: University of Alabama Press, 1992.

Mutz, Diana. *Hearing the Other Side*. New York: Cambridge University Press, 2006.

Nozick, Robert. "Coercion." In *Philosophy, Science, and Method*, edited by Sidney Morgenbesser, Patrick Suppes, and Morton White. New York: St. Martin's Press, 1969.

Nunberg, Geoffrey. *Talking Right*. New York: PublicAffairs, 2006.

Nussbaum, Martha. *Upheavals of Thought: The Intelligence of Emotions*. Cambridge: Cambridge University Press, 2001.

Olafson, Frederick A. "Habermas as a Philosopher." *Ethics* 100, no. 3 (1990).

Orwell, George. "Politics and the English Language." In *Collected Essays*. London: Secker and Warburg, 1961.

Peabody, Robert L., Susan Webb Hammond, Jean Torcom, Lynne P. Brown, Carolyn Thompson, and Robert Kolodny. "Interviewing Political Elites." *PS: Political Science and Politics* 23, no. 3 (1990): 451–55.

Penning, James. "Pat Robertson and the GOP: 1988 and Beyond." *Sociology of Religion* 55, no. 3 (1994).

Pettit, Philip. "Consequentialism." In *A Companion to Ethics*, edited by Peter Singer. Oxford: Blackwell Publishers, 1991.

———. "Democracy, Electoral and Contestatory." In *Designing Democratic Institutions*, edited by Ian Shapiro and Stephen Macedo. New York: New York University Press, 2000.

———. "Depoliticizing Democracy." *Ratio Juris* 17, no. 1 (2004).

———. *Republicanism*. New York: Oxford University Press, 1997.

Plato. "Gorgias." In *The Essential Dialogues of Plato*. New York: Barnes and Noble Classics, 2005.

Popper, Karl. *Objective Knowledge*. New York: Oxford University Press, 1972.

Putnam, Robert D. *Bowling Alone: The Collapse and Revival of American Community*. New York: Simon and Schuster, 2000.

———. *Making Democracy Work: Civic Traditions in Modern Italy*. Princeton: Princeton University Press, 1994.

Rawls, John. "The Idea of Public Reason Revisited." In *The Law of Peoples with "The Idea of Public Reason Revisited."* Cambridge: Harvard University Press, 1999.

———. *Political Liberalism*. New York: Columbia University Press, 1993.

———. *A Theory of Justice*. Rev. ed. Cambridge: Harvard University Press, 1999.

Rorty, Amelie. "Explaining Emotions." In *Explaining Emotions*, edited by Amelie Rorty. Los Angeles: University of California Press, 1980.

Rudinow, Joel. "Manipulation." *Ethics* 88, no. 4 (1978).

Rushkoff, Douglas. *Coercion: Why We Listen to What "They" Say*. New York: Riverhead Trade, 2000.

Sacks, Harvey. "Everyone Has to Lie." In *Sociocultural Dimensions of Language Use*, edited by Mary Sanches and Ben G. Blount. New York: Academic Press, 1975.

Sanders, Lynn M. "Against Deliberation." *Political Theory* 25, no. 3 (1997).

Schiemann, John W. "Meeting Halfway between Rochester and Frankfurt." *American Journal of Political Science* 44, no. 1 (2000).

Schumpeter, Joseph A. *Capitalism, Socialism, and Democracy*. New York: HarperPerennial, 1976.

Shapiro, Ian. *The State of Democratic Theory*. Princeton: Princeton University Press, 2003.

Skinner, Quentin. *Reason and Rhetoric in the Philosophy of Hobbes*. Cambridge: Cambridge University Press, 1996.

Smith, Christian. *American Evangelicalism*. Chicago: University of Chicago Press, 1998.

Sniderman, Paul M., and Sean M. Theriault. "The Structure of Political Argument and the Logic of Issue Framing." In *Studies in Public Opinion*, edited by Willem E. Saris and Paul M. Sniderman. Princeton: Princeton University Press, 2004.

Sparrow, Bartholomew H. *Uncertain Guardians*. Baltimore: Johns Hopkins University Press, 1999

Spender, Dale. *Man Made Language*. New York: HarperCollins, 1990.

Stanton, Glenn, T. *Why Marriage Matters*. Colorado Springs, CO: Navpress Publishing Group, 1997.

Stanton, Glenn T., and Bill Maier. *Marriage on Trial: The Case against Same-Sex Marriage and Parenting*. Downers Grove, IL: Intervarsity Press, 2004.

Stasser, Garold, and William Titus. "Hidden Profiles: A Brief History." *Psychological Inquiry* 14 (2003).

———. "Pooling of Unshared Information in Group Discussion." *Journal of Personality and Social Psychology* 48 (1985).

Stout, Jeffrey. *Democracy and Tradition*. Princeton: Princeton University Press, 2004.

Sunstein, Cass. "Beyond the Republican Revival." *Yale Law Journal* 97, no. 8 (July 1988).

———. "Deliberative Trouble? Why Groups Go to Extremes." *Yale Law Journal* 110, no. 1 (2000).

———. *Infotopia*. New York: Oxford University Press, 2006.

———. *Republic.com*. Princeton: Princeton University Press, 2001.

Thompson, Dennis F. "Hypocrisy and Democracy." In *Liberalism without Illusions*, edited by Bernard Yack. Chicago: University of Chicago Press, 1995.

Thucydides. *The Peloponnesian War*. New York: Free Press, 1996.

Tocqueville, Alexis de. *Democracy and America*. Translated by Arthur Goldhammer. New York: Library of America, 2004.

Walzer, Michael. "Deliberation and What Else?" In *Deliberative Politics*, edited by Stephen Macedo. New York: Oxford University Press, 1999.

Wardy, Robert. *The Birth of Rhetoric*. New York: Routledge, 1998.

Ware, Alan. "The Concept of Manipulation." *British Journal of Political Science* 11, no. 2 (1981).

Weber, Max. "Objectivity in Social Science and Social Policy." In *The Methodology of the Social Sciences*, edited by E. A. Shils and H. A. Finch. New York: Free Press, 1949.

Westbrook, Robert B. *John Dewey and American Democracy*. Ithaca, NY: Cornell University Press, 1991.

Wilcox, Clyde, and Carin Larson. *Onward Christian Soldiers?* Boulder, CO: Westview Press, 2006.

Wittgenstein, Ludwig. *Philosophical Investigations*. New York: Prentice Hall, 1999.

Wolterstorff, Nicholas. *Religion in the Public Square*. New York: Rowman & Littlefield, 1997.

Wuthnow, Robert, James Davidson Hunter, Albert Bergesen, and Edith Kurzweil. *Cultural Analysis*. Boston: Routledge & Kegan Paul, 1984.

Young, Iris Marion. "Communication and the Other: Beyond Deliberative Democracy." In *Democracy and Difference*, edited by Seyla Benhabib. Princeton: Princeton University Press, 1996.

———. *Inclusion and Democracy*. New York: Oxford University Press, 2000.

Index

~

About the Author

Nathaniel J. Klemp is assistant professor of political science and philosophy at Pepperdine University. Klemp holds a BA in philosophy from Stanford University and an MA and a PhD in politics from Princeton University. Klemp is the winner of the 2006 Association for Princeton Graduate Alumni Teaching Award as well as the 2010 Howard A. White Award for Excellence in Teaching at Pepperdine University. Klemp's essays have appeared in *Polity*, *Politics and Religion*, *The Journal of Public Deliberation*, *Outlines*, and edited volumes such as *Conservative Christianity and Democracy in America* and *Manipulating Democracy*.

CPSIA information can be obtained at www.ICGtesting.com
Printed in the USA
BVOW062246260212

283695BV00003B/2/P